WILD ABOUT FLYING!

Dreamers, Doers, and Daredevils

WILD ABOUT FLYING!

Dreamers, Doers, and Daredevils

DAVID MARSHALL & BRUCE HARRIS

FIREFLY BOOKS

Publisher	Gordon Cheers
Associate publisher	Margaret Olds
Art director	Stan Lamond
Project manager	Jayne Denshire
Cartography	John Frith
Cover design	Stan Lamond
Index	Glenda Browne
Production	Bernard Roberts
Foreign rights	Sarah Minns
Publishing assistant	Erin King

Special thanks to ADG Don Glover – World War II R.A.F. Beaufighter pilot, businessman, aircraft buff, and omnivorous reader. His enthusiasm and care over our words and pictures was the tonic we needed.
THE AUTHORS

Captions for paintings in the preliminary and section opening pages:

Page 1: The Avro 504, designed in 1914 with Roy Chadwick's involvement

Page 2: McDonnell F4E Phantoms, 1970

Page 3: Sikorsky's 1930s Cierva C-30 Autogiro, reconditioned after World War II

Page 4 (below): The Airspeed Ferry, 1934

Page 4/5 (right): Sidney Cotton's Lockheed 12a

Page 6 (left to right): The French Bernard Ferbois V-2 racing monoplane, 1924; a Pan-Am Sikorsky S-42 Clipper, Samoan Ciupper, 1937; the Me. 262 Schwalbe (meaning "Swallow") jet-fighter.

Page 7 (left to right): Roy Chadwick's ill-fated Avro Manchester; Sperry's Aerial Torpedo, 1915–1919; the Boeing B-47 Stratojet.

Page 8: Supermarine Seagull III, 1927

Page 9: The Lockheed U-2, 1955

Page 11: The Do. 31-E-I VSTOL

Page 69: The magnificent Mirage IV-A, 1959

Page 141: The Bristol Beaufighter, 1941

Photographs are acknowledged on page 232.

A FIREFLY BOOK

Published by Firefly Books Ltd. 2003
© Global Book Publishing Pty Ltd 2003

First printing

Publisher Cataloguing-in-Publication Data (U.S.)

Marshall, David, 1929-
    Wild about flying! : dreamers, doers and daredevils / David Marshall & Bruce Harris. ----1st ed.
[240] p. : ill. , photos. (chiefly col.) , maps ; cm.

Includes index.

Summary: Biographies of inventors, aviators, designers, engineers and navigators involved with aviation; and whose stories trace the history of flight from its inception to the present day.

ISBN 1-55297-849-4

1. Aeronautics -- Biography. 2. Aeronautics -- History. I. Harris, Bruce, 1924- .
II. Title.

629.13/0092/2 B 21   TL539.M37 2003

National Library of Canada Cataloguing in Publication Data

Marshall, David, 1929-
    Wild about flying! : dreamers, doers and daredevils / by David Marshall, Bruce Harris.

Includes index.
ISBN 1-55297-849-4

    1. Aeronautics--Biography. 2. Aeronautics--History. I. Harris, Bruce, 1924- II. Title.

TL539.M37 2003   629.13'0092'2   C2003-903220-5

Published in the United States in 2003 by
Firefly Books (U.S.) Inc.
P.O. Box 1338, Ellicott Station
Buffalo, New York 14205

Published in Canada in 2003 by
Firefly Books Ltd.
3680 Victoria Park Avenue
Toronto, Ontario, M2H 3K1

Printed in China by Midas Printing (Asia) Ltd
Film separation Pica Digital Pte Ltd, Singapore

O, I have slipped the surly bonds of Earth
And danced the skies on laughter-silvered wings;
Sunward I've climbed, and joined the tumbling mirth
Of sun-split clouds—and done a hundred things
You have not dreamed of—wheeled and soared and swung
High in the sunlit silence. Hov'ring there,
I've chased the shouting wind along, and flung
My eager craft through footless halls of air.
Up, up the long, delirious, burning blue
I've topped the windswept heights with easy grace
Where never lark, or even eagle flew;
And, while with silent, lifting mind I've trod
The high untrespassed sanctity of space,
Put out my hand, and touched the face of God.

High Flight by **John Gillespie Magee**

(killed in action with the Royal Canadian Air Force)

Contents

INTRODUCTION

At altitudes of up to 40,000 feet, sleek, powerful aircraft carry thousands of passengers across oceans and continents—around the world. Today's airliners evolved from ancestors so frighteningly flimsy it's a wonder they could fly at all. Yet they did—because of men and women with foresight, courage, and remarkable creativity.

The focus of aviation's development so often rests with the aircraft—the structures of wood and canvas, and the engines made of plastics and metal—but what of the people? What of the individuals who planned to fly, who did the math, who built the machines, and who flew them—sometimes to hell, but not always back.

They are aviation's dreamers, doers, and daredevils: extraordinary humans with towering skills, personalities, and bravery. All of them made contributions—sometimes in peace, often in war. Many converted vivid dreams into reality. Others improved the possibilities with a leap forward in aircraft design, or by inventing instruments that became essential to flight. Adventurers jumped at the chance to burst the boundaries, to fly higher, faster, further—whatever the consequences. Never before in human history have such amazing and rapid achievements changed the way we live, think, work, and travel as those that have occurred in just over 100 years.

From those pioneers who first took to the air in the late nineteenth century, to the astronauts now pushing out of Earth's orbit, come the stories of the dreamers, doers, and daredevils who have made it all happen. Alongside them, captured in story-telling colour paintings and archival photography, are the magnificent flying machines they designed, developed, and flew.

THE DREAMERS

Meet the visionaries who dreamed their own dreams, and created answers to the problems that had kept people earthbound. Critics said they were mad: "If God wanted us to fly, he'd have given us wings." The dreamers knew they could fly. Once the conquest of the sky began, a ferment of creativity produced dozens of prodigious idealists whose soaring dreams captured the imaginations of generations and inspired some of the most dramatic events of the twentieth century.

OTTO LILIENTHAL

IS IT A BIRD? IS IT A HANG GLIDER?

Otto Lilienthal

In the late nineteenth century, Europe was swarming with birdmen. It seemed that the promise of heavier-than-air flying machines fascinated the whole of the continent. In Britain, Sir George Cayley was developing curved lifting surfaces and experimenting with a remarkable triplane, said to have flown successfully in 1849. Some aviation historians still regard Sir George as the true inventor of the modern airplane.

Among Cayley's followers were British, French, Swedes, and Germans—names such as Hensen, Stringfellow, Ader, Penaud and Mouillard, Chanute, Langley, and in far-off Australia, Hargrave. They wanted to do better than the balloonist followers of the Montgolfier brothers who had made their first manned hot-air ascent in 1783. A balloon could take fliers high into the sky, but its direction was difficult to control. All over Europe adventurous minds were grappling with the problem of how to make effective, controlled flights.

This frantic search for answers influenced a young German engineer named Otto Lilienthal. The prospect of flight had fascinated Otto since his school days. He had observed birds in flight, and correctly deduced that the curvature of a bird's wing held the secret to its lifting properties. He constructed gliders with wings shaped like those of a bird, and used ribs to create and maintain the curved wing profiles. He engineered strong but light structures of bamboo and willow for the ribs, and stretched cotton fabric tightly across this frame for the wings. A fixed vertical and horizontal tail unit was mounted on a short bamboo extension at the rear.

Otto built a cradle in the midsection of the wing so that he could hang from the center by his arms when he was airborne. He was the original hang glider. But Lilienthal had no movable controls in his gliders. He could only fly straight and level in a certain direction by shifting his body and weight within the confines of his "cockpit." Starting in 1891, he made over 2,000 successful flights in a number of esthetically beautiful gliders, some of which were biplanes. However, his reliance on body weight control methods was to be his undoing.

He realized that to progress further he would need an engine. He favored a device that would power flapping wings, similar to the workings of his prototypes, the birds, but he did not focus on developing really effective control systems for his aircraft. On his last glider flight in 1896, while soaring in one of his inventions, a gust of wind lifted the nose of the craft. The glider stalled and Lilienthal was unable to right her. He crashed so heavily that the specially designed bamboo fender built to protect him (and often his savior in previous spills) was unable to absorb the shock. Tragically, Otto died from unsustainable injuries.

Left: Lilienthal usually flew his gliders from a specially constructed conical hill at Rhinover in Germany. In favorable conditions he was able to soar above his starting height as well as glide down the steep slope. It was here at Rhinover that he crashed and was killed.

Above: It was difficult (and potentially dangerous) for Lilienthal to use body movements to control his gliders.

Sacrifices must be made.

A FAVORITE PHRASE OF LILIENTHAL

Right: Between 1891 and 1895 Lilienthal built several gliders. Most were monoplanes and had wingspans of approximately 20 feet (6.1 meters). With their wings covered in white cotton fabric, the gliders were an unforgettable sight as they soared, with the wind humming through the rigging, low over the heads of onlookers at the "speed of a racehorse."

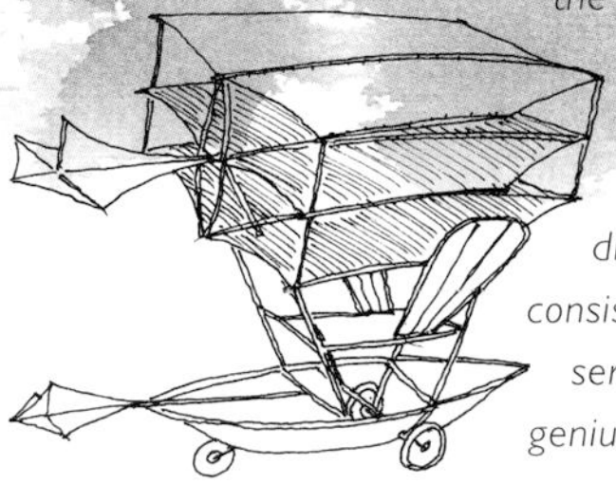

Right: Sir George Cayley experimented with curved lifting surfaces and discovered the stabilizing effect of giving wings dihedral—tilting them up to create an angle between the wing's surface and the horizontal axis. He used rudders to change direction up and down as well as left and right. He also believed that a steam or a reciprocating engine could drive a propeller, which would then power the machine into the air. He even thought of using biplane wings and of introducing streamlining to reduce drag. Cayley constructed and flew two gliders. One of his triplanes had tail surfaces consisting of horizontal stabilizers and vertical rudders. It is reported that Cayley put his servant in this machine and launched it successfully across a valley—a prophetic genius indeed. His influence was widespread and fundamental.

LAWRENCE HARGRAVE

FLYING A BOX KITE

During the dying days of the nineteenth century and the beginning of the twentieth, Europeans knew they were at the center of the universe and that any worthwhile development in science must, of necessity, originate from Europe. It had for centuries. The first sustained, powered flight in France, therefore, became one of the greatest moments in European aviation history. The fact that it had already occurred in America was either ignored or forgotten; it was a French happening and every Frenchman knew that.

In Paris, the populace took a diminutive Brazilian, Santos-Dumont, to their hearts because of his daring exploits flying around the city and the Eiffel Tower in dirigible airships. Santos-Dumont was convinced of success in his next venture. He would design and fly the first powered flying machine! The excited Parisians didn't know their idol was about to get off the ground, thanks to an innovative thinker living in Australia, literally on the other side of the world: the explorer and scientist, Lawrence Hargrave.

In the late 1890s Hargrave turned his mind to flight. He had been fascinated by the idea since childhood. He started designing different sorts of wings, experimenting with curved profiles. He made tiny steam engines to power models and is credited with designing the first rotary engine. The French used rotary engines as the basis of power plants for their World War I aircraft.

What makes Hargrave's efforts remarkable is that he carried them out almost in isolation, half a world away from the intellectual ferment and excitement in Europe. He was working alone, from his home in Sydney, in the British colony of New South Wales.

He generously made his findings available to anyone who was interested via the Scientific

Left: Dr. Alexander Graham Bell (right), the inventor of the telephone, with Lawrence Hargrave. Bell, an influential aviation enthusiast, regarded Hargrave's work as the basis of aviation knowledge at that time.

Left: Lawrence Hargrave made many models from 1885 onward and became interested in wing profiles in 1893. One of his most successful flying models was Number 82. Hargrave carved this model from redwood; the span was about $3\frac{1}{4}$ feet (1 meter).

Opposite page: In 1896, during a series of experiments on his property south of Sydney, Australia, Hargrave linked four of his box kites together and, because of the box kites' inherent stability, rose in a fresh breeze to about twenty feet (6.1 meters) with complete safety. The concept was incorporated into early European aircraft design and may have led pioneers such as American designer, Octave Chanute, to the idea of a straight biplane wing as opposed to a bird-shaped structure.

Royal Society in England. He also corresponded with fellow designer, Octave Chanute in America, advising him of his progress. Chanute was the man who later had considerable contact with the Wright brothers.

As with many other early inventors in this new science of aviation, Lawrence Hargrave was still looking at birds for his inspiration. Initially he thought that flapping wings must hold the answer to powered flight. Yet his primary contributions were distinctly unbirdlike. His most important practical invention was the box kite. The Hargrave box kite proved to be a stable flying platform. Without it, the first powered flight of a European airplane could not have taken place. Three years after the Wright brothers had flown at Kitty Hawk, Santos-Dumont took to the air in 1906. The French welcomed his efforts as the ultimate breakthrough.

OCTAVE CHANUTE

BORN FRENCH BUT DREAMED AMERICAN

Although Octave Chanute was born in France in 1882, he lived mostly in America as an American citizen. A railway engineer by profession, he dreamed of flying. Chanute was so interested in the theory of flight that he became a kind of father figure—an authority and mentor to others who were searching for answers to the secrets of successful journeys in the sky. He published his own theories and those of other inventors, such as the Australian Lawrence Hargrave. It was not long before Chanute became one of the foremost authorities on aviation, with correspondents and thinkers from all over the world referring ideas to him. He freely gave wise counsel to all who asked for it. Among the many designers who had the benefit of his insights were the Wright brothers as they grappled with their own innovative experiments.

Chanute was a brilliant lateral thinker. He applied his knowledge of engineering principles to designing gliders with a difference. He broke from the birdwing shapes that until then had restricted progress, designing wings of constant chord and airfoil sections. Then, to maximize wing areas into the most manageable size, he mounted one wing on top of another, as Sir George Cayley in Britain had done. He made his structures strong by employing the same principles as those used in designing a box-girder railway bridge—he trussed wings together with struts and wires to produce a light, strong, boxlike construction—virtually what was later to be called a biplane wing.

Chanute may well have been inspired to develop his straight-wing concept from the Hargrave box kite, or from a young English clergyman, Wenham, who was a follower of Cayley.

With Chanute's progression of wing shapes it seemed he thought the more he departed from birdwing shapes, the more efficient the wings would become. Chanute worked with three other dedicated men—Avery, Butosov, and Herring—to design a series of gliders. Their designs progressed from bird shapes to geometric multistructures with fixed tail assemblies. Like the gliding pioneer Lilienthal, Octave Chanute relied on the pilot shifting their body weight to provide control.

Octave Chanute

Above: Octave Chanute, with his helpers Avery, Butosov, and Herring, designed a series of gliders in various forms. One of Butosov's gliders was clearly based on birdlike shapes. Chanute convinced Butosov not to fly it—just as well, as the ballasted version they then launched, crashed 100 feet (30.5 meters) to its destruction.

Opposite page: Chanute's most interesting and successful glider had a two-layered wing—a biplane wing—and a fixed, cruciform tail empennage with a shape similar to that on Professor Langley's Aerodrome models. Chanute's assistants flew his gliders alongside Lake Michigan from 1896 until 1901, as Chanute himself was too old for such athletic pursuits. Ribs were constructed across the chord of the wings to maintain a consistent airfoil section, rather than allowing the cotton fabric covering to take up an unpredictable, bowed shape in the air stream. There were no controls; a shift in body movement altered the center of gravity, similar to Lilienthal's approach in his gliders.

(Two of my machines) have taken hundreds of glides ... without the slightest incident.

CHANUTE'S LETTER TO LAWRENCE HARGRAVE, SEPTEMBER, 1896

Left: Chanute's own early attempts featured curved wings, in a multi-layered form.

CLEMENT ADER

DID SHE OR DIDN'T SHE?

It has been sometimes claimed that Frenchman, Clement Ader made the first "heavier-than-air" flight. If an uncontrolled hop of about 140 feet (100 meters) can be called "flight" then perhaps there is a faint argument, but Ader's achievement didn't stack up against that of the Wright brothers.

At the turn of the century, in this time of much ferment, many inventors were striving to "fly." Otto Lilienthal was gliding into history. He had keen followers such as Scotsman Percy Pilcher and Frenchman Henri Ferber. Both men experimented with gliders based on Lilienthal's designs but neither added significantly to his theories or achievements. Clement Ader, however, was attempting to fly in a powered aircraft, using a very unusual machine indeed. Ader seemed dedicated to trying to emulate the birds. The whole appearance of his plane was batlike, with two propellers which resembled feathers and were driven by steam power. It was possibly just as well that Ader's strange machine achieved only one uncontrolled hop, as he was totally enclosed within the bowels of his machine with no way of seeing where he was going.

Clement Ader's experiments, while imaginative and daring, did little to open new paths to controlled and sustained powered flights. He epitomized those experimenters who could not free themselves from the siren calls of their feathered friends.

Clement Ader

Above: *Frenchman Henri Ferber's early gliders reflected traditional birdwing shapes, but after seeing representations of the Wright brothers' Flyer, Ferber made his own version of a biplane glider with limited fore and aft control from a forward elevator. The wings had no ribs or wing warping and the structure was very simple when compared to the sophistication of the Wrights' gliders. Ferber helped France become preeminent in early aircraft production.*

Right: *It is often said that if an airplane looks right, it is right. To a layperson, Ader's version didn't and wasn't. But then neither did many other flying machines of the time. At least this one hissed and whirred its way off the ground for a few seconds.*

PERCY SINCLAIR PILCHER

HE MADE IT A TWO-HORSEPOWERED FLIGHT

Percy Pilcher, a Scot, was inspired by the flying feats and the gliders Otto Lilienthal created. Pilcher built gliders of his own design, attempting to improve on the lead shown by the Germans. He made several successful flights in his gliders and is regarded as the most distinguished British aerial pioneer after Sir Arthur Cayley.

Pilcher took up engineering after a career in the Royal Navy, and was appointed assistant lecturer in Naval Architecture and Marine Engineering at Glasgow University. He also became an active council member of the Aeronautical Society. With the enthusiastic assistance of his sister, Ella, he built and experimented with a number of glider designs, but his most elaborate was his last creation—the Hawk. A unique feature was its wheeled undercarriage, developed to assist in takeoff and landing. Unlike Lilienthal, who constructed an artificial hill to launch his gliding attempts, Pilcher was towed into the air by two strong horses attached to a line, passing through a pulley with a line-release mechanism on the glider. For lightness and strength, the Hawk was built of bamboo, wood, and fabric. Once he could be assured of the Hawk's satisfactory gliding abilities, Percy was planning to build a machine similar to the Hawk, but with the addition of an engine and pusher propeller.

Pilcher's plans were cut short when he was putting the Hawk through its paces in 1899. While he was airborne—gliding over 30 feet (9.15 meters) in the air—a bamboo rod snapped, causing the movable tail surface to collapse. The resulting crash killed Pilcher at the young age of 32, a grievous loss of a key contributor to the developing theory of flight.

Right: Where Lilienthal's gliders were launched from the slope of an artificial hill, Pilcher used the bare landscape of the local area. Here, he prepares to launch his Hawk from the side of a hill around 1898.

Percy Pilcher

Left: Scotsman Percy Pilcher was inspired by Otto Lilienthal and made several flights in gliders of his own design. He is regarded as the most distinguished British pioneer since Sir Arthur Cayley. Pilcher was killed flying his Hawk glider when a bamboo rod snapped at 30 feet (9.15 meters) causing the movable tail surface to collapse. A unique feature of this glider was its wheeled undercarriage. Unlike Lilienthal, who built an artificial hill to glide from, Pilcher was towed into the air by two horses attached to a line passing through a pulley. His untimely death cut short his plans to fit an engine with a pusher propeller to a glider similar to the Hawk, as was any further contribution he could make to contemporary theory of flight.

SAMUEL LANGLEY

THE IDEAS THAT SANK IN THE POTOMAC

Sam Langley was a professor, an ideas man, and the secretary of the Smithsonian Institute in Washington. From 1891 he worked on his theories of flight, making models, and testing ideas, all financed by the Institute. He constructed many large models to develop his theories. One of these, a steam-powered Aerodrome model made several successful flights. Langley, like some others at the time, had freed himself of the idea that a flying machine should look like a bird. Indeed, to a casual observer, the appearance of his models is very much like a modern aircraft; two sets of straight wings with ribs to maintain the wing profile, and a movable tail.

In 1903 he had a full-sized version of one of his most successful models ready to fly. It was fitted with a brilliant,

lightweight, five-cylinder petrol engine, designed by Charles Manly, who was also destined to pilot the ill-fated Langley plane.

The first flight was to take place from a launching pad set up on a houseboat on Washington's Potomac River. The beautifully constructed machine, with its engine firing sweetly and its pilot tense in the cockpit, was catapulted off the launchpad. It dived straight off the end of its rails into the river, "like a bag of wet cement," commented one observer.

If that was not embarrassing enough, the next attempt a few days later was simply catastrophic. On leaving the ramp, the plane made a sudden vertical ascent. While Charles Manly struggled frantically to depress the plane's nose, which was now pointing vertically upward, the wings shuddered, flexed, then crumpled. The tail collapsed and the whole sorry mess slid tail-backward into the cold Potomac. The courageous Manly, near drowning, managed to struggle free but the airplane was wrecked beyond repair.

For someone of such strong scientific background it is almost unbelievable that Professor Langley had failed to calculate the stresses on the scaled-up airframe, which was simply not strong enough. In retrospect, neither had he fully understood the behavior of the forces created when the air moved over the curved wing surfaces. Langley had certainly

Professor Samuel Langley

Right: Langley's flying machine was launched from a platform mounted on the roof of a barge in the Potomac River. Its wing structure distorted and sent it plunging into the water "like a bag of wet cement," said one commentator. Apart from its structural problems, Langley's beautifully crafted machine, with its tandem wing and movable tail surface, still lacked a system with good control about the rolling axis. The upswept wings gave good lateral stability but, had the machine flown on its completion in 1903, it still would not have been able to make a properly banked turn. Glenn Curtiss later made fundamental modifications to this design and flew it successfully as a seaplane.

not carried out exhaustive studies of various wing sections as the Wright brothers had, nor had he learned from the death of Lilienthal, which highlighted the necessity of devising a fully tested control system before attempting to fly.

After this failure, the Institute withdrew all financial support for the project. The sad spin-off from that decision was that Charles Manly's superb radial engine was shelved and forgotten—a design that could well have changed the course of airplane engine development.

Left: Charles Manly's remarkable radial engine, whose design Glenn Curtiss—a devotee of Langley's cause—would have studied in detail before producing his own series of highly successful radial engines.

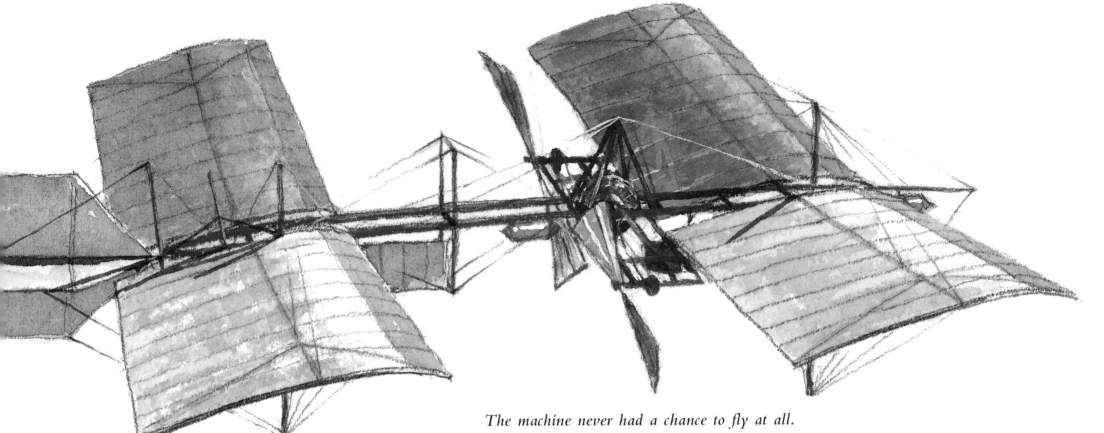

The machine never had a chance to fly at all.

A BROKEN-HEARTED LANGLEY AFTER HIS SECOND AERODROME SANK
IN THE POTOMAC RIVER, 1903

Right: The luckless pilot, Manly, (left) alongside the proud designer, Samuel Langley, aboard the launching barge on the Potomac River where the pair prepared to launch Langley's Aerodrome.

Far right: A crucial moment was captured during the first, unsuccessful flight of Langley's Aerodrome. The front wing had already distorted from its correct angle of attack. The aircraft had only one way to go from there— downward to disaster.

THE WRIGHT BROTHERS

FROM GLIDERS TO FIRST POWERED FLIGHT

Since boyhood, Americans Orville and Wilbur Wright had been interested in flight, but it was only in the dying years of the nineteenth century that they began their own serious study and experimentation. It was then that they first wrote to the Smithsonian Institute in Washington D.C. to gather the latest research findings and developments on the subject of flying.

The Wright brothers had the true Yankee "can do" spirit. They combined a natural inventiveness with the practical engineering abilities they had learned through their bicycle manufacturing business, refusing to accept at face value information provided from other sources. Instead they conducted their own experiments, compiled their own tables of results, and checked and tested previously accepted results that failed to deliver rational outcomes.

Over a period of four years from 1899, the hard-working duo progressed relentlessly—from models to kites, kites to full-scale gliders, and eventually to their first powered aircraft. Carefully and methodically they tested and retested ideas, often coming close to despair until a word of encouragement or a fresh spark of creative thinking set them striving again.

Wilbur and Orville realized that whatever craft they intended to fly could not be just a stable platform for the pilot, but had to be controllable—a craft that could be corrected and restored quickly to an even keel, should it be affected by wind turbulence or a shift in balance. They followed the pioneering work of German Otto Lilienthal and his successful glider flights, and knew of his untimely death when he crashed after a gust of wind threw him off balance. Lilienthal's gliders had no means of correction or control. The Wrights agreed that

Right: The Wrights' Glider No. 2 of 1901 had a wingspan of 22 feet (6.7 meters) compared to the 17 feet (5.2 meters) of Glider No. 1. The camber of the wings was increased to give more lift. Its disappointing performance presented complicated problems for the Wrights to solve.

the pilot of their machine should be able to control the plane's attitude, direction, and speed by operating built-in controls that didn't rely on the pilot shifting his weight.

Before the Wright brothers began to build their first glider, they realized that if they made one large wing out of wood, the strength would be in doubt, and its size would make it unmanageable. So they agreed to adopt a biplane wing, which would achieve the desired wing area needed to lift a human body.

They also discovered one of the fundamentals of controlled flight. Based on an observation of bird flight recorded by Moulliard in France in 1890, they reasoned that to keep the wings on an

Left: Wilbur and Orville Wright were a quite remarkable pair. Together they spent hours discussing and dissecting a topic, arguing back and forth until in the end, neither knew who had thought up an idea in the first place. They designed and built their own wind tunnel. They even designed and made the sturdy petrol engine to power their famous Flyer. When they went to the bleak, sandy hills of Kitty Hawk to test-fly their gliders, the resourceful pair constructed the building in which they were to live and work.

even keel the tips should be capable of being twisted up or down, thereby increasing or decreasing the lift. Already, the brothers were a jump ahead of their contemporaries.

During 1899 the Wrights made and tested a model kite near their home in Dayton, Ohio, to trial this idea (called "wing warping") of keeping their test kite on an even keel.

Their Glider No. 1 was based on this model and flown at Kitty Hawk, North Carolina, in 1900. In testing it, the Wrights concentrated mostly on controlling the plane's attitude, should it be tipped sideways or up and down by gusty wind currents. They were not able to contemplate maneuvering or even soaring. Instead they glided down the slopes of the dunes, studying how the craft performed. When they returned home to Dayton, they had sufficient findings to enable them to work on a number of design modifications over the next few months.

In 1901 Wilbur and Orville were back in Kitty Hawk with Glider No. 2—a larger machine—that incorporated many new design ideas and features. They were to face depressing evidence. The new airfoil section in the wing design didn't result in the lift they had anticipated. Their wing-warping invention proved to be of only limited value. After so much hard work they were dismayed to find that where they expected to control the wings—returning to a level position after one wing had dropped—the lower wing dragged back, pulling the glider off course, or worse still, causing the wing to drop even more. They began to feel that they would never solve the mystery of achieving full control. However, influential French-born American Octave Chanute, who had already successfully flown his double-decker glider,

*... average speed through air 31 miles
longest 59 seconds inform press
home christmas ...*

**TELEGRAM SENT BY ORVILLE WRIGHT TO HIS
FATHER, DECEMBER 1903**

*Below: The chance twisting of an old bicycle inner tube
box gave the Wrights the idea that they could induce
a similar helicoidal twist to their wing structure
without jeopardizing its structural integrity. On their
airplanes the center section of the box structure would
remain rigid; only the outer portion would be warped
(by controlling wires attached to wing struts). This would
increase or decrease the angle of the outer
wings (and likewise the lift) and thus bank the
aircraft. The action would allow the airplane to execute
a banked turn or would restore it to an even keel.
The Wright brothers patented this
"aileron" principle which later
led to much litigation.*

HOW WING WARPING WORKED

*The Wrights experimented with various control methods. On the Flyer, shown here in
diagram form, the pilot adopted a prone position across a small sliding cradle in the
middle of the lower wing to which the wing-warping control wires were attached. On a
previous glider the rudder controls were foot-controlled, but on the Flyer the cradle was
linked to harmonized rudder control wires.*

*By sliding his cradle slightly to one side or the other with his hips, the pilot was able to
control lateral stability. The elevator lever was hand-controlled. It was an awkward system
that was later simplified. A normal sitting position for the pilot was adopted later on.*

*To turn to the right, the cradle (shown in black) was made to slide
to the right. This pulled cable A, attached to the top left-hand strut
and lowered the trailing edge of the wing. This gave more lift, with
the opposite effect happening on the other wing. Simultaneously,
auxiliary cable B, attached to the lower outer struts, automatically pulled up
the rear strut of the down-going wing, giving less lift.*

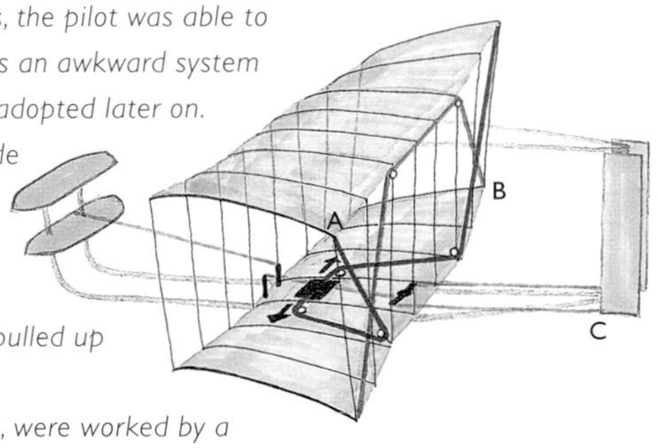

*Rudder control cables C, shown here as a hand-operated system, were worked by a
lever fixed to a bar on which rudder wires were attached. These were linked to the cradle
to give the pilot less work.*

Glider No. 1, 1900

had traveled to Kitty Hawk to witness the Wrights' attempts. His presence and subsequent suggestions greatly boosted their waning confidence, and they returned to Dayton encouraged to start again.

They thought they could fix the wing-dropping factor by installing a vertical fin at the rear of the glider. The lack of lift in the wing airfoil proved much more difficult. Doggedly, the brothers reviewed Lilienthal's tables, and then set about testing over 200 airfoil shapes in a wind tunnel they designed and built. Eventually, these tests were pivotal—proving that Lilienthal's calculations were inaccurate and misleading. They started crafting new wings.

In September 1902, with Glider No. 3, the Wrights were back at Kitty Hawk once more. The newly shaped wing wasn't the only change. This time, the glider was built with two vertical fins at the rear—quickly modified and transformed into movable rudders shortly after trials began. A controllable biplane elevator built at the front of the glider was another design innovation.

Glider No. 3 was a huge success. Enthusiastic but still learning, Orville and Wilbur made over a thousand flights in it. This time, they didn't simply glide down over the sand

Right: The Wrights made over a thousand flights in Glider No. 3. This aircraft had a better gliding angle than previous models and they had changed the way the controls were operated, but it still had potentially dangerous control problems. They found that if a dropping wing were not corrected enough the wing warping would not lift it. Instead, the aircraft skewered itself into the ground—"well digging" as they called it. Their vertical, fixed fins seemed only to add to the problem—tipping the nose down into the ground when the wings were tilted. Their answer was to replace the fixed fins with movable rudders to counteract the turning movement of the tail. This was successfully achieved and the Wrights now knew they were ready to install an engine.

hills. They soared high, sometimes higher than the point of takeoff. Potentially dangerous control glitches were detected then solved by trial and error as the hard-headed twosome were buoyed by their positive results. By the end of the flying season, the Wright boys were sufficiently confident in their development that they could move with renewed assurance to the next stage. They installed an engine and in doing so, fulfilled their overwhelming dream of powered flight.

Satisfied with the performance of Glider No. 3, sure that with their efforts they had developed an effective system of controlling an airplane in flight, the brothers headed back to Dayton to get moving on the next hurdle—to perfect a powered flying machine. They started the search for a suitable power plant. Unable to find an engine to meet their requirements, they decided to build their own. The result was a simple four-cylinder petrol engine, designed by

Left: The Wright brothers experienced some trials and tribulations in Glider No. 3 on the way to solving the problems of powered flight.

them, and made by Charlie Taylor—a mechanic employed in the Wrights' bicycle workshop. It developed 12 horsepower, and it was linked by chain to two pusher propellers.

Propellers were a problem in themselves. Some inventions had made flat, paddle-shaped blades, while others had flat, twisted blades to achieve more thrust. The brothers Wright were the first to realize that the propeller was really a wing moving on a spiral course, and should have an airfoil shape just like a wing. They came to appreciate that the shape and angle of the airfoil would need to vary according to its distance from the hub, because all points along the propeller would be moving at different speeds along different spirals. After days of complex calculations, they finally produced two beautifully carved specimens from laminated spruce wood, capable of generating better power from their engine.

On December 14, 1903, they were back in Kitty Hawk with their first flying machine. It was named *Flyer*. It was a flimsy biplane, covered with muslin, with a wingspan of 40 feet (12 meters). The little engine was fastened to the lower wing beside the pilot. At the rear were two movable rudders, and the movable front elevator was a small biplane structure. To save weight, the plane had no undercarriage. Instead, the Wrights laid out a monorail with a small carriage upon which the *Flyer* rested ready for takeoff.

There were a few setbacks, a lot of tension, and a number of last minute adjustments, but at last they were ready for their first attempt to fly up from the cold, windswept sand hills. The brothers tossed a coin—Wilbur won. He climbed aboard and warmed up the engine. The wire restraint was released and, with Orville steadying the wing tip, the *Flyer* moved slowly along the rail. It gained speed, and after traveling about 40 feet (12 meters), Wilbur lifted it off the rail carriage. She was airborne under her own power—but

not for long. The *Flyer* climbed only a few feet before Wilbur lost his grip of the control. It stalled and hit the ground, damaging the wing.

On December 17, three days later, the Wrights had the *Flyer* repaired and ready to go again. This time the honor was Orville's. He released the wire that held the aircraft to the monorail and the *Flyer* ran along the track before taking off. Orville kept her airborne for about 12 seconds, though it was still rather up and down because of the

unbalanced elevator control. But she flew! The Wright brothers knew that they had won. With each successive flight, they gained more skill and confidence until, on the fourth attempt on that memorable day, Wilbur stayed airborne for 59 seconds, and covered a distance of 582 feet (177.5 meters).

The Wright brothers had made the first controlled, sustained, powered flight in a heavier-than-air machine. It is hard to find an equivalent event in the human story.

After the first attempt to fly under power that ended with a damaged wing, the Wright brothers returned to Kitty Hawk with the repaired Flyer on December 17, 1903. This time, they achieved their goal. From the first short, but successful flight with Orville at the controls, Wilbur followed and three flights later, he was air-borne for nearly a minute, flying a distance equal to about twice the wingspan of a modern jumbo jet. The Wright brothers knew they had achieved their dream. It was a pivotal day in the human conquest of the air.

ALBERTO SANTOS-DUMONT

A FRENCH CONNECTION

Alberto Santos-Dumont brought a lively, Brazilian beat to Paris, capturing the hearts of even the most cynical of Parisians. He was almost impossible to ignore. A diminutive Brazilian expatriate, he first gained their attention in the early 1900s through his daring aerial exploits over the city in his dirigible airships. Alberto's sixth airship, which flew

from Saint Cloud to the Eiffel Tower and back, won him a handsome prize. When the news of the Wright brothers' first flight was flashed to Europe in 1903, it was generally greeted with disbelief and skepticism. Among the serious unbelievers was Santos-Dumont, who was convinced that he would be the first to make a successful flight in a powered airplane.

He had based his aircraft designs on the principle of the Hargrave box kite. He knew of the completely different approach the Wright brothers had taken with their aircraft, but Alberto believed that he knew better. His latest flying machine, No. 14, had quite a strange back-to-front appearance, looking—as some wit later remarked—"like a set of box kites flying in close formation."

A forward mounted box kite gave directional and fore-and-aft control. Lateral stability was achieved by giving the aft set of kites dihedral, or a pronounced upward tilt. The wings had no airfoil section other than that resulting from the natural ballooning effect of the air stream passing over it—in short, like a box kite.

To test his unique, ungainly-looking craft, Alberto hung it under one of his airships. As the aircraft did not perform to his expectations, he unhooked it and with a nonchalance which typified his daring airship flights, decided to fly it alone and unaided.

Right: Alberto Santos-Dumont, who made Europe's first flight in a powered, heavier-than-air machine.

Left: In 1901 Alberto Santos-Dumont captured the hearts of the Parisians, as well as a 100,000-franc prize, by flying his little dirigible airship around the Eiffel Tower.

Above: It wasn't just the air enthusiasts' love of flying that gave France the lead in aviation. The French government set out to make France preeminent in the new field of heavier-than-air flight in an effort to combat the perceived growing militancy of Germany and the success of Count Zeppelin's massive airships. Perceptive Frenchmen, such as Captain Ferber suspected rightly that the Zeppelins would be used as bombing machines.

Opposite page: In 1906 Santos-Dumont's 14bis made the first flight of a powered airplane in Europe. His engine drove a pusher propeller, which, unlike that of the Wright brothers' engine, was really little more than a crude paddle. The influence of Hargrave's box kite pedigree is also very strong.

In 1906, in front of a small crowd of aficionados in Paris's Bois de Boulogne, Santos-Dumont stepped into his wicker cockpit and started his engine. With great enthusiasm he took off in splendid flight a few feet above the ground. After covering a couple of hundred feet, he slewed off-line and landed to the spontaneous applause of the watching crowd. Alberto Santos-Dumont, with the craft he called *14bis*, had made Europe's first-ever flight in a powered, heavier-than-air machine. There never was another aircraft that looked like the *14bis* but that memorable flight in the Bois de Boulogne stirred France into a flurry of activity that was to give her the lead in world aviation until the end of World War I.

Santos-Dumont designed and built more aircraft after his machine, *14bis*, but later became horrified by the use of military airplanes in World War I. At the end of the war, this man who had thrilled the people of Paris with his inventions and spirit of adventure, became more and more depressed about the future of the world. Eventually, he returned to his homeland Brazil and on July 23, 1932 took his own life.

CLAUDIUS DORNIER

ZEPPELINS TO VTOLS, FLYING BOATS TO JETS

As a young man training to be an architect, Claudius Dornier had a sudden flash of inspiration when he stood by Lake Constance in 1900. He was there to witness the history-making first flight of the mighty, gas-filled dirigible, conceived and built by Count Ferdinand Graf von Zeppelin. It was a momentous and thrilling moment, raising hopes and fears for the future of flight. Apart from an awesome demonstration of German ambition and might, the Zeppelin had a profound effect on young Dornier. He decided to drop architecture and turned enthusiastically to the study of engineering.

As soon as he graduated, Claudius headed for Friedrickshafen, where his dream machine, the Zeppelin, was built. Dornier applied to join the Zeppelin company and was elated when he was accepted, being employed to help build the huge passenger-carrying dirigibles. Dornier proved to be of exceptional value to the Zeppelin company.

He quickly devised a method of more effectively joining metal spars in the complex web of girders that held the great gasbags within the airship—a method that also reduced metal fatigue and allowed the construction of even larger airships. Because of his knowledge of the behaviors of metals—a subject he had found particularly absorbing—he was appointed director of testing. One of the most successful passenger airships to come out of the cathedral-sized sheds at Friedrickshafen was the Dornier-designed *Viktoria Luise*. She was to carry over 8,000 passengers in nearly 400 flights between 1909 and when World War I broke out in 1914.

By 1914, Claudius had embarked on designing his first airplane. He chose to build a flying boat, made entirely of metal. The prototype was to fly from Lake Constance—where Dornier had watched the first Zeppelin flight—but a sudden storm destroyed the craft before it could be trialled. The RS II, the second prototype, did fly, and was followed by an all-metal monoplane, the RS III. This was a radical-

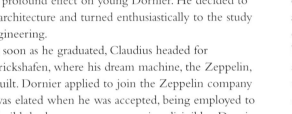

The RS III of 1916 showed Claudius Dornier's great lateral thinking in arranging significant parts of the airframe to ride clear of spray on takeoff and landing. The end result was hardly beautiful, but the RS III performed well with its four 245-horsepower Maybach engines mounted in tandem between the hull and the overhead tail boom.

looking machine with four engines, but mounted in tandem, with two propellers pushing and two pulling. The engines were housed in dual pods between the hull and the overhead wing, which was high above any damaging spray created during takeoff. This unorthodox and ungainly-looking aircraft proved to be an important stepping stone to Dornier's future.

By now, World War I had started making demands on the Zeppelin company. All airships including the *Viktoria Luise* were called into war service. They were converted for military reconnaissance and bombing operations. The worst fears of other European nations became a nightmare when these huge, menacing machines began night-bombing sorties.

After 1918, Dornier suffered along with the Fatherland. The Treaty of Versailles banned production of planes in Germany so he moved to Italy, eventually setting up in Marina da Pisa, where he started designing an entirely new airplane—a triumph indeed. Claudius named his sensational new flying boat the Wal, meaning "whale." It proved to be the most successful airplane ever designed up to that time and long after.

The Wal was a high-winged metal monoplane with two "push-me-pull-you" engines mounted in tandem above the wing. Being made of metal she was immensely strong and could handle rough conditions at sea. Dornier introduced sponsons—stub-winglets, which protruded from the sides of the hull at the waterline to keep it laterally stable on the

Left: The Dornier RS I of 1913, a large, all-metal flying boat, was Claudius Dornier's first design for an airplane. No doubt, after designing huge airships, Dornier didn't regard it as particularly big. This RS I was wrecked on the slipway in a gale, so a second craft was constructed.

Right: Amundsen and his crew transfer his polar expedition supplies to a second Dornier Wal. The first aircraft was holed after hitting an ice floe when it landed 150 miles (241.5 kilometers) short of the North Pole.

water. These were instead of the wingtip floats used on other machines, which could break off in a heavy sea—something which happened to a Curtiss flying boat on the first Atlantic flight in 1919. Dornier's sponsors gave enormous strength to the center section of the hull while providing excellent stability on the water.

Dornier's Wal was first flown in 1922 and the orders started pouring in. Many variations were made, including a four-engined Superwal. In all, about 300 of these superb machines were built and sold all over the world—both in commercial and military configurations. One of the purchasers of the Dornier Wal was the famed Norwegian explorer, Roald Amundsen. He bought two of them, and in a heroic Arctic flight, one of his Wals saved his life and the lives of all in his team.

Claudius Dornier's financial stability was assured. The Wal created many world records, and Amundsen's heartfelt testimonial after his North Pole attempt, "I owe my life to Dornier!", all helped to cement the reputation and success of the Dornier marque.

Amundsen was attracted to the Earth's poles, North and South. All his life they were magnets that drew him in. While the Wright brothers were still flying their kites, Amundsen was planning to become the first seaman to navigate the Northwest Passage. In 1909 he was preparing to go to the North Pole, but American Robert Peary beat him to it. Frustrated, he sailed for the Antarctic, intending to be the first person to reach the South Pole. With four men, sleds, and dogs, Amundsen made it, beating the doomed British expedition led by John Falcon Scott. The sympathetic note he left for the Brits at the South Pole was found when the bodies of Scott and his companions were recovered.

Roald Amundsen

In 1925 Roald Amundsen decided to strive for another first—to reach the North Pole by air. With two Dornier Wal flying boats, Roald and his expedition flew from Spitzbergen, Norway. It was to become an epic journey of endurance. When landing 150 miles (241.5 kilometers) short of the Pole, one of the Wals was holed by an ice floe. The crew struggled to transfer equipment and supplies to the second flying boat. Heroic efforts were needed to build a snow runway suitable for the undamaged plane's takeoff.

Overloaded, with two crews on board, the pilot showed superb airmanship to get airborne. The splendid, reliable Wal demonstrated its powers by making the long, perilous flight back to Spitzbergen.

Unfazed, Amundsen tried again, this time recruiting Italian explorer Umberto Nobile, and using his gas-filled dirigible to achieve his goal. On May 12, 1926, they flew serenely over the North Pole, becoming the first team to cross it in a dirigible. But three days earlier, on May 9, American Admiral Richard F. Byrd, with pilot Floyd Bennett, had beaten them to it, flying over the Pole in a Fokker triplane. In 1928, just two years later, as a cruel coincidence, Amundsen lost his life in a flying-boat crash while attempting an air rescue of his fellow explorer, Umberto Nobile. Nobile's dirigible had floundered while he was flying— this time on his own—over the Arctic wastes.

Claudius Dornier

By 1927, the Allied ban on the production of aircraft in Germany was lifted. Dornier moved his factory back to his homeland Alterheim, beside Lake Constance, where he was first inspired. Here he would oversee the flight of his next airborne miracle.

Dornier believed the way to link continents by air was via flying boats. He argued that flying boats would be able to use existing port facilities without requiring new, sophisticated airfields big enough to accept huge land planes weighed down with passengers and freight. Moreover, existing land planes—usually biplanes—simply didn't have the range or carrying power to make long transocean flight economically viable.

Other exponents were obviously coming to the same conclusion. Encouraged and financed by Juan Trippe of Pan American Airways, Igor Sikorsky had begun, in America, to design a series of original and successful flying boats, which were proving that the idea was feasible and practical. With the success of his Wal series, Dornier started planning a scaled-up metal flying boat, which he hoped would be an ideal solution—the aircraft of the future. He was chiefly concerned with whether he would find engines powerful enough to lift his flying boat off the water. He set about designing and building the largest commercial flying boat of the time.

He called the flying boat the Dornier X and it was a colossus. By comparison with the strutted and wire-braced biplanes of the day, it looked deceptively simple. It was an enormous monoplane with a conventional fin and rudder at the end of a long hull. Like the Wal, it was fitted with sponsons rather than wingtip floats. Above the massive wing, Dornier fitted 12 engines, mounted in the preferred Dornier style of six tandem pairs. The power plants were controlled and monitored by an engineer seated in his own control room behind the two pilots in their fully enclosed flight deck. The pilots had no throttles, instead—as on an ocean liner—when the captain called for the power he needed the engineer and his assistant pulled the levers.

With its enormous proportions the huge wing provided relatively light wing loading, which meant that once aloft, the plane would be easy to handle without the flightiness

and surprises of even modern airplanes. So there on Lake Constance, in 1929, Claudius Dornier watched his latest brainchild taxi out for its trials. Imagine the scene: the huge silver machine bigger than any flying boat ever built, with its myriad whirling, flickering propeller blades catching the light; the engineer runs up each engine separately, checking temperatures, oil pressure, engine revolutions, and ticking off other technical data, then gives the thumbs-up to the pilot for takeoff; once properly cleared, the pilot calls for full power and behind him the engineer advances the 12 throttle levers. The two pilots keep the mighty craft straight and level with their big steering wheels and rudder pedals. The Do. X, with its wingspan of 157 feet (47.9 meters) and 12 engines roaring in unison, increases its speed, building a wake of foam from her hull.

On the shore, with racing heart, Dornier held his breath as the captain eased firmly back on the control column and the big machine lifted, then gracefully climbed away from the water at about 80–90 miles (128–144 kilometers) per hour, the engines thrumming like a formation of bombers. For Dornier, that successful takeoff was the crowning moment of his life.

It must be said that the Do. X was neither a beauty to the eye nor a boon to her maintenance crews. Her robust lines proclaimed her Germanic strength and purpose, but reliability was another matter. From the start, the Do. X was plagued by problems—not surprising perhaps as it had 12 power plants to maintain. Despite critical press reviews that followed her whenever she took to the air, Dornier dispatched the Do. X on a world tour in 1931. She was designed to carry about 70 passengers but she could cram in up to 100

or more. With a full load, she set out on a luxury demonstration tour from Amsterdam to South America and back. The trip turned out to be 10 months of technical trouble.

Dornier's brave technology proved to be a step ahead of practicality. Nevertheless, to Germany it was like a repeat of the golden days of the Zeppelins. The big flying boat became a symbol of leadership for a country stirring itself to again become the most powerful nation in Europe. While it would be nearly 10 years before large flying boats would cross big oceans with regularity or reliability, in the early thirties the Do. X was a flying aerial banner for Germany which proclaimed, "We're back!".

At the same time, Germany was making great strides with smaller flying boats. Along with Dornier's Wal, other makers—Junkers, Blohm and Voss, and Heinkel—were providing mail links from Europe to South America and Africa. German ships, anchored off the coast of Brazil and Africa to provide basic refueling facilities for the aircraft, were equipped with large catapults. It was an ingenious way to thrust flying boats, carrying heavy loads they could never lift off the water under their own power, into the air. In 1938, Dornier's Wal set one of its many records. Catapulted from a ship anchored off England's Devon coast, the Wal flew from Britain to Brazil nonstop.

LAKE CONSTANCE TO RIO DE JANERIO FLIGHT, 1931

Calshot · Amsterdam
Bordeaux · Lake Constance
A Coruña · Santander
Lisbon

North Atlantic Ocean

Las Palmas

Cape Verde Islands · Buraque

Natal

South Atlantic Ocean

Rio de Janeiro

Opposite page: The huge Do. X makes a spectacular takeoff in a fresh breeze before making her trouble-plagued flight from Amsterdam to Rio de Janiero in 1931. Even though the Do. X was fitted with new, more powerful engines for this historic transocean epic, the great machine could barely climb to more than a few feet above the ocean for the 12 hours of the momentous 1,300-mile (2,093-kilometer) flight from the Cape Verde Islands to Natal.

Below: Originally designed as an airliner, the Do. 17 was considered too cramped for passenger use because of its small diameter fuselage. The German Air Ministry immediately ordered it as a high-speed bomber because it was faster than fighter aircraft of the day. It was first blooded in 1937 during the Spanish Civil War and later in the Battle of Britain, when it was dubbed The Flying Pencil because of its slim fuselage. It was greatly modified to become the Do. 215, then the Do. 217, the latter becoming a very effective medium bomber and night fighter.

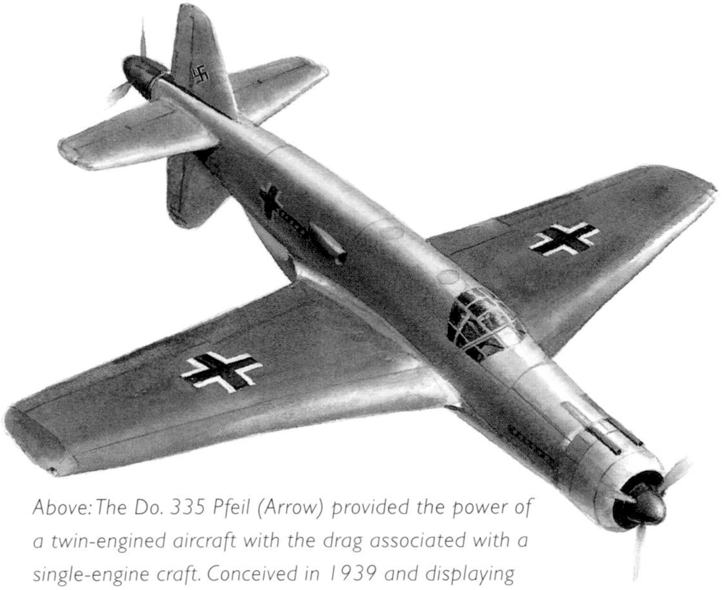

Above: The Do. 335 Pfeil (Arrow) provided the power of a twin-engined aircraft with the drag associated with a single-engine craft. Conceived in 1939 and displaying Dornier's penchant for "push-me-pull-you" engine installations, it first flew in 1943. Its superb performance was the best of any piston-engined fighter of World War II. Its maximum speed was 477 miles (767 kilometers) per hour and it was the first production aircraft ever fitted with an ejector seat.

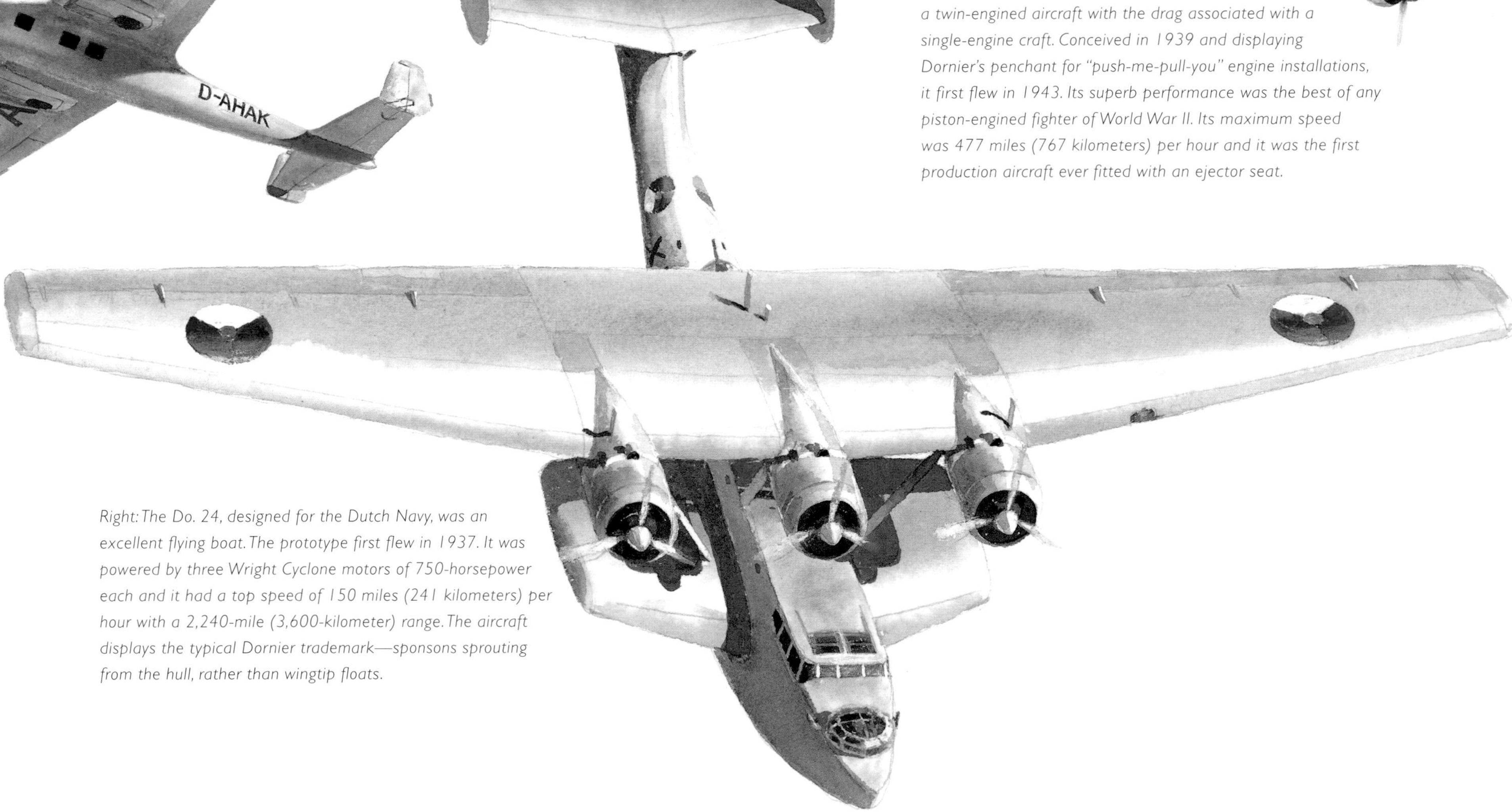

Right: The Do. 24, designed for the Dutch Navy, was an excellent flying boat. The prototype first flew in 1937. It was powered by three Wright Cyclone motors of 750-horsepower each and it had a top speed of 150 miles (241 kilometers) per hour with a 2,240-mile (3,600-kilometer) range. The aircraft displays the typical Dornier trademark—sponsons sprouting from the hull, rather than wingtip floats.

With the rise of the Nazi Party in Germany and knowing Dornier's towering reputation in the field of aviation, it is not surprising that he played an important role in the design and the development of German air power. His exact relationship with the Nazi Party is not known although it is suspected that, like many others of the older generation, he was more a patriot than a Nazi.

Quite early, when the military was covertly building its armed strength, Dornier submitted a streamlined design for a fast civil airliner to Lufthansa. It was rejected because it was too cramped. But the Air Ministry saw potential in the slim machine and immediately ordered its production in the form of a very efficient, twin-engined bomber. Compared to the machines being produced by France and Britain at the time, the Do. 17—dubbed *The Flying Pencil*—was a very advanced aircraft. Its design became even better when it was modified to become the Do. 217 during World War II.

Throughout the rearmament period, Dornier's company produced some excellent military machines. His love affair with flying boats continued when the three-engined Do. 24 appeared, described by pilots as the best of all boats to fly. In 1942, Dornier changed direction and started work on a remarkably fast, twin-engined fighter, which revived his fascination with the in-tandem engine configuration. His unique Do. 335 contained two powerful engines in the one fuselage, with propellers front and rear. Though it looked dangerous, it was safer to fly than the jet and rocket fighters being turned out by Messerschmitt. Called the Dornier Pfeil, meaning "arrow," it was produced too late in the war to become operational in large numbers.

With the end of World War II in 1945, Dornier faced a re-run of his 1918 downfall. Once again on the losing side, along with his German rival Willy Messerschmitt, Dornier was sentenced to two years' jail as a war criminal. Once released and while restrained from rebuilding his aircraft business in Germany, Claudius again looked for refuge in a sympathetic country. Spain welcomed him, so he opened a

The Do. 31-E-I VSTOL passenger transport was powered by two banks of Rolls-Royce lift jets, mounted in pods at the wingtips, and by two Bristol Siddeley Pegasus vectored thrust jets, conventionally mounted under the high wing. The Do. 31 made many successful flights and could fly at 460 miles (740 kilometers) per hour.

small Dornier factory there to produce light aircraft. In 1955, when the ban on German aircraft production was lifted, again repeating his earlier life, he returned to the country of his birth. Now 71 years old, with a factory at Munich, he began producing the Dornier 27—a light, general-purpose transport plane—before turning his mind to the challenge of short takeoff and landing aircraft.

In Europe and America huge sums of money were being invested in the development of both piston-engined and jet-engined VTOL (vertical takeoff and landing) machines. Dornier threw his hat into the ring with the Do. 31 VSTOL (vertical short takeoff and landing) machine. The intention behind this flurry of activity was to try to overcome the massive landuse demands, and the vast expense of huge airfields that normal jet airline operations used. As well, designers were trying to find ways to minimize the noise factor—a major source of irritation and indignation in main population centers. Once again, Claudius demonstrated his vivid conceptual thinking and imaginative answers to aviation problems. His innovative Do. 31 was the only

passenger-carrying aircraft that could successfully make the transition from vertical takeoff to horizontal flight. But though it worked and was well tested and proved, there were no takers. The aircraft terrified passengers as well as the airline executives who had to make the decisions.

Yet Dornier continually produced interesting solutions to unusual problems during the postwar years, mostly with smaller aircraft. He remained head of his company almost to his death at the age of 85 in Zug, Switzerland, in 1969. Eventually, in 1996, control of the Dornier company passed to the American Fairchild company, which bought 80 percent of the shares.

Although twice caught on the defeated side in two major wars, Dornier was a brilliantly creative designer and a most gifted man. He was also one of the rare few who, born in the nineteenth century, helped propel the world to move from slow, cumbersome, gas-filled dirigibles to sleek, fast, jet airliners—a very rare and inspiring talent.

IGOR IVANOVITCH SIKORSKY

THE TURN OF THE SCREW

Igor Ivanovitch Sikorsky was born in Kiev, Ukraine, in 1889. He was educated at the Russian Naval College at St. Petersburg, then in Kiev and Paris. In 1913, at the age of 24, while the threatening clouds of the great European war were beginning to gather, Igor designed and started to build the world's first four-engined aircraft.

The S-22, a massive biplane powered by four 100-horse-power motors, took to the air for a successful flight in January 1914. There were openings each side of the fuselage to allow mechanics to check the engines while the plane was flying, and behind the pilot's enclosed cockpit was a large passenger cabin with windows, and a smaller private cabin and washroom. In June 1914, Sikorsky flew a record-breaking 1,600-mile (2,576-kilometer) round trip from St. Petersburg to Kiev with four stops in the plane he named *Ilya Mourometz* after a tenth-century Russian folk hero who rode a winged charger.

Sikorsky's historic achievement was overshadowed by the assassination of Austrian Archduke Franz Ferdinand at Sarajevo on the eighteenth day of the same month—the killing which flared into the start of World War I. But Igor's landmark flight resulted in the Russian Army ordering the immediate construction of 10 of his S-22 planes. In World War I, 80 of the aircraft were produced, some as bombers and some as observation planes at the front line.

In 1919, Igor Sikorsky fled the political turmoil which was rending Russia and arrived in the United States on March 30. Inspired by the successes of Thomas Edison and Henry Ford he had great plans. His passport of the times shows he entered New York "to construct aircraft." It was not to be. Following World War I there was a glut of airplanes on the American market and Igor's hopes were dashed when he was told that aviation was a dying industry and his skills would not be required.

Left: Igor Sikorsky flew his first successful airplane, the S-2, in 1910 and went on to make 50 flights in this model. The previous version, the S-1, failed to fly because its 15-horsepower Anzani engine was not powerful enough, unlike the S-2, which had a 25-horsepower engine.

Below: There were many versions of Igor Sikorsky's Ilya Mourometz 113-foot (34.5-meter) wingspan bomber. Some aircraft were outfitted with seven machine guns; one version had an additional 2-inch (50-millimeter) quick-firing cannon. They carried an accurate bomb sight, and a typical bomb load would have been ten 35-pound (15.9-kilogram) bombs, which were delivered by lobbing them over the side. A variety of different engine types were fitted in many different ways—Sunbeam, Mercedes, Renault, and Argus engines were predominant—and normally a crew of seven was needed to operate the giant machine. With the 1917 revolution, production of this amazingly advanced aircraft ceased.

For nearly three years Sikorsky struggled to support himself, teaching mathematics, then astronomy, and aviation theory to immigrants. But his drive and creativity remained strong. In March 1923, just over four years after his arrival in the U.S.A., he set up the Sikorsky Engineering Company at Long Island N.Y., and started to build his newly designed S-29A. Things were looking up for this determined player.

Sikorsky's first commercial success was a twin-engined plane, the S-38. It was an amphibious machine, able to take off from land or water and with a crew of two, could carry nine passengers with baggage. It had a top speed of 130 miles (209 kilometers) per hour, and could fly on one engine. A prototype flew in July 1928, and within two months of official performance data being published, Igor had orders for the first series of 10 aircraft. Before long the S-38s were operating throughout the world. They pioneered executive travel, and established the first regular airmail and passenger air routes. The Sikorsky Aviation Corporation was born.

Above: The Sikorsky Type S-29A, 1923

Above: 1928 saw the first in a line of successful Sikorsky amphibian flying-boats, the S-38. Pan American Airways used this type, with its Curtiss-style hull and twin-boom layout, to open up links with Latin America. Charles Lindbergh made the inaugural flight to Panama, which took six hours, carrying two crew and eight passengers. The S-38 had a maximum speed of about 130 miles (209 kilometers) per hour.

Below: The Sikorsky Type S-40 was a 40-seat flying boat, designed by Sikorsky in 1931 specifically for Pan American Airways. In 1934 Sikorsky designed his S-42 flying boat for Pan American's long-distance ocean routes, particularly those in the Pacific. Individual stages on the route were often 1,200 miles (1,920 kilometers), the longest being 2,410 miles (3,856 kilometers). All flights were in daylight. The development of these transocean air routes was one of the most far-reaching and magnificent achievements in aviation history.

Igor hadn't finished yet. After designing flying boats for the emerging Pan American Airways, he then set about planning and building America's first practical helicopter. Sikorsky had started to design helicopters when he was 19 years old, but it was the successful work of Don Juan de la Cierva in producing his popular C-30 Autogiro in England in the 1930s that was said to have inspired Sikorsky to return to the challenge of designing a practical helicopter.

He would have been aware of the success of the Fa-61 in Germany. Dr. Heinrich Focke's model Focke Achgelis Fa-61, the first successful helicopter, flew in 1937 and it created height, speed, and distance records. Mass production of a military version was curtailed by the defeat of Hitler's Germany after World War II and the U.S.A. took the lead in helicopter design. The Focke design was not as maneuverable or as flexible in operation as Sikorsky's model.

The Focke Achgelis Fa-61, 1937

A 1930s Cierva C-30 Autogiro, reconditioned after World War II

Right: Igor Sikorsky built his first helicopter in 1909. It was too heavy to fly, as was his second, so he put his ideas on hold until the 1930s.

Sikorsky's helicopter design featured the first perfected combination of single main rotor and tail rotor, and it took to the air—although tethered to the ground—on September 14, 1939. After further testing and finessing, Sikorsky free-flew it in May 1940. Then, a year later, he piloted his VS-300 helicopter to achieve a world endurance record of 1 hour, 32 minutes, and 26 seconds. There were still many changes to be made before the VS-300A took to the air in its 1942 configuration featuring its single main lifting rotor, with full cyclic-pitch to control both roll and pitch, and a single tail rotor for directional control and anti-torque. This machine could be controlled very precisely.

Once again Sikorsky's achievement was overshadowed. The day before the celebratory flight of the perfected helicopter on December 8, 1941, the surprise attack on Pearl Harbor devastated the American fleet and the nation. Nevertheless, the development of the VS-300 led to the design and production of the Sikorsky VS-316 (R-4), the model which pioneered the world's helicopter industry. In a tribute to his hero, Sikorsky presented the original VS-300 to Henry Ford's Edison Museum in 1943. Igor Sikorsky died in 1972 at the age of 82, leaving a name much revered in the history of aviation.

I always believed that the helicopter would be an outstanding vehicle for life-saving missions.

FROM A LETTER DICTATED BY SIKORSKY AT AGE 82, THE DAY BEFORE HE DIED

Above: The VS-300 provided the basis for the Sikorsky R-4, which was the first military helicopter produced in the U.S.A. The R-4 was virtually the same as the VS-300 but the R-4's fuselage was redesigned to carry a crew of two as well as rescue facilities. It was produced in some numbers to serve with the Allied Forces in World War II, setting the standard for future helicopter design.

Right: The great Igor Sikorsky lived a long and creative life. He was an exceptional pilot as well as a highly inventive designer. He reportedly said wryly, that a designer should always be the test pilot of his own planes because then one gets only good designers!

Left: One of Sikorsky's early prototype helicopters was the VS-300A. By the time this machine appeared in 1942, control problems had been solved so it could be flown very precisely.

Opposite page: The S-61 Sea King was delivered to the U.S. Navy in 1961 and is a direct descendant of the famous R-4. It demonstrates how far helicopter technology has advanced in 20 years since the first flight of the VS-300.

The Sea King is a very sophisticated, all-weather, amphibious helicopter for anti-submarine warfare, also used for search and rescue. It features a boatlike hull with two small pods, which give additional stability and allow the craft to alight on water.

In Vietnam, the S-61R Jolly Green Giant version performed many dangerous, long-range rescues of downed airmen. The President of the United States is often seen alighting from a Sea King on the lawn at The White House, courtesy of the Executive Flight Detachment in Washington.

The Sikorsky Sea King made an amazing long-distance rescue while serving with the British commandos in the 1991 Gulf War, landing at night in the middle of a tank battle to rescue two wounded soldiers. The pilot, Lt. Peter Nelson of the Australian Navy, was awarded the Air Force Cross by the British Royal Air Force for his astonishing feat of airmanship. He had flown at night, low down, through a sandstorm, most of the way in zero visibility.

FRANCESCO DE PINEDO

THE ITALIAN MARQUESS WHO EMULATED MARCO POLO

Francesco de Pinedo, a young marquess and Italian Air Force officer, had fought with distinction as a pilot in World War I. When the war was over, Francesco turned his thoughts toward peace. He became deeply interested in, and began to espouse, the cause of the flying boat, arguing that it had the potential to fly and alight on water, where no land-based aircraft could dare go.

By the early 1920s de Pinedo was Chief Staff Officer in the Italian Regia Aeronautica, and Vice Commandant of an air squadron. People in high places listened carefully to what the marquess had to say. He had demonstrated the value of his beloved flying boat by taking a couple of newsworthy flights— one was a long-distance haul from the Italian city of Brindisi to Constantinople (now Istanbul) in Turkey. By 1925, with a paper delivered to The Royal Aeronautical Society in London and an article published in the *National Geographic* magazine, de Pinedo was becoming Italy's leading authority on aeronautical matters, particularly in relation to flying boats and amphibious craft. He argued with great passion that not only could the craft operate from landing fields, but they could also set down on sea, rivers, and lakes. This, he claimed, would connect flight to areas bereft of suitable landing fields. According to de Pinedo, flying boats would open up long-distance air transportation to the world. Moreover, the world's major cities were all centered around seaports or major rivers. In 1925, with the courage of his convictions, de Pinedo set out to prove his vision from the cockpit by taking an extended flight halfway around the world, through three continents, to Asia and back.

At 35, by then a seasoned leader, Francesco arranged for a Savoia-Marchetti S 16ter flying boat with an open cockpit— modified from a 1923 five-seater model from Regia Aeronautica—to carry him as pilot, with his chosen mechanic,

Ernesto Campagnelli. The wooden fuselage was converted to carry freight, water and food supplies, timber and canvas for running repairs, and a compact, portable workshop for any carpentry or mechanical work that might be needed on the way. He named the craft *Gennariello*.

On April 20, 1925, the marquess from Naples, with Campagnelli sitting proudly beside him, took off from Sesto Callende in Northern Italy for their first hop to Brindisi. They spent a couple of days in Brindisi fixing faults and rearranging the load to improve the aircraft's handling. Then they were really on their way, crossing the Adriatic and Aegean seas to Leros in Greece, then on to Turkey, Iraq, the Persian Gulf, and India. Along the way they fixed a damaged float and a leaking oil tank, but generally, the little flying boat performed superbly well. In India, they flew into strong winds, then monsoon rains, which enveloped them as they flew on to Burma (now Myanmar). At Rangoon they needed to repair the engine, and for three days worked in a constant downpour before flying to Siam (now Thailand) where de Pinedo reported a further delay: "tremendous storms and heavy rains prevented us from getting along as quickly as I had hoped."

In Batavia, Java (now Jakarta, Indonesia), they overhauled the engine meticulously, in preparation for their next destination

Above: Francesco de Pinedo was a quintessential Italian aristocrat. A marquess, as was his father before him, de Pinedo first served in the Italian Navy where he developed his love of the sea and ships. In 1917, during World War I, he transferred to the Corpo Aeronautico Militaire where he won distinction as one of those daring young men in their flying machines. In times of peace, as a pilot and navigator he had few equals, and rightfully deserves his place as one of the greatest aviators of the twentieth century.

I suppose we shall soon travel by air vessels ... and at length find our way to the moon.

LORD BYRON, 1882

Left: The Savoia S 16ter of Francesco de Pinedo and his mechanic Campagnelli at a halfway point in what was to be, in 1925, the longest air journey in history. The wooden flying boat is flying near Mount Fuji, Japan, ready to return across uncharted country to Rome. Pinedo's extraordinary achievement was only equaled by the staying power of his rugged aircraft.

The Savoia S 16ter had a wingspan of 50 feet (15.24 meters) and was only 32 feet (9.75 meters) long. The standard S 16ter power plant was replaced with a more powerful 400-horsepower Lorraine Dietrich engine. The biplane's wings were constructed of wood and covered with doped fabric. De Pinedo also designed a jib sail that could be rigged, as well as a large rudder in case they were forced into the sea through engine failure. The flying boat, which de Pinedo named Gennariello, had a top speed of about 120 miles (193 kilometers) per hour and a cruising speed of 93 miles (149.6 kilometers) per hour. This gave her a range of 850 miles (1,367 kilometers). With a little coaxing she could fly at a ceiling of 9,800 feet (2,987 meters).

41

after leaving Timor, which was the long haul of 550 miles (885 kilometers) across open sea to Australia. Five weeks and two days after leaving Italy, the arrival of the sturdy little flying boat brought a surprise to the isolated pearling port of Broome on the northwest coast of Western Australia.

In easy hops, the trusty Savoia flew along the coastline of the great, sprawling, island continent, winding up in the city of Melbourne, where de Pinedo planned to overhaul his flying boat with supplies and spare parts he had had sent to Melbourne ahead of him. In Melbourne the Royal Australian Air Force offered de Pinedo and Campagnelli the use of a seaplane hangar at Point Cook, the R.A.A.F.'s number one flying training school. With help from their engineers, the engine was stripped down, examined, and re-built, needing only minor reseating for one valve. The aircraft itself was also tended, demonstrating it had suffered little damage, with very few minor replacements necessary. On July 10, 1925, the Savoia was rolled out in its reconditioned glory, with the addition of a R.A.A.F. crest and "Point Cook, Melbourne" written on both sides of her bow. De Pinedo

was delighted. He had been welcomed to Melbourne by crowds of over 30,000 people when he first arrived. He stayed for five weeks and later proclaimed: "Among all the cities I visited during my journey, it is the one to which I have great longing to return."

On they went, first to Sydney, where they arrived in time to welcome battleships, cruisers, and destroyers of the visiting American fleet with a one-plane flyby. The marquess then planned to head for Tokyo, a course never before attempted by any aircraft. The Savoia flew in stages up the north coast of Queensland to Thursday Island and Dutch New Guinea before flying over long 500-mile (804-kilometer) ocean stretches to Manila in the Philippines. From North Luzon Island they flew to Formosa, on to Shanghai, China, then to Korea and finally Tokyo, arriving in a heavy storm on September 26, 1925.

In Tokyo, de Pinedo fitted a new engine before heading for home, and replaced the lower starboard wing, which had taken

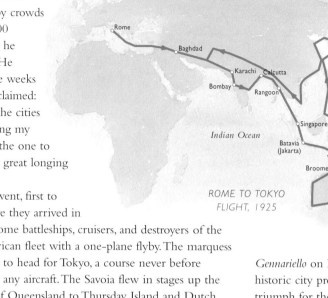

ROME TO TOKYO
FLIGHT, 1925

some hard knocks on the 52 days and 90 flying hours racked up since the flying boat had left Sydney. On the homeward legs, the *Gennariello* was to fly back across China to Hong Kong, Indo China, Siam (now Thailand), Burma (now Myanmar), India, the Persian Gulf, Iraq, and back to Pinedo's beloved Italy, to Naples where he received a hero's welcome. But it was on November 7, 1925, when he and Campangnelli landed the well-traveled *Gennariello* on Rome's Tiber River, that the citizens of that historic city provided a traditional Roman procession of triumph for the dauntless pair. Thousands upon thousands lined the bridges and streets. An ambitious, up-and-coming, political strongman Signor Mussolini, Premier of Italy's coalition government, gave them an official welcome.

As a twentieth-century Marco Polo, his 1925 flight to and from Asia in the *Gennariello* marked a high point in his aviation achievements. He had flown over the continents of Europe, Asia, and Australia, covering 33,500 miles (53,915 kilometers) in 142 days, recording 360 flying hours. In 1927, he tackled the Americas in the same pioneering way.

De Pinedo's second great flight took him across the South Atlantic to South and then North America. He was accompanied by Cmdr. del Prete and mechanic Zacchetti. It was an eventful and demanding trip but the rugged, twin-hulled S 55 stood the test well—that is, until they reached Phoenix, Arizona, of all places. Neatly moored on a reservoir, the *Santa Maria* was the center of attention in Phoenix until a careless smoker flicked a smoldering cigarette, setting the craft alight. A second machine had to be shipped in so the intrepid crew could continue their interrupted voyage. They flew 4,350 miles (7,000 kilometers) across the United States and Canada before leaving Newfoundland for a transatlantic

Left: De Pinedo salutes the American fleet in Australia's Sydney Harbour, 1925

passage that would take them to Rome via the Azores. But, starved of fuel, they were forced to put down 200 miles (320 kilometers) short of Horta, a principal seaport in the Azores. The S 55 had to be towed in the open sea for seven days, but proved her toughness by withstanding all the hammering that rough seas threw at her. After refueling at Horta, de Pinedo flew back to where the crew were forced down before flying on to Rome, just to prove the capability and endurance of his trusty flying boat.

The gallant marquess died in 1933 when he forsook flying boats and attempted to take off from New York in an overloaded Bellanca landplane with the aim of flying across the Atlantic and the Mediterranean nonstop. The landlocked plane refused to lift off the ground, veered, and crashed into a fence before bursting into a fury of flames from which there was no escape.

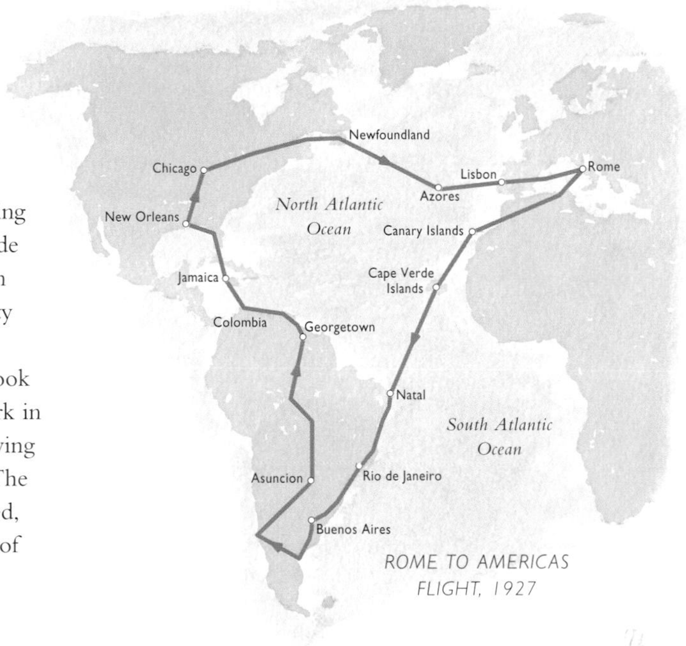

ROME TO AMERICAS
FLIGHT, 1927

Below: The Savoia-Marchetti S 55 Santa Maria, was the flying boat flown and navigated by the marquess, now General, de Pinedo, in 1927— two years after his ground-breaking flight from Italy to Asia and back in the smaller Savoia S 16ter biplane flying boat. In the S 55, de Pinedo was again proving his theory that flying boats had the unique ability to open up isolated communities by being able to land and take off on water.

The Savoia-Marchetti S 55, 1927

43

JOHN KNUDSEN NORTHROP

THINKING BEYOND THE SQUARE

John Knudsen Northrop was young, tall, sandy-haired, and shy. He was also interested in airplanes, and when he noticed an aircraft being built in a small motor-car garage in Santa Barbara, California, he couldn't resist talking to the owners, Allan and Malcolm Loughead, and asking questions. This meeting was to etch two of the most memorable names on the honor board of U.S. aviation. Northrop wanted a job and the Lougheads (who later became known as the "Lockheeds") checked his credentials and took him on. He was given the task of designing a huge 71-foot (21.7-meter) wing of what was to be—in 1914—the biggest flying boat in the world.

Northrop was exceptional; his aptitude for physics, mathematics, and chemistry was outstanding. Add to this his excellent mechanical drawing skills as well as a knowledge of stress analysis, and it is easy to see what had impressed the brothers Loughead.

John—better known as Jack—began to stride ahead from his first full-time job with the Lougheads to become one of the most influential thinkers in aviation development. For 50 years (half of the entire history of powered flight) Northrop dreamed up radical design and construction techniques that form the basis of practically every aircraft that flies today.

He was an early exponent of the idea of streamlining. With the Loughead brothers and Anthony Stadiman, he patented a new system of making immensely strong wooden fuselages—labeled "monocoque"—with a smooth, stream-lined surface. No struts or bracing wires were necessary and the company developed a way to produce them in a tenth of the time taken by earlier French designers who had first dreamed up the monocoque concept.

Jack Northrop's first design, the S1, was a working man's private plane but with so many ex-wartime Curtiss Jennies then on the market, there were no sales. The company was

John (Jack) Northrop

broke, and Northrop had to leave. He worked for three years with another up-and-coming aviation man, Donald Douglas, before approaching Allan Loughead again with design ideas for a new airplane. Loughead liked what he saw. The Lockheed Aircraft Company was formed—Jack was co-founder and chief engineer of the company.

He called this creation his dream ship and it became a flight classic: the Lockheed Vega. It quickly turned into a must-have plane, sought after by the growing list of aviators who had become international stars. With the Vega many aviators went on to create new world records.

The Vega was a streamlined beauty displaying a monocoque fuselage and a cantilevered monoplane wing, with no supporting struts. A Wright Whirlwind or Pratt & Whitney Wasp engine drove the airship at a top speed of 135 miles (216 kilometers) per hour. Though Jack left the Lockheed company some years later to form his own company, the Vega was further developed by Lockheed into a larger machine they named Sirius.

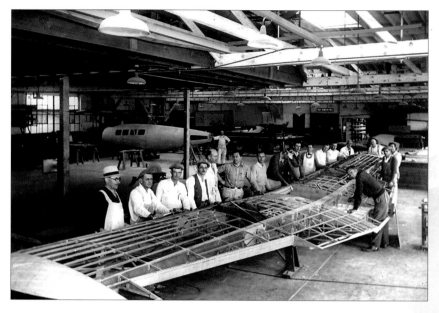

Above: Jack Northrop's revolutionary Lockheed Vega, under construction in the Burbank factory in California.

Right: The first monocoque fuselage design was seen in the smooth, streamlined body shape of this superb French Deperdussin monoplane. It was not only drag-reducing but immensely strong. Similar models to the Deperdussin took out world speed records, the last of which was recorded in 1913 at 126.3 miles (203.2 kilometers) per hour. The aircraft is preserved in le Musée de l'Air et de l'Éspace in Paris.

The revolutionary Lockheed Vega, conceived on the drawing board of young designer Jack Northrop, was the first of its kind to be produced. The life of this model was very short as it took part in the historic and disastrous 2,439-mile (3,902.4-kilometer) Dole Race from San Francisco to Honolulu in August 1927. Named Golden Eagle (despite its bright orange color scheme), this airplane was fitted out with special features, which allowed it to stay afloat for 30 days. No one knows whether or not it did, because pilot Jack Frost and his navigator Gordon Scott took off, headed out to sea, and were never seen again.

Every major airplane has some Jack Northrop in it.

DONALD DOUGLAS SR., 1938

Right: In the factory in Burbank, California, the monocoque Lockheed Vegas, designed by Jack Northrop, took shape. Northrop's manufacturing technique made for quicker manufacture of an otherwise uneconomic task. Northrop laid overlapping timber lathes in a female concrete mold, which had been made to the shape of a fuselage half. The lathes were covered with glue and then compressed with a concrete, matching male mold until the glue dried. Fuselage halves made in this manner were then glued onto frames to complete the fuselage. Window and door openings for the Vegas were then cut according to need.

Jack Northrop was also enthusiastically considering another revolutionary idea—designing a machine with no fuselage at all in order to reduce drag. The first plane that emerged from the Northrop stable was the all-metal Avion Experimental No. 1, with a shape the press immediately dubbed "The Flying Wing," even though it had a small tail empennage. It was Jack Northrop's first attempt to make his vision work and it was not going to be his last.

The restless young designer was also thinking of replicating in metal what he had achieved in wood. Northrop claimed that his most important contribution to aeronautics was his development of the metal-skinned monocoque fuselage. His designs utilized a stressed skin of metal taking much of the structural load, instead of a maze of internal bulkheads, bracing wires, and struts. The German designers Hugo Junkers and Dr. Adolphe Rohrback had been early exponents of metal construction, where the use of rolled metal sheets, riveted together on light metal formers, produced cross-sections that had no flat areas to buckle. The skin could then take some of the stress off the supporting frame. Gradual developments, mostly in America through to World War II and beyond, saw the introduction of still greater refinements in stressed skin construction, eventually allowing the skin to carry more than 50 percent of the load of the total structure. In his book

Right: This Jack Northrop design of 1929, the Avion Experimental No. 1, was where the stealth bomber began. It was an experimental craft, flown to test the possibilities of a thick-sectioned wing and would eventually form the basis of a true flying wing. After initial testing it was put aside by Northrop until he could find time to develop its exciting potential.

about Northrop's aircraft, Richard Allen quotes him as saying (with justification): "That which was developed on the Alpha was really the pioneer of every airplane in the sky today."

That statement still applies in the new millennium, and the Northrop Alpha was first designed in 1930. It was a low-winged monoplane displaying a cantilevered wing without struts. The Alpha and its successors proved to be speedy, reliable, and highly successful in the race for faster intercity transportation in the U.S.A. The three-seat version—there was also a six-passenger version—was one of several operated by Transcontinental and Western Air, later to become T.W.A.

In 1939, Northrop Aircraft Inc. was formed, with Jack Northrop as President. For much of World War II the company produced airplanes for the war effort, including designing and building a reconnaissance bomber for the Norwegian government. It was also a time when Jack's

creative juices were flowing freely, and he returned to designing a truly efficient flying wing. Flying wings had been tried as early as 1914 when English designer J. W. Dunne had flown his tail-less machine from London to Paris. Jack Northrop's spectacular, visionary aircraft, dispensing with fuselage and tail assembly, began taking shape in 1940. He planned that fuel tanks, undercarriage, engines, freight, all control surfaces, and even passengers, should be incorporated within one thick, but very efficient wing structure.

His futuristic-looking machine was unveiled in 1940—the bright yellow NM I. It had no vertical fins or rudders. Elevators, normally on a tail assembly, were placed on the wing with ailerons to give control in all axes. As its engine was too small to carry it high enough for testing, NM I was towed as a glider for research purposes. With the test results in, Northrop made bigger and more powerful machines with two engines. Then in July 1946, his amazing XB 35,

The Northrop Alpha, 1930

Left: The all-metal, stressed-skin Alpha was one of the most significant airplanes ever built. The aircraft was the result of cellular construction, using attendant rivets. Another noticeable feature was the streamlined engine cowling. Air-cooled radial engines usually had their cylinders exposed for maximum cooling, but this incurred a drag penalty. Engineers of the National Advisory Committee for Aeronautics designed a streamlined cowling that reduced drag and improved cooling. Northrop incorporated one of them into this aircraft.

a four-engined bomber with a wingspan of 170 feet (51.9 meters), took to the sky above the airfield for the Northrop Corporation in California.

No one had seen anything quite like the XB 35. The man who had designed the streamlined Vega and the all-metal stressed-skin Alphas had done it again. Northrop said his flying wing could fly faster and more economically, and with more payload than equivalent conventional aircraft. The awesome eight-jet version of his XB 35—designated YB 49—had a speed of 500 miles (800 kilometers) per hour and made an endurance flight of nine hours and more without refueling. Soon after production of this promising jet bomber started in 1949, the whole project was aborted in favor of a huge but conventional Convair B 36. It is still not clear

Right: The 38-feet (12-meter) NM 1 flying wing, nicknamed "The Jeep" after a cartoon character, was the first true flying wing to be built in the United States. It was constructed of wood so that alterations could be made quickly. Test pilot Vance Breeze made its first flight on July 3, 1940.

Northrop patented the design, which allowed its details to become public knowledge, accelerating, it is said, Nazi Germany's efforts in developing the Horten brothers' brilliant, jet-engined flying wing. Fortunately for the Allied war effort but not, perhaps, for aviation generally, the prototype German machine was destroyed in a bombing raid and could not be finished in time to take part in World War II.

why the Northrop YB 49 was never produced, although Jack Northrop claimed, to his dying days, that the decision was politically motivated.

Not that the flying wing was without its problems. Pilots found that there were occasions when they could not react quickly enough in order to control the unusual behavior patterns of a flying wing. A yaw in a flying wing produces a pitching down of the nose, which the pilot must correct very quickly, unlike a yaw in a conventional aircraft, which will induce a rolling movement. Some spectacular accidents had occurred during testing. Control problems such as this were overcome by the application of the first power-boosted controls along with the Minneapolis-Honeywell invention known as SAS (stability augmentation system) that reacted to changes in flight patterns better and faster than any pilot could.

The solutions that Northrop applied helped point the way to the modern fly-by-wire systems used in modern jets. Instead of control lines, electronic impulses were used to move the controls, reacting many times per second to the minutest changes in flight patterns not detectable by the pilot. In turn, these answers led to the design of military aircraft, which otherwise would have been inherently unstable.

Above: Jack Northrop's last big project was the XB 35 in 1946. This astonishing four-engined, propeller-driven, long-range intercontinental bomber was designed to attack Europe from the United States without refueling. Several aircraft were produced for the U.S.A.F. and were undergoing conversion to an eight-jet version, designated the YB 49, when production ceased in favor of the more conventional Convair B 36. Also never to be realized were Jack Northrop's visions of large passenger-carrying flying wings.

The flying-wing testing revealed another vital factor. The testers found that it gave a significantly reduced radar signature, allowing the aircraft to penetrate radar defenses more efficiently. From there, it was not difficult to reach the conclusion that undetected penetration of radar defense could be more important than the speed of attack, although conventional military thinkers took a long time to fully appreciate the concept.

In Germany, the brilliant Horten brothers discovered after they developed their jet-engined, tail-less bomber in the 1940s that radar defenses could be confused by the use of radar-absorbent construction materials. They used sawdust, charcoal, and glue in a wooden airframe. Stealth aircraft were later designed using more modern radar-absorbent materials both in basic structure, and as a covering. A low radar cross-section was achieved by using a flying wing format.

British Prime Minister Stanley Baldwin said prophetically in 1932: "The bomber will always get through!" At the start of the new millennium, that statement seems truer than ever. In theory, the stealth bomber doesn't rely on the expensive deployment of teams of aircraft sent in advance of a bombing force to jam enemy radar, and knock out missile sites and air force bases. It doesn't require fighter planes to search for enemy fighters sent to intercept bombers, as was the experience in previous wars.

This point was proved when a Grumman-Northrop B2 Spirit bomber was successfully deployed to fly across the Atlantic Ocean to bomb targets in Yugoslavia for N.A.T.O. in 1999 and returned safely to the U.S.A. without any fighter force running interference.

Above: In Germany the Horten brothers were renowned for their work on tail-less aircraft. They developed the Horten Ho IX. This beautiful machine was decades ahead of its time. It was not only futuristic in shape but it was powered by two jet engines. It could fly so fast and so high that it could outstrip the fastest fighter planes produced by the Allies. Fortunately for the Allied forces, full development was stalled and only prototypes were flown. The Ho IX remains one of the most remarkable machines ever to take to the air.

Right: Englishman John William Dunne designed the first successful flying wing. Work was carried out in secret from 1907 and was backed by the British Government. Dunne's D 5 model was successfully flown in 1910 with a sweep back of 45 degrees—amazingly, the design was inherently stable. His third model, the D 8, taking off in 1913 from Eastbourne, Southern England, on a successful trip to Paris, is a dramatic demonstration of his extraordinary machine. Despite the U.S. Navy also taking up the idea and experimenting with the design as a seaplane, military development was not continued.

Opposite page: Jack Northrop designed flying wings with thick profiles and these reacted badly to supersonic flight. Supersonic flight was considered to be the key to the bomber getting through. However flying wings give low radar signatures and thus provide better protection than conventional machines.

This feature was highlighted when Grumman-Northrop B2 Spirit stealth bombers were selected by the U.S.A.F. to bomb Serbia from America on April 1, 1999. Flying from the Whiteman Air Force Base in Missouri and refueled by air tankers en route, these bombers made history with their successful nonstop, 30-hour mission. All got through; none were lost.

SIR ALAN COBHAM

FLYING FOR THE EMPIRE

Alan Cobham

The end of World War I left many footloose pilots wanting to recapture some of the adventure and excitement they had tasted as warriors in the air. One of these was Alan Cobham, who made the transition from being a military pilot in the Royal Flying Corps to using his flying skills in a time of peace. It says much for his character that he carved a reputation for organization, courage, and great energy in advancing the cause of air travel. A grateful nation eventually honored him for his achievements by making him a knight of the realm.

What a realm it was. In those exuberant days between two World Wars, it was said that the sun never set on the British Empire. The world map was splashed with countries printed in red, owing allegiance to the greatest colonial power the world had ever seen. For Britain, it was a time to exploit every means available to shorten the lines of communication to these vast and sprawling territories. There was an economic need to shrink distances, to bring closer the cosmopolitan mix of people making up what was to be called "The Commonwealth."

Most important of all, with the war to end all wars behind it, there was a need to preserve and improve the Empire's power, to keep it as a cohesive entity so that no other world power could threaten it. Efficient lines of communication were essential and the airplane was seen as one of the most practical means to that end.

Cobham was there, in the right place, at the right time, with the right skills. His vision of using airplanes to stitch the Empire together may seem jingoistic now, but in the heady climate of the 1920s and 1930s he could see nothing but a glittering future for air travel. He visualized the British Isles as the hub drawing together India, Africa, Malaya, Singapore, Hong Kong, Australia, New Zealand, and

Arthur B. Elliott

Canada, with air routes as the strong, unifying threads.

Alan Cobham became a pilot in an air taxi service in the early 1920s and soon took one hirer on an amazing and memorable 5,000-mile (8,000-kilometer) tour of Europe. With a growing reputation as a courageous pilot, faultless organizer, and impressive demonstrator of sound judgment in adverse conditions, he was approached once more to make an effort for king and country.

Sir Sefton Branckner, Director of Civil Aviation in Britain, asked him to take on the task of surveying air routes throughout the Empire. Cobham accepted the task with enthusiasm and, for seven hectic years, between 1924 and 1931, he ranged the world in airplanes.

In a three-seater, single-engined De Havilland 50 biplane Alan made the first flight from Britain to Cape Town and back. He flew to India and back, then he tackled the longest flight of all, to Australia and back—surveying the best air routes to connect Britain with her colonial outposts. Next he moved into the big, new, fashionable flying boats, and flew all around Africa. Then later, in a large seaplane, he went deeper into Africa into what was still known as "the dark continent."

Those pioneering Cobham flights were conducted against enormous logistical odds. In those days, the countries he had to pass through were lacking technical expertise and their facilities were poor to nonexistent because flights such as his were both rare and unusual.

Typical of his vision was the idea to make in-flight refueling a part of commercial airline operations. In Cobham's time it had been tried only for specific tasks such as breaking endurance records but he experimented with his own ideas and could visualize them saving time and costs on regular mail and passenger routes. His attempts to consolidate a plan for a nonstop England to U.S.A. route across the Atlantic were cut short by World War II. In-flight refueling never took off for commercial air routes but has become a vital element in military flying.

Cobham's achievements were awesome. His flights were trailblazing, and he pointed the way for present-day air routes. The fact that many of these routes are now followed by the independent countries, once part of the Empire for which he served, is surely a lasting tribute to this great aviator.

LONDON TO CAPE TOWN FLIGHT, 1925–6

London
Marseille
Rome
El Sollum
Cairo
Khartoum
Malakal
Kisumu
Tabora
Bulawayo
Pretoria
Johannesburg
Kimberley
Cape Town

Opposite page: When Alan Cobham and engineer A.B. Elliot were flying over the Tigris river in their de Havilland De H 50 seaplane from Baghdad to Bushire, Elliot was badly wounded from a bullet fired by one of the Arab villagers in the Marshlands. Elliot died from his wounds.

Short Singapore I, 1928

Left: This Short Singapore I was the flying boat Alan Cobham chose for his air-survey flight around Africa in 1927. She was powered by two Rolls-Royce Condor engines of 650 horsepower. Flying boats were ideal as survey aircraft because there was a lack of prepared landing grounds for normal aircraft in "the wilds of Africa." It was considered that a flying boat could always put down on a coastal waterway, river or lake. As any sailor knows, wind and water can never be taken for granted, which Cobham and Elliot found out to their cost early into the flight. When they arrived in Malta the aircraft was caught out in strong winds and heavy seas while being towed across open water. She was rolled off a wave and lost her port lower wing. Cobham and his crew's heroic efforts to balance on the opposite wing got the crippled machine back to shelter. However repairs delayed them for nearly two months while new wingtip floats and a lower wing were sent from England as replacements.

As if there was not enough for him to do on this very arduous operation, Cobham was asked to do a survey within a survey. The British Colonial Office asked him to backtrack some 2,700 miles (4,347 kilometers) from Lake Victoria in Africa in order to discover the possibilities of running an airmail service there via the Nile Valley.

The total distance covered by the Singapore I was a very creditable 20,000 miles (32,200 kilometers). She was considered a large machine in her day with a wingspan of 93 feet (28.4 meters).

Right: Lady Cobham takes her place aboard the Short Singapore I flying boat. Cobham had included his intrepid wife among the six crew as his secretary and aide when visiting local dignitaries to discuss air routes, infrastructure, and base facilities.

The first Short S 23 C Class flying boat, Canopus, 1936

Above: Sir Alan Cobham's in-flight refueling methods were being refined before World War II began in 1939. Cabot, a British Empire Airways Short C class flying boat, lines up for refueling from a Handley Page Harrow tanker on a test flight over Southampton Waters in southern England. Because flying boats were not powerful enough to take off with a full load of passengers, mail, and fuel, Cobham's idea was for them to take off with minimum fuel then, once airborne, take on a full fuel load from a tanker aircraft. They could then fly the Atlantic nonstop. These plans were aborted when World War II broke out.

Right: In 1931, the Short Bristol three-engined seaplane was the largest of its type, sporting a wingspan of 107 feet (32.6 meters). She was capable of being converted to a landplane if required. Alan Cobham used this craft for a detailed survey of air routes from England to Lake Kivu, in Africa. His previous survey aircraft, the Singapore I, was a flying boat, not a seaplane. (A flying boat has a boatlike hull and wingtip pontoons or floats as distinct from a seaplane which normally had its fuselage supported clear of the water by two large pontoons.) A distance of 12,300 miles (19,790 kilometers) was covered without serious problems, creating another successful survey flight for the adventurous Cobham.

Short Bristol seaplane, 1931

HUBERT WILKINS

A COLD-WEATHER MAN

Hubert Wilkins pursued weather in a plane. He was the first man to fly over the Arctic continent and the first to fly in the Antarctic. As a dedicated meteorologist, Wilkins knew that the world's weather patterns were initiated at the Poles. He dreamed of being there, to see these icy pressure points for himself so he could better understand their pivotal nature. He was well prepared.

Hubert Wilkins trained as an electrical engineer, but became a photographer, war correspondent, aviator, and navigator. His interest in meteorology was lifelong and deeply ingrained. As a young son of a farmer in South Australia, Hubert had watched cattle and sheep die from prolonged drought, and wondered why it was not possible to predict weather, then move stock to richer pastures to ensure their survival. Searching for adventure, he ran away to sea, and in the early 1900s spent some years living with the Inuit people in Alaska. Later in Britain he worked as a photographer, taking aerial photographs from balloons and airships. During World War I, he joined the Royal Australian Flying Corps and continued to make hazardous cinematic sorties recording battle scenes from the air.

In 1925, after World War I, Wilkins followed with interest, the Norwegian explorer, Amundsen's ill-fated attempt to fly to the North Pole. Then in 1927, with Carl Eielson as pilot, Wilkins made his first attempt to reach the North Pole. It was a disaster. Their plane crashed, and the two walked for 13 days through ice and snow in appalling arctic conditions in search of safety. It was Wilkins' previous experience living with the Inuit people, and his navigational skills that brought them to safety.

One year later he was at it again, this time in a new Lockheed Vega monoplane. With Carl Eielson again at the controls, they flew across the Arctic from Barrow, Alaska, to Spitzbergen, off the Norwegian coast.

Two years earlier the Americans, Lt. Comdr. R. E. Byrd and F. G. Bennett were reported to have flown to the North Pole and back. However, Wilkins was the first to cross the Arctic continent by airplane. In December 1928, flying the same Lockheed Vega and accompanied by another similar monoplane, Wilkins successfully made the first flight in the Antarctic.

In 1931 the extraordinarily adventurous Wilkins initiated and navigated the first underwater attempt to cross under the North Pole in the submarine, *Nautilus*. The first attempt was unsuccessful and was not achieved until 1958 by a U.S. Navy submarine with the same name. Because of his reputation as a navigator and polar explorer, Wilkins was to finish his career in a leading role with the Research and Development Command of the United States Army.

Left: Hubert Wilkins in the hatch atop the fuselage of his Lockheed Vega—the aircraft in which he and Carl Ben Eielson flew across the Arctic in 1928. In the same year, Wilkins took this same aircraft and another Vega to make the first-ever flight in the Antarctic.

Opposite page: After being forced down on the arctic ice by a blinding storm on the Island of Spitzbergen, having flown for 20 hours from Barrow in Alaska, Wilkins and Eielson sheltered for four days in their cockpit, in sub-zero temperatures. While there, the airplane's skis froze onto the ice. In order to take off, Wilkins tried to free the skis while Eielson gunned the engine, but he failed to climb into his hatch on top of the rounded fuselage in time and the Vega took off without him.

Eielson saw Wilkins on the ice and had to land again. This time, Hubert rigged a rope ladder to his hatch and rocked the skis free of the ice but was still unable to clamber aboard; instead he was hit badly by the tail plane as Eielson, feeling the weight of Wilkins being dragged through the snow, assumed he was aboard, and again roared off without him. Fuel was down to the last 20 gallons (91 liters) but there was nothing for it but to land again.

On the third try, Wilkins, still half-stunned and with his teeth loosened from the tail hitting his mouth, perched himself half-in and half-out of his hatch. He pushed and strained with his foot on a bulk of driftwood until, at last, the Vega moved off the ground. Wilkins collapsed, bruised and battered, into the hatch as the Vega took off. They finally flew the few miles that remained to complete their pioneering crossing of the Arctic continent.

Far left: In an arctic wasteland, Hubert Wilkins photographs the the Nautilus. In this converted World War I submarine, Wilkins made a quixotic attempt to cross the polar ice cap underwater in extremely cold, cramped conditions, but it was a dismal failure. The U. S. Navy succeeded where he had failed. As a tribute to Sir Hubert, following his death in 1959, the U. S. nuclear submarine, Skate, broke through the ice at the North Pole to ceremoniously scatter his ashes.

R.J. MITCHELL

CREATOR OF A KILLER FIGHTER

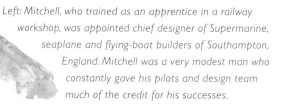

A young aircraft designer anxiously watched a small, silver floatplane hurl itself into the air from Chesapeake Bay, Baltimore, in a dangerous flurry of spray. No seaplane had ever looked like this one. It had a slim, one-piece, monoplane wing with no supporting bracing wires or struts. Its Napier Lion engine was closely cowled in a low-drag casing while its cooling radiators were spread out beneath the wings. The Supermarine S-4 was a streamlined beauty.

The pilot, Henry Biard, had already won the Schneider Trophy for Great Britain in 1922 but the Americans had won it back the next year. In 1925, the races were on again, this time over Baltimore Bay and Chesapeake Bay.

Biard turned to begin a speed trial, low down over Chesapeake Bay. He had already achieved a phenomenal record speed of 226 miles (361.6 kilometers) per hour in this airplane but now, as his aircraft streaked across the bay,

tragedy would strike. It suddenly smashed into the water at high speed. Miraculously, Biard survived but the designer's dreams were shattered along with his airplane. Reginald Mitchell, chief designer for Supermarine, had failed.

What Mitchell didn't realize, however, was that he had set himself on a course that was to make him the preeminent English airplane designer of the 1930s and who, as the outright winner for Britain of the Schneider Trophy, would go down in history as the creator of the famous Spitfire.

The British Air Ministry were aware that the potential high performance aircraft based on Schneider Trophy technology could produce excellent fighter aircraft. So they sent several aircraft manufacturers their specifications for a high-speed (250 miles/402 kilometers per hour), four-gun fighter. The new model 224 from Supermarine, though using much of Mitchell's racing seaplane technology (such as the complex evaporative cooling system for the craft's engine), was a conservative monoplane having a thick, gull-shaped wing with radiators along its leading edges. It failed to meet the specifications.

However, such was the faith of Vickers Supermarine and Rolls-Royce in the talents of R. J. Mitchell that they decided to produce their own private-venture "killer fighter." They believed that official specifications were too limiting. They would finance it provided that Air Ministry technical experts were not allowed to intercede.

Left: Mitchell, who trained as an apprentice in a railway workshop, was appointed chief designer of Supermarine, seaplane and flying-boat builders of Southampton, England. Mitchell was a very modest man who constantly gave his pilots and design team much of the credit for his successes.

Opposite page: Pilot Henry Biard banks the Supermarine S-4 into a tight, high G-turn low over the water in Chesapeake Bay before the start of the 1925 Schneider Trophy races. The aircraft crashed spectacularly into the bay with Biard lucky to escape with his life.

Left: A place of honor; R.J. Mitchell's Supermarine S-6A, which helped win the 1929 Schneider Trophy, on display in the Southampton Hall of Fame, England.

Above: It appears that R. J. Mitchell was not the only designer wanting to produce a "clean" airplane—the French Bernard Ferbois V-2 racing monoplane of 1924 had a thick-sectioned, unbraced cantilever wing and a closely cowled engine. Engine radiators were placed beneath the wings. Flown by test pilot Florentin Bonnet, this advanced machine achieved a record speed of 278 1/5 miles (448.2 kilometers) per hour.

The British Air Ministry considered that eight guns were necessary for a modern fighter plane in the late 1930s. Sqdn. Ldr. R. G. Sorley, an unusually prescient thinker in the Air Ministry, guessed rightly that future air battles would occur at such high speeds that a pilot would have only two seconds in which to aim and fire his guns. Hence he would need to pour many bullets into the target to destroy it in two seconds. Mitchell and the team agreed.

However, everything hinged on Rolls-Royce designing a new engine powerful enough to drive an eight-gun, streamlined fighter to a speed of about 350 miles (560 kilometers) per hour, twice the speed of contemporary service aircraft. After much testing and re-designing of existing engines, Rolls-Royce came up with the famous Merlin (named after the bird of prey, not the wizard). This powerful, reliable, liquid-cooled engine, in later more powerful variants, became the most successful power plant fitted to fighters and bombers during World War II.

Mitchell started work on his new designs in 1934, applying as many ideas as technically possible from his racing seaplanes to arrive at the Spitfire we know today—a beautiful airplane with a characteristic semi-elliptical wing that set it apart from other aircraft. The wing shape was not the whim of an individual who wanted an esthetically pleasing shape; it was an elegant solution to a tricky problem. The only way to fit all the machine guns into such a thin wing was to keep the wing as wide as possible, as far out as possible. Then to minimize drag, the remainder of the wing would be swept to a narrow tip.

Mitchell's dream machine took to the air in early 1936. "I want nothing changed," reported a satisfied "Mutt" Summers after his first test flight. The killer fighter had arrived.

Above: The Supermarine model 224, R. J. Mitchell's first Spitfire of 1934, failed to perform to specifications and met an inglorious end as a gunnery target. As a result the Gloster Gladiator was put into service with the R.A.F.

The Gloster Gladiator, 1934

Left: The original 1936 prototype Spitfire, with a wingspan of 37 feet (11.27 meters), retractable undercarriage, and a fixed pitch propeller, had a top speed of 364 miles (585 kilometers) per hour.

R.J. Mitchell was doomed never to see more than the prototype Spitfire. He died of cancer a few months after its first flight. Joseph Smith, a talented aircraft designer, joined Supermarine in 1921. He carried out all subsequent development and design work from the original Mk-1 in 1934 through to the Mk-24 and Seafire variants. The final variant, the Spitfire Mk-24, had a top speed of 454 miles (726.4 kilometers) per hour; it was fitted with a Rolls-Royce Griffin engine, driving a five-bladed propeller, and had virtually double the power and double the wing loading of the prototype. Through Smithy's efforts the Spitfire was the only fighter that remained in service throughout and after World War II.

Left: The Supermarine Stranraer of 1940 flying boat was on Mitchell's drawing board at the same time as he was designing the Spitfire. The difference in the design concepts of the two aircraft is generational.

Opposite page: There was a road bridge in Winchester, England, not far from where the Spitfire made its first flight. It was called The Spitfire Bridge because it was claimed that a Spitfire flew under it during World War II. The fact that the aircraft was a Curtiss Tomahawk made no difference; such was the extraordinary charisma created by the Spitfire that, to the British public, any single-engined fighter of the day was a Spitfire. For fighter pilots too, it was the machine they most wanted to fly; even Luftwaffe pilots thought so. These Spitfires are Mk-Vbs, seen over Darwin, Australia, in 1943 during one of the 64 Japanese bombing raids.

HAROLD GATTY

THE QUIET HELMSMAN WHO LED THE WAY AROUND THE PACIFIC

For all Gatty's extraordinary skills, encyclopedic knowledge, and practical abilities, people just didn't know this quiet Australian was there! The most accomplished aerial navigator of his day, Harold Gatty was known by very few. While American flier Wiley Post broke records circling the world in a Lockheed Vega and was feted as a hero wherever he landed, the public heard little about his navigator, Harold, who quietly sat checking his sextant, plotting on his charts, and pointing the way for Wiley to fly. It was 1931 and Gatty had organized Wiley's flight. He arranged the logistics, laid out the flight plan, and flawlessly navigated all the way around the globe. Yet his no-nonsense contributions received few accolades.

Gatty was deeply admired and respected by an inner circle of his peers. He was awarded the America Distinguished Flying Cross by presidential decree, in recognition of his trail-blazing work. But he never received the public acclaim that his aviation achievements so richly deserved. In his own country, he was frowned on by government officials who thought he was promoting U.S. interests rather than those of his native land.

Evidence of Gatty's brilliance as an aerial navigator showed up in an early flight. He and Canadian pilot Harold Bromley attempted to make the first nonstop flight across the Pacific in 1930. On this flight Gatty first used his ground-speed-and-drift sight—a device he had developed at his navigational school in Los Angeles with an American colleague. The sight was later refined and adopted by the U.S. Army Air Corps.

Harold Gatty (left) with
Harold Bromley

Above: Japanese Naval personnel pushed the Emsco Tacoma City of Tacoma onto the grass runway at Kusumigaura Naval Air Station near Tokyo. Bromley and Gatty were forced to fly from here, lightly loaded with fuel. They flew to the final takeoff point—a beach at the northern tip of Honshu Island—where they filled the tanks and took off from a steep ramp built by the locals to assist the heavily laden aircraft on its way.

Opposite page: Bromley and Gatty's Emsco monoplane dived flat out to sea level through a gap in fog, nearly colliding with a freighter. They had been forced to return to their starting point on what was to have been the first nonstop flight across the Pacific from Japan to North America in 1930. They had flown in or above fog from soon after takeoff. Now, after hours of flying virtually blind, Harold Gatty as navigator calculated that they should descend through a gap in the fog. What he didn't know was that the pilot, Harold Bromley, was hallucinating under the influence of carbon monoxide poisoning from a faulty exhaust system and when instructed to descend, simply poked the nose of their Emsco monoplane downward instead of making a throttled-back, controlled descent. The result was a hair-raising, high-speed dive that broke through the fog just above the sea and nearly sent the aircraft into the masts of a freighter. "I don't know who was more scared, the people on the ship or me," said Gatty.

As the monoplane flattened out, there ahead was the same lighthouse that marked the start of their flight 22 hours before—a wonderful example of Gatty's masterly navigational skills.

"... it was Harold who was the guiding hand of the Winnie Mae."

WILEY POST, AFTER HIS RECORD-BREAKING ROUND-THE-WORLD FLIGHT, 1931

Left: The Harold Gatty memorial in Campbelltown, Tasmania— Gatty's birthplace—featuring the Lockheed Vega on top of the globe.

Above: The celebrated American pilot Wiley Post chose Harold Gatty as navigator on his amazing eight-day flight around the world in 1931 in the Winnie Mae, a Lockheed Vega. Gatty's navigational skills and organizational ability made the achievement possible. In 1933 Wiley Post flew the circumnavigation solo, using the same Lockheed Vega monoplane and knocked 31 hours off the previous flight time.

Top: The strain shows on the faces of Harold Gatty and Wiley Post around the time of their epic flight of the Winnie Mae.

Harold Gatty moved on to navigational tasks of even greater importance. He started the groundbreaking challenge of developing airbases throughout the Pacific—from Tokyo to San Francisco, Hawaii to New Zealand—to connect new air routes for the growing and powerful Pan American Airways. Behind the scenes, providing covert backing, was the might of the United States Government. Already U.S. diplomats could foresee the importance of U.S. airbases should a future conflict with Japan arise. Led by the charismatic Pan American Airways Chief, Juan Trippe, pioneers such as Lindbergh and Gatty carved out wide-ranging Pan-Am air routes.

Years of survey work culminated in 1937. That year, Harold Gatty waited in New Zealand to welcome a big Sikorsky flying boat bearing the Pan-Am insignia as it landed after crossing the Pacific in a milestone flight from the Hawaiian Islands. Gatty's lobbying and planning made the flight happen, even though it raised the ire of officials back in Australia—his home country, which had ignored his talents for so long.

Harold Gatty's fascination with all aspects of navigation led him to write a survival book honoring those lost at sea and it was issued to all American airmen during World War II. A subsequent book by Gatty, published in 1958, detailed his observations of natural events and explanations of the navigational techniques used by early Polynesian navigators, providing practical survival hints for anyone attempting to sail in the South Pacific.

During World War II, Gatty returned to Australia to serve with the Royal Australian Air Force at General Macarthur's headquarters, but once peace was declared he decided to continue in the business he loved best. He set up his own company—Fiji Airlines—which would fly over his favorite ocean. Gatty's enterprise, now called Air Pacific, still flies today but Gatty does not. He died in 1978. This quiet achiever is little remembered in his country of birth. Only a modest column at Campbelltown, Tasmania, where he grew up, commemorates the life and times of Harold Gatty, aerial pioneer and superb navigator.

Left: A Pan-Am Sikorsky S-42 Clipper, Samoan Ciupper, at the end of the first proving flight on a proposed Pan-Am air route from Honolulu to New Zealand in 1937.

Sikorksy S-42, 1937

Left: Harold Gatty leads the crew to shore in Auckland, New Zealand. For Gatty, who did so much to establish air bases, particularly in the Pacific, it was one more landmark in a distinguished career as a navigator and airline executive.

CHARLES ULM

LET'S BUILD AN AIRLINE

Charles Ulm. 1934

Charles Ulm was a visionary who lived in a country aching for the advantages that flight could bring. Australia was an isolated continent, nearly the size of the United States of America, and surrounded by the Indian Ocean, the Great Southern Ocean, and the Pacific Ocean. It's no surprise that this country produced more dedicated airmen for its population than any other nation in the world. Ulm was one of the best, a man imbued with the idea of developing aviation in Australia—to organize air links both within the country, and with the rest of the world.

He had tasted the potential of the airplane when, in 1927, he joined Charles Kingsford Smith in a record-breaking flight around Australia, followed by the first-ever flight across the Pacific Ocean.

Fired with possibility, Ulm and Kingsford Smith registered a new airline, Australian National Airways Limited. For nearly two years the newly formed airline traded well. Then after many attempts to keep the A.N.A. planes flying, financial problems—made worse by the Great Depression—forced the company into voluntary liquidation.

In 1933 Ulm purchased one of the failed company's aircraft intending to continue to build a viable Australian airline. He bought an Avro X (a British-built Fokker FV II)—one of the small A.N.A. fleet—installed a re-designed wing and

larger fuel tanks, and gave it the name *Faith in Australia*. Ulm flew *Faith in Australia* to England, with Scotty Allen as copilot-wireless operator and P. G. Taylor as navigator-relief pilot, in an attempt to let the world know of his desire to expand air travel. He hoped to continue around the world, via America, but in Ireland, he came to grief. On Portmarnock beach, where he had intended to take off for Newfoundland, an undercarriage strut gave way while the fuel tanks were being filled, throwing a wheel awry and cracking the wing. The flight had to be aborted.

Back in Australia, in 1933-1934, *Faith in Australia* made passenger and unofficial mail flights to New Zealand, as well as the first official mail flight to New Guinea. Despite this and other demonstrations of Ulm's ability, the important Australia-to-Singapore mail tender was awarded to British Imperial Airways instead of to Ulm.

Undaunted and still determined to prove the value of aerial transportation, Charles Ulm formed a new company, Great Pacific Airways Limited. With this new company in place, he planned to make a demonstration flight across the Pacific as a precursor to providing regular air transportation from America to Australia. In Britain Ulm purchased a

twin-engined Airspeed Envoy and with this small, six-seater airliner, aimed to show that an air route from America to Australia was commercially viable. It was a bold decision to take. The odds were fearsomely stacked against him and the flying distances were long and dangerous, particularly as aircraft were still in their formative years. The Envoy was stripped down, seats were removed, extra fuel tanks and new radio equipment were installed, and it was shipped to Canada. Ulm and his crew flew the plane to Vancouver, and then on to San Francisco.

Only weeks before their planned flight, Charles Kingsford Smith and fellow flier P. G. Taylor successfully flew together from Sydney, Australia, to San Francisco in the U.S., in a single-engined, Lockheed Altair, but this was no guarantee for the success of Ulm's venture.

In Ulm's newly named *Stella Australis* and with he as pilot, George Littlejohn as copilot, and Leon Skilling as navigator, the crew planned to fly to Sydney. They took off on the first, long leg from San Francisco to Oahu in the Hawaiian Islands on the afternoon of December 3, 1934. They were scheduled to land at Honolulu early next morning. They never arrived. At 9:45 A.M. they radioed to say they were going to ditch and requested assistance, but that was the last ever heard of them. Though a huge and comprehensive search was mounted, they were never found.

In the late 1930s Juan Trippe of Pan American Airways pioneered air travel in flying boats—the Pan-Am Clippers designed by Igor Sikorsky. The great American flier Charles Lindbergh, Australian navigator Harold Gatty, and the U.S. Government assisted Trippe in planning comprehensive air routes that stretched from California to the Philippines, and later to New Zealand. Charles Ulm's vision of land planes crossing the Pacific was not realized for over 20 years with the development of large and powerful airliners such as the Super Constellation. The little *Stella Australis* didn't stand a chance.

Left: In March 1931, Australian National Airways Southern Cloud disappeared on a regular air run from Sydney to Melbourne and was not found for 27 years. Had she not been lost, A.N.A., the airline founded by Charles Ulm and Charles Kingsford Smith, may well have survived instead of going into liquidation in 1933.

Above: With engines starved of fuel and flaps down, the Stella Australis lines up for a ditching, somewhere near the Hawaiian Islands. Charles Ulm had been heard calling for the radio beacon in Oahu, but he never made contact. Charles and his crew had calculated that the aircraft would stay afloat for two days, so were hopeful of being rescued. Neither the plane nor her crew was ever seen again. Ellen Rogers, Charles Ulm's secretary, later remembered him talking about the impending flight across the Pacific in December 1934. He said: "I have no doubt in my own mind that I am at last standing on the threshold of vast possibilities of which I have dreamt and for which I have worked for many years." Those possibilities were not to be realized for another 20 years.

I think we are going into the drink. Hurry and send someone to fish us out.

ULM'S LAST RADIO MESSAGE,
SAN FRANSISCO TO HAWAII, 1934

HOWARD ROBARD HUGHES JR.

LAME DUCK OR A GOOSE WITH ATTITUDE?

Howard Hughes is remembered most for the gigantic (but beautifully designed) flying boat, which flew just once, almost by accident. It became known as "The Spruce Goose."

At 18, Hughes's father died, leaving him 75 percent of the Hughes business and one of the most wealthy orphans in the world. At 19, Howard Robard Hughes Jr. was in control of the Hughes Tool Company, which had a virtual monopoly in the supply of oil-drilling equipment, supplying him with almost unlimited financial resources. He moved to Los Angeles and with a driving interest in aviation, quickly learned to fly. Hollywood captured his attention, and before long he was financing, producing, and directing films, one of which is still a classic. Titled *Hells Angels* it told the story of World War I pilots in the Royal Flying Corps. Hughes acquired 87 wartime fighter planes: Spads, Sopwith Camels, and Fokkers, then set about filming some remarkable dog-fight footage over the sprawling area which became today's Los Angeles Airport. Three stunt pilots were killed during the filming, and Hughes was lucky to be pulled out alive after he crashed in his own scout plane. Released in 1930, the film was a box-office sensation.

Howard Hughes

Then he took to flying in earnest. Under an assumed name, Howard worked as an airline pilot, gaining experience of multi-engined aircraft. He went on to win every American aviation award possible. In 1935 he formed the Hughes Aircraft Company to develop new, faster planes. He soon had a successful aviation business, and was looking for new air speed titles to conquer. In 1938 he set a new round-the-world record of 3 days, 19 hours, and 14 minutes in a Lockheed 14.

During World War II American industrialist Henry Kaiser proposed to build giant cargo planes made of wood that could carry 700 troops or a load of 60 tons (62 tonnes) to overcome the losses caused by German U-boats sinking allied shipping. Hughes was enthusiastic, and in 1942 the U. S. Government contracted the development of the laminated wood aircraft.

Originally designated the HK-1 Hercules flying boat, it became the H-4 Hercules when Kaiser backed out of the project. Hughes's aircraft company designed a plane with a wingspan of 320 feet (97.6 meters), then three times larger than the largest aircraft ever built.

But the project fell way behind schedule. The U. S. Congress became critical of soaring costs. One senator lampooned it as "The Flying Lumberyard," which led to its nickname, "The Spruce Goose," even though it was made mainly of birch.

Two years after the war, in November 1947, the flying boat was ready for taxi tests. With Hughes at the controls, the eight Pratt & Whitney Wasp Majors—the biggest radial

Right: In 1935 Hughes captured the world land speed record of 352.39 miles (567 kilometers) per hour in this H-1 racer he designed. Flying experience plus shrewd business sense enabled him to create a thriving aviation business, later incorporating commercial and military helicopter design, weapons, and electronic systems—including the first communications satellite.

engines ever made—were revved up. Once the trial began, onlookers were amazed to see the flying boat lift off the Los Angeles Harbor to a height of about 70 feet (21.4 meters) and fly one mile (1.6 kilometers) in less than a minute, before making a perfect landing. The Spruce Goose taxied back to its huge hangar. There it stayed for 29 years, and, until Hughes's death in 1976, the plane was kept "flight-ready". Each month all its engines were run to keep them in good working order.

Over the years Hughes became withdrawn and increasingly reclusive. In 1973, in absentia, he was inducted into the Aviation Hall of Fame in Dayton, Ohio. Three years later, in 1976, Howard Hughes died in an airplane flying from Mexico, to a hospital in Houston, U.S.A. He was almost unrecognizable, seriously addicted to codeine, and died of heart failure.

The Spruce Goose was put on display as a Walt Disney attraction at Long Beach, California. In 1993, it was moved to the Evergreen Aerial Museum, Oregon—a final resting place to house Hughes's unique and historic aircraft.

Left: This Hughes XF-11 reconnaissance fighter is the second prototype. The first prototype featured contra-rotating propellers to absorb the power of its huge Wasp Major engines. One of the propellers reversed thrust in mid-flight causing the aircraft to plow through houses, exploding in a fireball. The near-fatally injured Hughes recovered within five weeks to resume flying.

Opposite page: November 2, 1947—the gigantic Hughes H-4 Spruce Goose with Howard Hughes at the controls, carves its way through a light chop on Los Angeles Harbor, past warships of the U.S. Navy and a multitude of spectator craft. With spray flying and one float still dragging the surface of the water, the huge wooden bird is about to become airborne.

THE DOERS

In the short, turbulent history of flying, these action men and women embraced the visions of others and flew with them. In a sense, they were the dynamos who wanted to rev up their engines and equipment, in an effort to probe the possibilities and extend beyond the perceived limits of men and machines. They were the engineers who wrought new miracles out of timber, fabric, plastics, metals, and motors—the aviators who wanted to vault over aerial frontiers to distant places. "Let's do it!" they said—and they did.

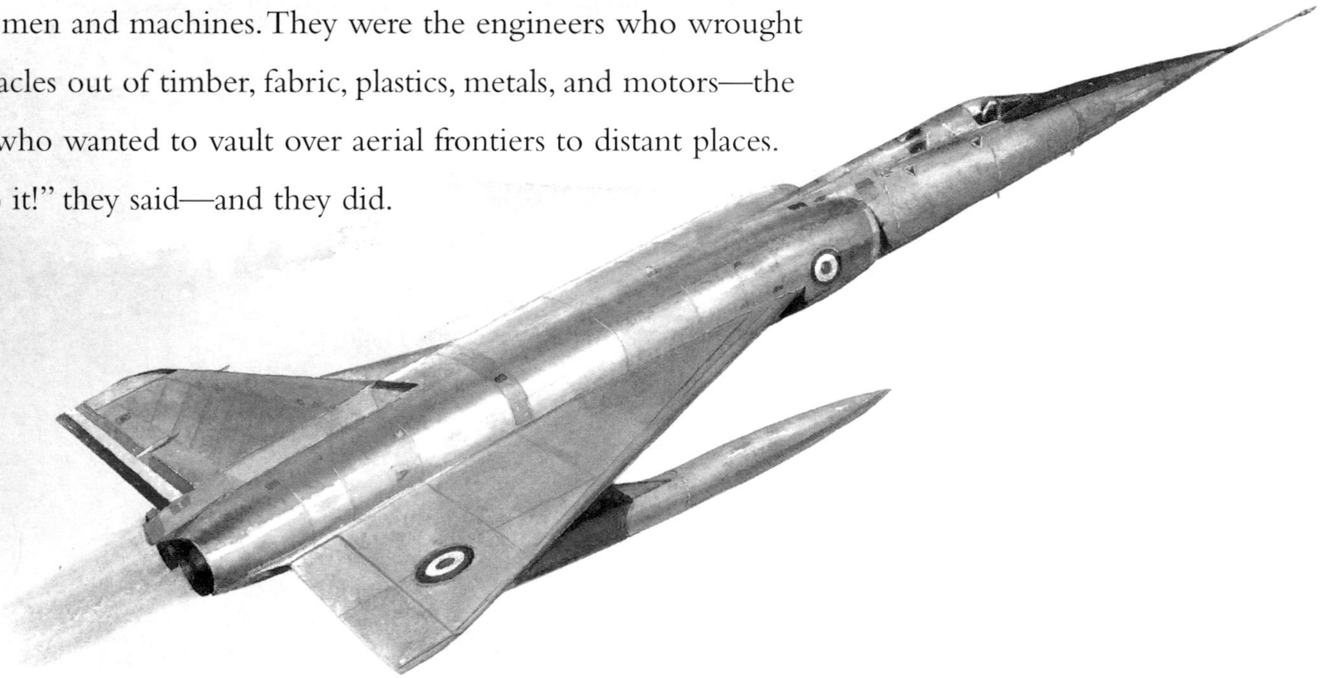

THE VOISIN BROTHERS, LEVAVASSEUR, AND FARMAN

OH WHAT A WEEK!

The wild excitement of Blériot's Channel crossing in July 1909 had scarcely abated when another occasion sent French enthusiasm for aviation soaring to giddy, new heights. This event changed the notion that flying was an indulgence for enthusiasts or some kind of esoteric sporting activity. Instead it became the promise of a burgeoning industry with immense potential. What was about to take place at Reims would awaken awareness of a potential new field for government and business investors. While individual genius was to play a major role in the development of the airplane, the real incentives and the direction for future efforts would be driven by those two major forces.

The event was The Great Week of Aviation held in August 1909 at a racetrack at Betheny near Reims. Big

cash prizes provided by major champagne growers of the region attracted thousands of spectators along with 28 pilots and 38 aircraft, and provided fierce competition, thrills, spills, and once-in-a-lifetime excitement.

People poured into Reims as never before, thousands of excited men and women. They watched in wonder as aircraft of all shapes and sizes competed in speed contests, height competitions, and maneuverability trials in the air, providing a great spectacle in full view of the amazed, enthralled onlookers. Presidents and kings, lords and ladies, and distinguished politicians rubbed shoulders with pilots, aviation designers, and innovative manufacturers. Most of the competitors were French, as were most of the machines. The Voisin and Farman brothers—highly successful as manufacturers and airmen—stood out along with Levavasseur, Latham, Blériot, and more. The Wright brothers were represented by several of their biplanes, made under license in France. The Wrights were not interested in racing; they did not take part. Glenn Curtiss was, and did!

The Voisin brothers, Henry Farman, and Leon Levavasseur were some of the many talented French designers and builders who attended The Great Week of Aviation at Reims in 1909.

Left: The Great Week of Aviation of 1909 was held at Betheny Racecourse near Reims, France. It was a gala event attended by the local populace, the fashionable, the wealthy, and royalty.

Henry Farman won most prizes during The Great Week, followed by the popular British-born Hubert Latham and the visiting American hero Glenn Curtiss.

The real winner was the airplane. Here, only six years old in this landmark week, the airplane was demonstrating it had become more stable and its engines were becoming more reliable. Despite the variety and effectiveness of individual control systems, a consistency was emerging that would result in standard control systems—a hand-operated, central column to move ailerons and elevators and a foot-operated, rudder bar to move rudders. Materials were becoming stronger and more durable. The dreams—that airplanes could be robust enough to travel across oceans and over mountains—soon became realities, enabling the planes to fly above bad weather. At Reims the dreams became distinct possibilities.

Let others amuse themselves with races if they want!

WILBUR WRIGHT, SPURNING THE OPPORTUNITY TO PARTICIPATE IN THE GREAT WEEK OF AVIATION AT REIMS, 1909

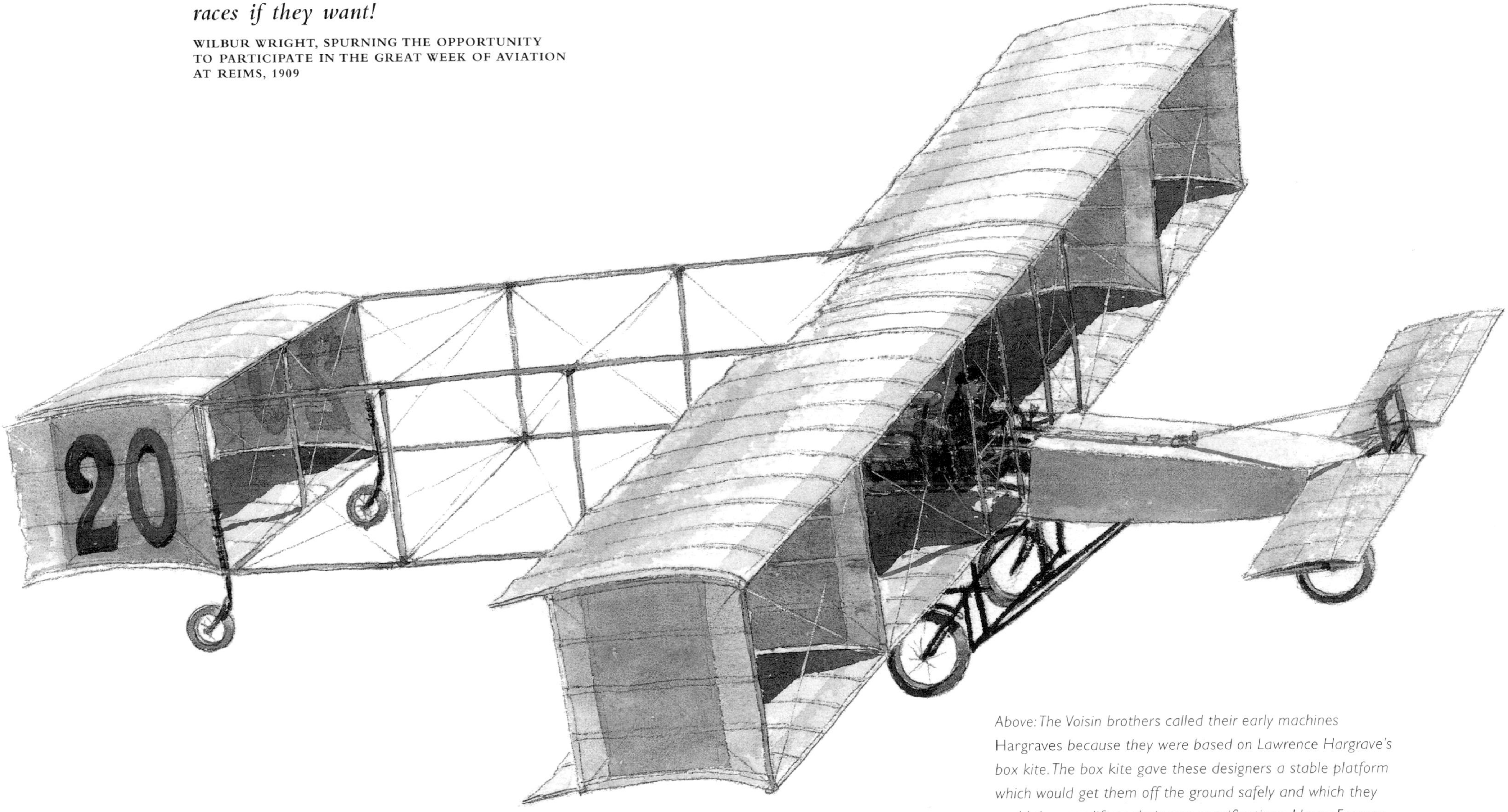

Above: The Voisin brothers called their early machines Hargraves because they were based on Lawrence Hargrave's box kite. The box kite gave these designers a stable platform which would get them off the ground safely and which they could then modify to their own specifications. Henry Farman, who also became a well-known flier and manufacturer, further modified the Voisin machines. There were many variations in the use and placement of the side curtains, both on the main planes and on the tail assembly.

Left & right: Hubert Latham, a very popular Englishman living in France, decided he would fly the English Channel in an Antoinette. He took off six days ahead of Blériot. This dashing young man was forced to ditch his lovely machine in the English Channel when the usually reliable Levavasseur engine failed. Yet his Antoinette was undamaged and Latham climbed out of the cockpit with only his pride dented. With unflappable sangfroid he sat on the wing of the floating aircraft smoking cigarettes while awaiting rescue. Not even his feet were wet.

Léon Levavasseur's Antoinette monoplane was a thing of beauty. This graceful, attractive airplane was the creation of someone with artistic flair. Leon had more than that. As well as a graduate of the Beaux Arts of Paris he was a boat builder, engineer, and inspired designer of flying machines. Antoinette was his masterpiece, one of the most advanced airplanes of the day. Its wings had a graduated section, thinner airfoils at the wingtips than at the roots, and carefully shaped under-curves to each rib. Antoinette's powerful V8 engine was also Levavasseur's own design. The engine developed 100 horsepower. The engine was originally designed for his motorboats and ran at high temperatures. For Antoinette he incorporated an ingenious cooling system into the engine— water evaporated as steam flowed through a series of horizontal pipes mounted along the sides of the boat-shaped fuselage, then returned to the engine as cooled water.

Twenty years later, Glenn Curtiss and R. J. Mitchell were using similar cooling systems on their Schneider Trophy racing seaplanes.

The Antoinette flew both with and without Curtiss-type ailerons. Originally fitted with a paddle-bladed propeller it was also used with more aerodynamic, Wright-type airscrews. The ailerons were not very efficient—they twisted the wings and turned the aircraft the wrong way when they were applied. They acted as servos to wing warping, the very action they were in place to avoid.

Levavasseur's later designs were typically advanced in thinking. He was the first designer to use a fully cantilevered wing and streamlined shapes.

At Reims, The Great Week of Aviation was not just a success; it was a remarkable pioneering public and trade exposition. Many theories of flight were put to the test. Designers, manufacturers, and pilots learned so much from seeing different aircraft designs put through their paces. The inevitable, in-depth discussions, arguments, and observations which followed sparked new creative fires to fuel the future of the flying machine.

Left: The Antoinette had a boatlike fuselage and superbly finished engine. The primitive, paddle-bladed propeller was fitted to the earlier machines while the Wright brothers' more sophisticated propeller design was fitted to later models.

Above & above left: Louis Blériot fought a valiant battle at Reims for the honor of winning the Gordon Bennett Speed Trophy, when he flew his powerful, new Blériot XII against Glenn Curtiss. His hopes were dashed when the machine crashed and caught fire. Blériot escaped serious injury, but Curtiss went back home to America with the prize.

Left: In January 1908 Henry Farman, an English expatriate artist living in France, completed the first ⅗-mile (1-kilometer) circuit flying his Voisin-designed airplane. Notwithstanding the success of this box kite type of machine—this one also completed a 18⅗-mile (30-kilometer) cross-country flight—they tended to skid around corners instead of banking safely in the coordinated, controlled manner of Wright and Curtiss airplanes.

Right: American Glenn Curtiss was not the only designer at Reims to fit ailerons to his machine. This red-painted monoplane, designed by Robert Esnault-Pelterie, made a feature of them in his futuristic-looking machine. The design did not perform too well at Reims although it had two years of successful flights behind it. The REP, as it was known, had a seatbelt fitted for its pilot. Other pilots simply sat, unrestrained, on benches or basic wooden seats.

RICHARD WILLIAM PEARSE

THIS KIWI WAS NOT A FLIGHTLESS BIRD

Richard William Pearse

In a letter he wrote to New Zealand's *Dunedin Star* newspaper in 1915, Richard Pearse advised that he had not satisfied his own requirements for a "proper flight." Yet years before, in 1903, a number of his neighbors and locals who had gathered on the Main Waitohi Road, in New Zealand's South Island, were surprised and impressed when, after a number of attempts, Richard Pearse's homemade two-cylinder engine affixed to a strange flying machine he had built, clattered into life. Pearse climbed into position above the tricycle undercarriage, and took off down the road in his handmade monoplane. The onlookers were even more amazed when his contraption of bamboo, wire, tubular steel, and canvas climbed into the air, whirring and shaking before it veered left and plummeted into the top of a matted gorse hedge growing alongside Pearse's farm. It was a pity that there were no "official observers" or photographers to record the flight, bar one who came the following day to photograph the crashed craft jammed in the bushes. Even that record of the crash was to be lost in a flood some time after. Neither Pearse nor anyone else recorded the specific date—it had to be decided circumstantially. There was agreement by some that the most likely date was March 31, 1903. Other aviation authorities suggest the year of his attempt was actually 1909.

Later, witnesses' reports varied. Pearse had flown 50 yards (46.2 meters) said one; others had different ideas, with distance claims stretching from 109 to 164 yards (100 to 150 meters), to an even wilder guess of 437 yards (400 meters). And there's the rub. Without a careful, trained observer, or a photographer to record the event (In Kittyhawk, the Wright brothers had both) all claims made for Pearse lacked scientific proof. What can be said, is that "Mad Pearse"—as some of the villagers called him—did take off in a powered heavier-than-air machine that anticipated some future aviation developments. It bore a surface resemblance to today's micro-light aircraft. It was a monoplane with a 25-feet (7.62-meter) wingspan, equipped with a kind of aileron for maneuvering, and it boasted a tricycle undercarriage with a steerable nose wheel.

Some of the farmers in Waitohi, in the South Island of New Zealand, thought that Richard Pearse was quite mad. Instead of working his 100-acre (40.5-hectare) farm effectively, Pearse spent days at a time in an old cottage on his land, which he had converted into a workshop. Here, the interests that had obsessed him as a schoolboy would be refined and tested. He had wanted to study engineering, but his farming parents couldn't afford it and he wound up as a farmer instead. As a voracious reader of *Popular Mechanics* and *Scientific American* as a boy, Richard kept in touch with the engineering and scientific developments in Europe and America. Farming took a poor second place to his driving ambition to create, invent, and fly.

In his workshop, Pearse toiled deep into the night, developing his engineering ideas by working with scraps of metal, building his own forge, designing and constructing his own lathe, and creating things out of metal off-cuts, cast-iron pipes, and even bamboo. By 1902 he had patented an ingenious bamboo-framed bicycle with all the trimmings—vertical-drive pedal action, rod and rack gearing, back-pedal rim brakes, and built-in tire pumps.

Earlier, in 1899, at the age of 22, he enlisted the help of New Zealand engineer Cecil Wood to put together a two-cylinder internal combustion engine he had designed. He made his own crankshafts, carburetors, and spark plugs. He produced a two-cylinder, horizontally opposed lightweight engine. It weighed about a quarter of motorcar engines at that time, but generated 25 horsepower. Pearse's aim was to build an engine that he could install in the airplane he had in mind. His driving ambition was to fly.

Certainly this reclusive, introspective man achieved some of his ambitions. The machine he constructed alone, in the workshop behind his gorse hedge and which he tested that day in Waitohi, left the ground for a short hop. But not well enough or for a far enough distance to satisfy his aim of sustained, controlled flight. He continued trying over subsequent years, achieving several powered takeoffs and some quite lengthy hops. These were witnessed, but none of them met Pearse's own, self-imposed standards. As he

Left: This replica of Richard Pearse's aircraft was built by Auckland's Museum of Transport and Technology to celebrate the centenary of Pearse's flight attempt. It is shown taxiing during a ground run at the original site in Waitohi, New Zealand, on March 31, 2003. The plane is recorded on the Civil Aviation Register as ZK-RWP, authorized for one experimental flight not to exceed 1,000 feet (305 meters).

later wrote, he never claimed to have beaten the Wright brothers yet it has been argued that he almost achieved as much as the Wright brothers did with their initial powered flight, which also came to grief at the first attempt. But Richard Pearse probably suffered from being a loner, from not having the healthy arguments and the battling over theories and possible solutions that typified the Wrights's working methods. Moreover, once the Wrights had overcome control problems with their aircraft, flying machines in the U.S. and Europe quickly roared ahead of the work of the lonesome genius so far away in New Zealand.

Pearse didn't give up. His lively mind kept creating new inventions, which were wide-ranging and innovative. He developed a motorized plow, a fertilizer applicator, sound recording and playback equipment, a harp, and an automatic potato planter. In the early 1930s he turned once again to aircraft. This time, instead of being a pioneer of powered flight, he wanted to build what he termed his "Utility Plane." This would be an aircraft for the people—one with fold-away wings that could be kept in a garage, able to "take off vertically on rough ground or limited areas" as it would have an engine that could be tilted for vertical takeoff and landing. He applied for a patent for his Utility Plane in 1943. After much stonewalling and argument, a patent was finally granted in 1949. But it was too late—Pearse's Utility Plane never flew.

Right: Richard Pearse's valiant attempt to fly ended atop the gorse hedge bordering his farm. The flat wing on his craft indicates that he had not gathered sufficient theoretical data to develop a curved profile in order to give his wing better lifting qualities.

"Mad Pearse" did finally crack. After a lifetime of reclusive, obsessive hard work, full of constant setbacks and financial hardships, he suffered a breakdown in 1951 and was admitted to Sunnyside Mental Hospital, where he died two years later aged 75.

In March 2003 in the South Canterbury town of Timaru, a full-scale replica of Richard Pearse's monoplane was on display. To celebrate the centenary of heavier-than-air powered flight, aircraft buffs in New Zealand carefully reconstructed replicas of Pearse's pioneering aircraft, including the unique two-cylinder petrol engine he had designed and built. One of the replicas is now displayed at the Museum of Transport and Technology in Auckland, New Zealand.

... I decided ... it was useless to try to compete against men who had factories at their back.

PEARSE'S LETTER TO *THE CHRISTCHURCH STAR*, 1928

ANTHONY FOKKER

"THE FLYING DUTCHMAN"

Anthony Fokker was born in 1890 in the Dutch East Indies—now Indonesia. His father was a rich colonial planter whose wealth was to be a factor in Fokker's future success. To ensure that their son would gain a European education, the family returned to live in Haarlem, Holland, when Anthony was 11 years old. He was a mischievous, adventurous boy, not dedicated to studying. "I found learning very boring. Only one subject appealed to me—handicrafts—at which I excelled," he later wrote. Anthony loved experimenting with making things, and specialized in building model trains, which he later set up and electrified in his attic playroom. He also devised his own security system by connecting the doorknob with a live wire, once nearly electrocuting a nosy niece who was trying to see what the young Anthony was up to.

After scraping through high school he went to Germany to attend a car-manufacturing school, but after only two days decided to move instead to a new course on a completely new subject—aviation. Part of the course required the students to jointly construct a plane. On completion, the aircraft was taken out to fly, manned by a pilot with little experience who, unable to fly it, crashed the plane, simultaneously bringing the course to an abrupt end.

Fokker then decided to build his own craft, and appealed to his father for money for the project. In 1910 he designed and built his first aircraft, which he called the *Spider*. It also crashed but Anthony learned a lot from his first attempt and designed and built the *Spider II*. This time he reported that he had fixed a proper rudder and constructed an improved elevator. As his own test pilot he started to make his *Spider* airborne. "When I taxied over the field after the adjustments, I found the plane had gained much in the way of control. Every time I revved up the engine we made a small jump in the air—first 3 and 6 meters, then 30- and 60-meter jumps. When I made a jump of a few hundred meters I felt like a bird," he recorded.

Fokker flew enough to test the plane's ability to maneuver

Left: Anthony Fokker in the driver's seat of his second Spin (Spider). Sitting in the center of a maze of wires and struts, Fokker said he felt like a spider—hence his name for the aircraft.

Left: Young Anthony Fokker loved flying and he was a great entrepreneur. His exuberant and lively display flying was only exceeded by his ability to promote himself and his cause on the ground. He never missed a sales opportunity and hated to be beaten by his rivals. When he set up his manufacturing company in Germany he met and teamed up with the brilliant Reinhold Platz, who became Fokker's designer and engineer. Over a long association, Platz was to create Fokker's most successful aircraft.

and circle around the field a number of times before landing. On May 16, 1911, after applying for his pilot's license, he flew in his plane and became a fully qualified, licensed pilot. Later he was asked by the citizens of Haarlem to give a demonstration to celebrate the birthday anniversary of the Dutch queen. He treated the town to a lengthy display of the aircraft's flying abilities, circling close to the cathedral tower. Fokker's flight resulted in an amazing outpouring of excitement, emotion, and jubilation from the townspeople who crowded the streets. His father was, for the first time, able to observe the fruits of the money he had advanced to his son.

Within months, Fokker had returned to Germany and, by the end of 1911, had formed the Fokker Aviation Company

I felt like Balboa when he sighted the Pacific.

**ANTHONY FOKKER, AFTER FLYING HIS
FIRST PLANE, 1910**

Anthony Fokker's first successful design was the Spider. There were several variations of this machine. This version is the one he flew over Haarlem, Holland, during 1911. With his name emblazoned on the wings, every citizen of Haarlem would have been aware of whose plane it was. Later in his career he often insisted that his name appear in large letters on the wings or fuselage of aircraft he sold to record-making pilots. With drive such as this, it was no surprise to see this young man running the world's largest airplane manufacturing business in the late 1920s.

Left: A close-up view showing a deflector plate and the position of the machine gun firing through the propeller arc of French ace, Jules Vedrin's Morane fighter.

with a small factory just outside Berlin ready to manufacture his Spiders. It was tough going for a couple of years, with few sales. Survival depended on demonstrations and joyrides. Then came the growing threat of war and Fokker's military versions of the Spider—the M-1 and M-2—won orders from the German military. In 1914, the day after war was declared, the German government took over all Fokker's available aircraft and ordered more.

Before long Fokker fighters became the scourge of the skies, and with Fokker's invention of the synchronized machine gun firing through the sweep of the propeller without damage, the Fokker became the deadliest weapon in the air.

From the moment air warfare made its debut at the start of World War I, no one built as good a reputation for daring, courtliness, dazzling flying, and deadly efficiency as the German fighter ace, Manfred von Richtofen.

Right: Roland Garros, the famous French flier, had become a popular figure in France because of his courageous pioneering flight across the Mediterranean in 1913. As a military pilot he soon became an air ace after he had mounted deflector plates on the propeller blades of his Morane fighter. When he fired his gun at the enemy, enough bullets would get through the spinning propeller, and the rest simply bounced off its metal deflectors.

The German high command, alarmed at Garros's success, asked Fokker to come up with a response. They got it in two days. Anthony Fokker devised the mechanism after being shown Garros's captured aircraft. It was a most efficient system and made the Fokker E-1 Eindekker, to which it was fitted, invincible in the hands of German masters such as Immelmann and Boelcke. The famous Fokker Eindekker was the first warplane to be fitted with interrupter gear so that a machine gun could be fired through the arc of the propeller.

The Fokker E-I Eindekker was fitted with
a single machine gun. A second version of
the Fokker fighter, the E-II, was fitted
with two Spandaus.

Above: Martin Kreutzer was the designer of the Fokker Eindekker. He
died air testing an aircraft in 1916. Reinhold Platz thereafter designed
all the Fokker machines well into the 1930s.

Manfred was the descendant of a wealthy Junker family, hailing from Prussian aristocracy. He loved taking risks. From his childhood days he grew up with a love of riding, controlling spirited horses, and hunting. Like many Junker males, to be a military man was his ambition. He quickly graduated from cadet to cavalry officer, and once war broke out, he saw duty scouting for the German army on the eastern and western fronts. In 1915, he transferred to the Flying Service, swapping horses for airplanes.

Richtofen was a natural. His fire and love of risk-taking, combined with Anthony Fokker's remarkably efficient and maneuverable fighter planes, made the Baron an overnight hero for the German side. On September 17, 1916, he made his first "kill," downing a cumbersome British plane. It was the first of 80 Allied planes which were to fall to his rattling Spandau machine guns and his mastery of aerial dogfights. Before long he led his own squadron, the Richtofen Circus, with handpicked pilots proud to be teamed with the fearless Baron. Richtofen was showered with decorations and became the leading ace of the war.

Opposite:This reconstruction shows the moment of truth when Richtofen, flying his red-painted Fokker DR-I triplane over British lines during World War I, was fired on by Australian Lewis gunners on a ridge overlooking the River Somme in France.

The triplane was hit first by the Lewis gunners on the right and immediately after by those on the left. Pieces flew off the aircraft. Richtofen whipped off his goggles and banked sharply to the right.This gave the gunner on the right a clear view of Richtofen as he fired. It is possible that the German ace was fatally hit at this point. He gunned the engine, flattened out, fired at the Camel, then suddenly cut the motor. The Fokker spiraled to the right, then crashed into a beet field. An Australian rifleman also shot at the plane just after the Lewis gunners. It is not known whether his shot or that of the Lewis gunners killed Richtofen.

The high command instructed Richtofen that the planes were to be camouflaged to make them difficult targets. The order challenged his Junker pride. He had all the planes in his squadron painted a flaming red. Renowned as The Red Baron in the recorded history of war in the air—a title used by friend and foe alike—his reputation for skill and bravery became legendary, so much so that it was feared his death would be a savage blow to the morale of German troops as well as civilians. In 1918, he was invited to retire.

He became depressed, partly it is said because of a serious head wound for which he hadn't allowed enough convalescence time before he climbed back into the cockpit. In his autobiography, he is quoted as saying, "I think of this war as it really is, not as people at home imagine, with a hoorah! And a roar. It is very serious, very grim." Manfred flatly refused to stop. He would keep flying, he said, as long as there were German troops in the trenches.

On April 21, 1918, in a new Fokker triplane, chasing an inexperienced pilot in a British Sopwith Camel, the Red Baron flew low over Allied lines. His own plane was being pursued by a Canadian fighter pilot, Roy Brown. Richtofen's career came to an abrupt end when he was over a ridge above the River Somme. Brown was given credit for shooting down Richtofen's plane, but forensic evidence shows that a single fatal bullet entered the Baron's lower chest on the right-hand side, and exited near his left nipple. It was most likely he was shot by ground fire, not by aircraft machine gun bullets. In his biographical book *Manfred von Richtofen*, first published in 1990, author David Baker provides evidence to suggest that Richtofen's nemesis was one of two Australian Lewis gunners or an Australian rifleman in the trenches who fired as the triplane pursued the Camel.

The loss to the German side was immense. Richtofen's opponents showed their deep admiration for this noble adversary. He was given a hero's funeral with full military honors at Bertangles, close to where he died. His legendary reputation will never be laid to rest.

Above: Reinhold Platz's most famous fighter, the Fokker D-VII, proved to be the best fighter aircraft of World War I. Its 160-horsepower Mercedes engine pushed it along at 124 miles (198 kilometers) per hour and was Ernst Udet's favorite mount. Ace Willi Gabriel flew this example.

Below:The Fokker Dr I Dreidekker was Anthony Fokker's best-known airplane. Reinhold Platz, who created Fokker's most successful machines, designed the DR I. Platz is seen standing to the right of Anthony Fokker on a half-assembled Dreidekker. Inspired by the very successful British Sopwith triplane, the Dreidekker was not fast, but it was highly maneuverable with an excellent rate of climb.

Immediately after the end of World War I, Anthony Fokker produced a series of airliners. One of the early models was the Fokker F-IV. It could carry 10 passengers. The thick, clean, cantilevered 80-foot (24.4-meter) wing showed it came from designer, Reinhold Platz. It was driven by a single 400-horsepower Liberty engine, which gave it a cruising speed of around 90 miles (145 kilometers) per hour.

The U.S. Army used two of Fokker's models, designated the Fokker T-2 and, in 1923, one of them was used to create the first, nonstop flight across the United States. The pilots were Lt. John Macready and Lt. Oakley G. Kelly. The two pilots left from Roosevelt field, taking so long to get airborne they lurched off the end of the runway and jumped a bluff onto the runway next door in Hazelhurst airfield! The flight was relatively free of trouble, apart from the fact that Kelly in the front cockpit who, while flying along at 1,000 feet (305 meters), had to reset the points in the voltage regulator to cure the rough running of the Liberty. Nevertheless, it was a tour de force and they landed, exhausted, in San Diego after taking 26 hours and 50 minutes for the 2,470-mile (3,952-kilometer) trip.

Left: Lts. Macready and Kelly were the victorious pilots of the U.S. Army who flew the Fokker T-2 (below) on the first, nonstop flight across the American continent. There was only a single-seat cockpit, set right up against the exhaust stacks of the howling Liberty engine. There was, however, another pilot's position inside the main cabin. The two pilots took it in turns to fly from the front cockpit, the man in the back holding the plane steady while the swap took place.

Fokker T-2, 1923

Right: The Fokker F-VII created aviation history. It was the first airliner to fly from Holland to Batavia (now Indonesia) for the Dutch airline, K.L.M., in 1924. The flight was a nostalgic event for Fokker because he had been born in Batavia, his parents having returned to Europe when he was a boy to give him better schooling.

Designer Reinhold Platz based the F-VII on a previous airliner that grew out of his powerful Fokker D-VIII parasol monoplane fighter. Its characteristic triangulated tail plane and thick, cantilevered wing are evidence of its pedigree. In turn, this airplane gave birth to the famous Fokker trimotor series—the incentive for Fokker was his desire to set up his company in America. With his usual flair for judging the market, he gave the American version of the F-VII more power with three engines. It was an immediate success and the Fokker F-VII3m became the machine of choice for airlines and long-distance exploration. It made Fokker the world's biggest airplane manufacturer.

Right: Anthony Fokker wishes the K.L.M. crew of the F-VII "bon voyage" on the departure of their historic flight to Batavia on October 1, 1924.

Far right: The passenger cabin of the Fokker F-VII

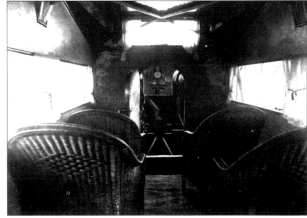

ROSS AND KEITH SMITH

"GOD 'ELP ALL OF US"

*Left: L to R, Jim Bennett, Ross Smith,
Keith Smith, and Wally Shiers*

This memorable quote was said half in jest, half seriously. It all had to do with a £10,000 prize for an air race to be awarded to the first airplane manned by Australians to fly from England to Australia. Australian Prime Minister "Billy" Hughes put forward the challenge in 1919, shortly after a similar prize offered by the English newspaper, *The Daily Mail*, had resulted in the first-ever nonstop flight across the Atlantic. Prime Minister Hughes (known affectionately as "The Little Digger") had participated in the Versailles Peace Conference and felt Australia should play a more important part on the world stage. He believed that the air race would attract positive, international press for Australia via the popular interest in aviation, while encouraging a number of Australian wartime aircrew still in England to return home by flying their ex-service planes.

One of the seven craft to take up the challenge was a twin-engined Vimy bomber entered by Vickers Limited, makers of heavy bombers in World War I. The registration

letters on the plane were: G-EAOU, which the crew said stood for "God 'Elp All Of Us." The competitors would need all the help they could get as it was the biggest challenge ever faced by flying machines at that time. The entrants were looking at a 12,000-mile (18,500-kilometer) journey across land and sea, with harsh climate change and confronting conditions for takeoffs and landings in countries which had either very little or no previous experience with aircraft. No plane had ever set out to fly such a long distance before.

One of the starters was a Frenchman, who knew he couldn't win because he wasn't an Australian, yet he was keen to show that France's enthusiasm for aviation had not been dimmed by a war which, in terms of air force standards, had left Great Britain on top. He was Etienne Poulet, who, with his navigator and engineer, Jean Benoist, intended to fly a Caudron twin-engined biplane. Howell and Frazer would fly a single-engined Martynside; Matthews and Kay chose a similar plane to the Sopwith Atlantic; Douglas and Ross flew an Alliance Endeavour with a fully enclosed cockpit, and Rendle and Wilkins opted for a twin-engined Blackburn Kangaroo. Late starters were Parer and McIntosh flying a single-engined De Havilland 9. Ross Smith would fly the G-EAOU Vimy, with brother Keith as navigator. Sgt. Wally Shiers and Sgt. Jim Bennett joined them as crew, maintaining airframe and engines.

On November 12, 1919, one day after the first anniversary of the Armistice which ended World War I, the heavily laden Vimy lifted off from Hounslow in London. Ross Smith had something of an advantage over his competitors. He had previously flown from Cairo to Calcutta on a survey flight

Left: The Smith brothers' Vickers Vimy had an exposed, open cockpit for the pilot.

Opposite page: The air route from England to Australia was pioneered by an air race. It was organized by the Australian Government in 1919 to help promote Australian aviation. In the 1970s, jets took over from piston-engined airliners and flying boats, shrinking the flight time to under 24 hours. This Qantas Boeing 707–338c, City of Parramatta, pictured over Rome, was one of the popular early jets to fly the route. Very few travelers today know of the debt they owe to the sterling work of Ross and Keith Smith who flew the winning Vickers Vimy twin-engined biplane that won the infamous air race, taking 27 days.

in a Handley-Page bomber. He knew what to expect. Yet the flight was put to the test early.

On the first leg to Lyons in France, the team were met with strong frontal conditions with icing, strong winds, and poor visibility. Bitter cold and lack of blind-flying instruments made this one of the most challenging sections of the whole flight. Sitting in open cockpits, the crew were clad in heavy leather flying suits with helmets and goggles, but the cold and the deafening racket of the Rolls-Royce Eagle engines made it a trying time for pilots and crew. It was just the start. The Vimy was to make over 20 refueling and rest stops, many of them dangerous.

The competition took its toll early. Douglas and Ross were killed in England only a few minutes after takeoff. Howell and Frazer, in their Martynside, crashed and drowned in the Mediterranean. Rendle and Wilkins crashed their Kangaroo in Crete; Matthews and Kay, despite their speedy progress, crashed in a Bali banana plantation only one day's flying from Darwin, the target finishing point in Australia's north. The unofficial French entry gave the Vimy solid competition. In a contest conducted with goodwill and

Right: A French Caudron G4 was very nearly the first airplane to fly across the world to Australia from Europe in 1919. It was flown by the famous French flier, Etienne Poulet and his navigator and engineer, Jean Benoist. It actually arrived in Rangoon only one hour after Ross Smith's Vimy, though it had set out from Paris many days before the Vimy left London. Because of engine and propeller problems their gallant attempt in this ex-wartime light bomber finally ended in Moulmein, Burma.

Like the Smith brothers, Poulet and Benoist flew in an open cockpit, exposed to everything the weather could throw at them. The cockpit of the Smith brothers' Vimy (below) had virtually no instruments apart from an altimeter, compass, and airspeed indicator. Flying this aircraft required strength, as there was no automatic pilot and it had to be flown "hands-on" all the time.

Opposite page: Latitude 10° 57'S, Longitude 128° 14'E, the Smiths fly the Vickers Vimy low over H.M.A.S. Sydney. The cruiser, placed on station in the Timor Sea to render any help necessary on the final stretch of the flight from England to Darwin, picked up a small parachute weighted with a bottle which had been thrown from the Vimy. The bottle contained a message, reading, in part: "Very glad to see you. Many thanks for looking after us. Going strong," and signed by Ross and Keith Smith, Jim Bennett, and Wally Shiers.

Above: After their pioneering flight across half the globe, Ross Smith and his crew board their Vickers Vimy near Ross Smith's hometown of Adelaide, South Australia. The public's imagination was fired up by their success, so the victorious crew, with famous wartime photographer, Frank Hurley aboard, made a triumphant tour of the southeastern states of Australia in 1920.

gentlemanly rivalry, the two planes often flew the same stages together for their mutual assistance. Poulet and Benoist had to pull out of the race at Moulmein, Burma (now Myanmar), only a few days away from the Darwin finishing line.

The Vimy plowed on. They had many hairy moments—flooded airstrips were a hazard. Short runways meant that Jim Bennett had to invent a perilous braking technique, which consisted of him climbing out of his cockpit between the wings, then sliding back along the top of the fuselage to the plane's tail so his weight would dig the tailskid into the ground and shorten the landing run. In Indonesia, the local villagers turned out to lay a runway of matting on a muddy airstrip for the bogged Vimy's takeoff. The final stages of the historic flight were to take the Vimy from the island of Timor, across the shark-infested Timor Sea to Darwin.

Early on December 10, 1919, they left Alamboe, Timor, and after flying hours over the Timor Sea, were excited to see the big Royal Australian Navy cruiser, H.M.A.S. *Sydney*, loom out of the haze, lying right on station as promised, in the area of their proposed route. Ross took their big biplane low over the warship to acknowledge the officers and crew

who were cheering on deck. As they passed the ship, the aviators dropped a thank-you note tied to a small parachute before turning back on course. They flew the last 180 miles (290 kilometers) of their extraordinary flight, arriving in Darwin to an enthusiastic welcome. They made their landing 27 days and 20 hours after leaving London. One of the requirements of the contest was that the flight had to be no more than 30 days. Ray Parer and his observer John McIntosh were the only other entrants to finish, and their time was outside the 30-day limit.

For their triumphant flight, the brothers Smith were appointed Knights Commander of the British Empire. Bennett and Shiers were promoted to honorary lieutenants. On April 13, 1922, Sir Ross Smith and Lt. Jim Bennett were both killed flight-testing a Vickers Viking amphibian, in which Ross and Keith were planning to circumnavigate the world. The Vickers Vimy, which made the prize-winning flight, is still in mint condition, well preserved in the city of Adelaide, South Australia, where the Smith brothers were born. The flight was the start of many world-famous flights by pioneering Australian aviators.

WRIGLEY AND MURPHY

A FUNNY KIND OF WELCOME

When the famous Vickers Vimy aircraft of Ross and Keith Smith completed the first-ever flight from England to Australia in December 1919 it was greeted, albeit two days late, by a small, spindly looking, ex–World War I reconnaissance aircraft. The BE2E two-seater plane was flown by Capt. H. N. Wrigley DFC and Sgt. A.W. Murphy DFC of the Australian Flying Corps. Their arduous flight was the first crossing of the Australian continent. They took off from Point Cook near Melbourne to follow a tortuous route north to Darwin in the Northern Territory.

Even today, with fine airfields to provide good servicing and solid runways to land on, a flight of that nature would not be undertaken lightly by a small airplane carrying all the latest navigational aids. In 1919 such sophistication was not to be found. Wrigley and Murphy's flight from the bottom of Australia to the top was a prodigious feat of airmanship.

MELBOURNE TO DARWIN FLIGHT, 1919

Darwin
Katherine
Alexander Station
Townsville
Cloncurry
Winton
Longreach
Charleville
Cunnamulla
Brisbane
Bourke
Narromine
Forbes
Sydney
Adelaide
Cootamundra
Melbourne

The trip took 46 days, flying 2,500 miles (4,000 kilometers), and because of the limited range of the BE2E, extra fuel tanks were fitted beneath the upper wings of the aircraft. Despite this Wrigley and Murphy had to make 17 stops before arriving at Port Darwin. Their route had only recently been pioneered on the ground. Maj. R. S. Brown and Lt. A. R. McComb were responsible for the southern section, while P. J. McGinness and Hudson Fysh (with George Gorham as their mechanic) drove and pushed a Ford motor car over the wild and inaccessible terrain from Charleville to Darwin.

The crew of the BE2E was briefed to land at the various staging posts so they could assess them for future use as landing grounds. The victorious Vickers Vimy later used the route to fly south via the eastern states to Melbourne where Ross Smith and his crew were to receive the £10,000 prize for winning the Great Air Race from England to Australia. But the survey was not just for the benefit of the Vimy; Darwin was seen as the natural entry point for any future international air route so the establishment of an internal airway linking the far north with the population centers of the eastern and southern states was fundamental. So it proved to be—Hudson Fysh, who had helped pioneer this link, later became one of its principal users as a pilot and Chief Executive of Qantas Airways.

Above left: The route of the BE2E from Point Cook in Melbourne to Darwin encompassed 2,500 miles (4,000 kilometers). Wrigley and Murphy received little credit from the public for their pioneering efforts, however, their peers recognized the 46 hours flying time as a wonderful tour de force and a great pioneering achievement. Wrigley was to become an Air Marshal and Murphy a Group Captain in the R.A.A.F.

Left: The BE2E alongside the Vickers Vimy in Darwin, 1919

Opposite page: December 12, 1919. Wrigley and Murphy fly over Ross and Keith Smith's Vickers Vimy in Darwin after the Vimy had won the England to Australia Air Race.

GOBLE AND MCINTYRE

"THE FINEST FLIGHT IN THE HISTORY OF AVIATION"

To survey the largest island in the world was a momentous undertaking for Wing Comdr. Stanley Goble and Flt. Lt. Ivor McIntyre. After the event these two adventurers were praised as having won a special place in the records of flying achievement. Together in 1924, they surveyed the coastline of Australia—the world's largest island continent. As members of the Royal Australian Air Force (R.A.A.F.) the pair had convinced the Australian military planners and politicians that they could carry out a survey of the eastern seaboard much more economically than the original intention of sending a warship equipped with an airplane. At a time of worldwide depression there was little dissension. Goble—then acting chief of staff of the R.A.A.F.—was mainly responsible for arguing the case, and he was appointed leader and navigator of the expedition. Ivor McIntyre was the pilot. As well as surveying the eastern coastline for possible military base sites, they were to establish whether seaplanes could deliver mail to isolated areas of Australia as part of normal flying services. They also had to test the suitability of the airplane and the viability of the materials used in its construction.

The airplane chosen for the expedition was a British Fairey III-D, one of several ordered for the Australian Navy and then transferred to the R.A.A.F. It was a single-engined biplane fitted with floats and equipped with an extra 40-gallon (182-liter) fuel tank. Other precautions were taken to protect the fabric skin and the wooden airframe from the hazards of tropical conditions. Fuel dumps, supplies of spares, and extra engines were set up at selected points across Australia, along the proposed route. Goble and McIntyre were both World War I naval fliers who faced this daunting adventure with the confidence born of having survived the cauldron of the European air war.

Their flight started in April 1924 when they flew out from the R.A.A.F. base at Point Cook, south of Melbourne in the state of Victoria. As Goble said later, "Our troubles began early..." Indeed they did. Soon after leaving, a problem arose with the auxiliary fuel tank and they had to put down at Wilson's Promontory at the southeastern corner of Australia. Then McIntyre's compass burst, showering him with alcohol. Not long after that, they were hit by 35-miles (55-kilometers) per hour headwinds. Because they cruised at just over 80 miles (120 kilometers) per hour, their ground speed was painfully slow. They were forced down to 250 feet (76.25 meters) above the sea in blinding rain and realized they were not going to make it to Sydney in one hop. They decided to break the flight and refuel at Eden, a small fishing port on the New South Wales south coast.

In alighting on a heavy swell, they damaged a float but they were off to Sydney within two hours. Conditions had worsened—the little seaplane was forced to fly for 90 miles (144 kilometers) in visibility so thick that McIntyre, with his compass broken, strayed off course. He had to bank sharply to avoid ramming into cliffs on the coast just south of Sydney. A bit chastened, the pair pressed on to arrive in Sydney at 1600 hours.

Stanley "Jimmie" Goble (left) and Ivor McIntyre (below) wore pith helmets on their pioneering flight, a common practice for R.A.A.F. aircrews working in hot conditions. The crew must have wondered why they chose this headgear when much of their flying was carried out in cloudy conditions with heavy rain.

Opposite page: Stanley Goble and Ivor McIntyre used this wood and fabric spotter and reconnaissance aircraft on the first aerial circumnavigation of Australia. It was a Fairey III-D with a wingspan of 46 feet (14 meters) and an economical cruising speed of 80 miles (120 kilometers) per hour. In still air this gave her a range of only 550 miles (886 kilometers) necessitating the large number of stops on her round trip of 8,450 miles (13,520 kilometers). Goble and McIntyre ran up against depressingly adverse weather conditions. Rain and atrocious visibility forced them down to 150 feet (45.7 meters) approaching Sydney, and they nearly slammed into cliffs at one point. Things did not improve after their stop in Sydney Harbour. As they flew north from Sydney scuds of low cloud presaged the start of a 57-miles (92-kilometers) per hour wind that was about to hit them; the associated mist and rain forced them to an emergency landing farther up the coast. The flight turned out to be a rugged circumnavigation of the world's biggest island continent.

Left: At Gladstone, Queensland, Goble and McIntyre had to check leaking floats, working up to their necks in water off the beach.

End of day one … 43 days would follow. Clearly this trip was to be no picnic. The two men soon learned that looking after their seaplane was a constant grind. After each day's flight they were putting in seven hours labor just baling floats, cleaning plugs, adjusting valve springs, humping drums of petrol to refuel; refueling entailed straining every drop of petrol through a chamois leather filter. Typically, at Gladstone they could only refuel on the beach, and this took them from 8:00 A.M. until 3:00 P.M., up to their necks in water. Their floats leaked constantly so there was a lot of patching to be done with red-lead paint and canvas. At Thursday Island they fitted a fresh set of floats, which had been shipped in. To do that, they had to lift the 2.5-ton (2.55-tonne) aircraft on makeshift 50-feet (15.25-meter) sheer legs

provided by a local pearl fisherman. This was one of only three places around the coast of Australia where they were able to lift the machine out of the water to carry out maintenance. No surprise then that Goble commented after the survey was complete that the most depressing part of their trip was the total lack of facilities along most of the route.

Above: The standard Fairey III-D seaplane featured old-style pontoons (called "floats" by British airmen). Visible are the three cockpits—pilot in front, navigator in center, and air-gunner at the rear. Goble navigated his machine from the rear cockpit. The center was fitted with an extra fuel tank.

Right: R.A.A.F. Sgt. Gottschalk finalizes the replacement of the Fairey III-D's Rolls-Royce Eagle engine at Carnarvon, Western Australia.

Far right: A typical beach stopover—at Southport, Queensland, the crew service their seaplane, surrounded by interested locals.

Right: At Darwin, in Australia's Northern Territory, facilities were in place to lift the Fairey III-D out of the water for a full service.

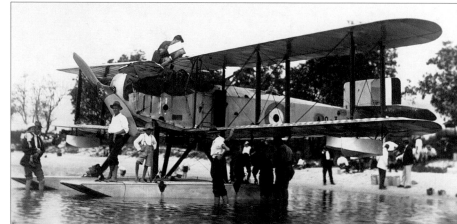

The R.A.A.F. crew's problems were not all technical and weather related. In the tropics, mosquitoes and sand flies drove both men to distraction as they worked on the aircraft or tried to get a good night's rest. At one point, McItyre's legs and ankles were so swollen from insect bites he could hardly operate the controls; his face became so puffed up that he could hardly see. However, their spirits rose whenever they stopped at small settlements because the local residents always showered them with kindness and generosity.

The flight was an extraordinary accomplishment of the period. Goble and McIntyre surveyed the coastline of a country the size of the United States in 44 days. They logged 90 hours of flying time and covered 8,450 miles (13,520 kilometers) of territory—2,500 miles (4,022 kilometers) of which was through appalling weather conditions, often with close to zero visibility. Other than having to replace the Rolls-Royce Eagle VII engine when they reached Western Australia, the Fairey seaplane served them well. It was a trailblazing achievement without parallel at the time. It inspired one of Britain's top aviation experts to say: "This is the finest flight in the history of aviation."

Above: The Fairey III-D sits high and dry on a beach at Elcho Island in Australia's far north during a break in the seven-hour daily servicing ritual.

Above: Enthusiastic onlookers of the Fairey seaplane on the Swan River in Perth, Western Australia—especially children—put the safety of the seaplane at risk. At one fueling stop, the crew caught children swinging on control wires. On another occasion, a vandal untied safety-locking wire on a fuel cap, causing a fuel tank to run dry without warning, which in turn, forced a landing in rough sea.

Left: Goble and McIntyre were amazed at the enthusiastic welcome they received when they returned to their base at Point Cook. Top officials and senior politicians came to pay their respects to these two tired and disheveled men, as they were carried shoulder high in their well-worn and crumpled uniforms. Aviation experts in Australia and half the world away in England, applauded the flight. Goble was awarded £500 and McIntyre, £250 and the duo became part of aviation history when they won The Britannia Trophy for the best flight of 1924.

Below: In 1926, Ivor McIntyre featured in another great flight as pilot of the R.A.A.F. De H 50 seaplane. It was the first flight outside of Australia by an Australian-based aircraft. Captain Williams was in command and Flight Sergeant Trist was the mechanic. The trio completed a 10,000-mile (16,090-kilometer) trip from Point Cook to Tulagi in the British Solomon Islands, over 31 days, and in a flying time of just over 126 hours. McIntyre was awarded the coveted Oswald Watt Gold Medal for the best flight of the year. Sadly, he crashed and died soon after, while performing aerobatics over Parafield aerodrome in Adelaide, South Australia.

COUTINHO AND CABRAL

MEET CAGO THE NAVIGATOR

In the glory days of Henry the Navigator, Vasco de Gama, and other great conquerors of the sea, Portugal was the world leader in the art of navigation. In 1922, Vice Adm. Cago Coutinho aptly demonstrated that the ancient skills of Portuguese navigators could be practiced most effectively in the air.

Three years after Alcock and Brown had crossed the Atlantic nonstop in a Vickers Vimy bomber, Vice Adm. Coutinho and his pilot, Comdr. Sacadura Cabral, both of Portugal's defense forces, decided to conquer the South Atlantic. Spain and Portugal, with their strong historical links to South America, urgently wanted to open up air routes in this area—routes which had been ignored up until now by the major European powers.

The Atlantic has never been an easy ocean to cross. Cabral and Coutinho took three heroic attempts and lost two aircraft in their drive to reach their target. Portugal had no aircraft industry so the men turned to Britain to choose their plane, a Fairey III-D seaplane. Perhaps they shouldn't have named her *Lusitania*, remembering that the ill-fated ship of that name was sunk by a U-boat in World War I.

They flew *Lusitania* from Lisbon in March 1922, first to Las Palmas in the Canary Islands. After delays because of poor weather, they then took 10 hours to fly to Saint Vincent in the Cape Verde islands. There were more delays as they faced adverse weather before leaving Porta Pria—in the south of the archipelago—heading for Fernando de Noronha, with a planned refueling stop at St. Paul's Rock. There the unpredictable ocean wrecked the machine as she lay at the mooring. Hopes that they would reach Rio de Janeiro were dashed.

But just over a month later, on May 11, they were flying the route again, in another Fairey III-D seaplane.

They repeated their previous achievements, but this time successfully taking off from St. Paul's Rock. Sadly, on the long ocean crossing fate struck again. The Fairey's engine died and the crew were forced to put down in the sea. Eight hours later, still in their machine, they were rescued by ship, but the seaplane was destroyed while being hauled aboard.

Another month later the two adventurers were at it again. This time, on 5 June, 1922, in yet a third Fairey seaplane, they again flew their chosen path. With consummate courage both of them clung to their original intentions. Coutinho, a tough, responsible 52 year-old, was a masterly navigator and used some of his own inventive methods to keep on course. Cabral, a brave and very capable pilot, prepared to overcome the dangers they both faced and decided to ride the seaplane to its ultimate destination. On June 17, they finally alighted in the harbor of Rio de Janeiro—a victory of fortitude and memorable courage.

It was fitting that when a huge Dornier Do. X flying boat, powered by 12 mighty engines, made its maiden Lisbon to Rio de Janeiro passenger flight in 1931 Vice Adm. Cago Coutinho was invited to fly as an honored guest. But Sacadura Cabral was not on board the flight—in November 1924 he had vanished off the Belgian coast in a thick fog while he was on a delivery flight in a Fokker airplane, never to be seen again.

Lisbon

Las Palmas

North Atlantic Ocean

Cape Verde Islands

Fernando de Noronha

Recife

South Atlantic Ocean

Rio de Janeiro

LISBON TO RIO DE JANEIRO FLIGHT, 1922

Above: L to R: Comdr. Sacadura Cabral and Vice Adm. Cago Coutinho

Left: Cago Coutinho took this route on the first air crossing of the South Atlantic in 1922. A masterly navigator, he used a specially modified sextant and calculated drift by observing smoke bombs.

Below: The enormous 12-engined Dornier flying boat, the Do. X, flew from Lisbon to Rio de Janeiro in 1931. It was the first commercial use of the South Atlantic route pioneered by Cago Coutinho. The huge aircraft carried 150 passengers on its memorable flight, one of whom was a distinguished guest, Vice Adm. Coutinho.

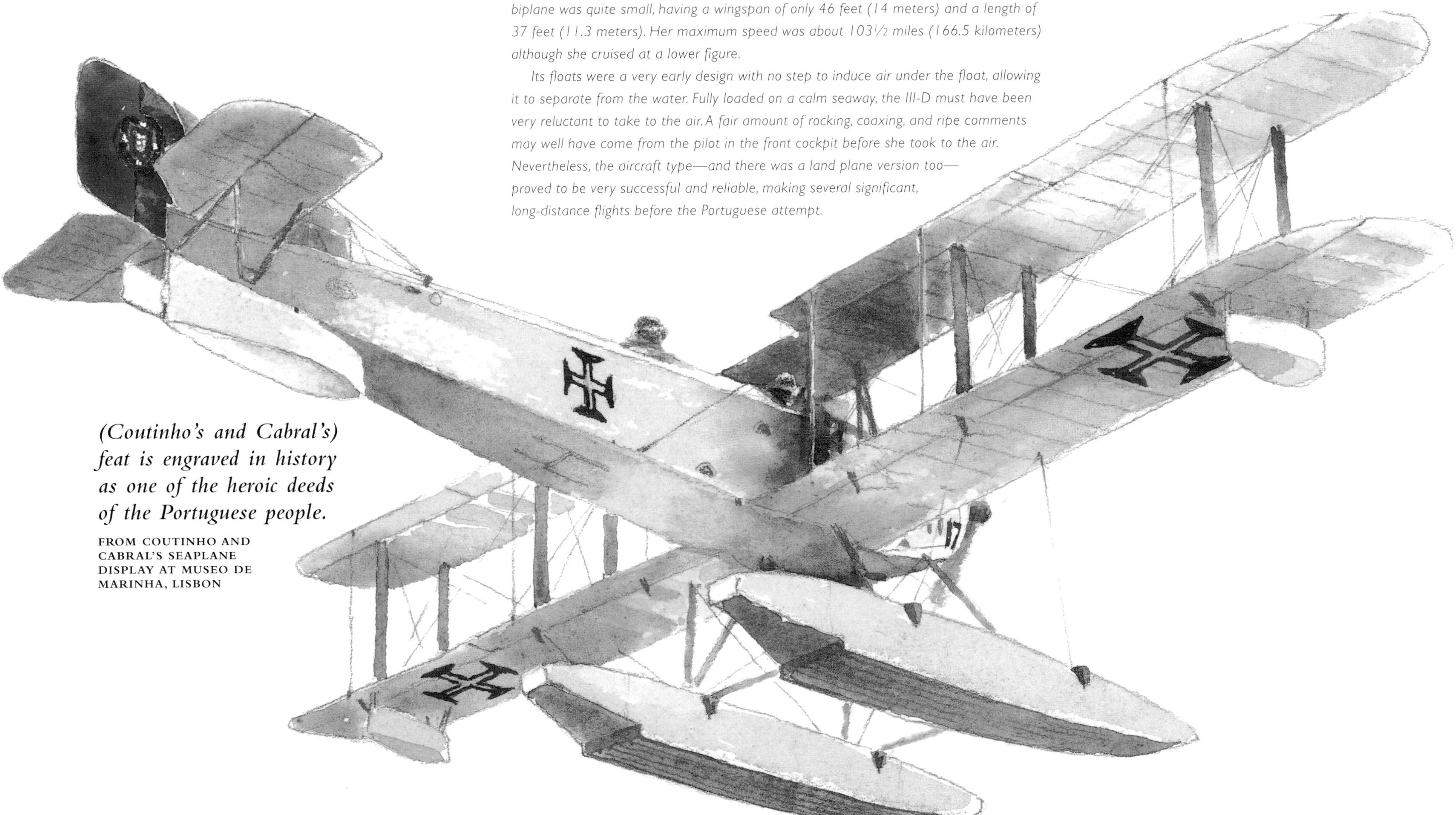

In 1922 Cabral and Coutinho flew the three-seat spotter reconnaissance Fairey III-D across the South Atlantic. The flying machine was powered by a Rolls-Royce Eagle engine of about 360 horsepower. As with so many of the pioneering airplanes, the Fairey biplane was quite small, having a wingspan of only 46 feet (14 meters) and a length of 37 feet (11.3 meters). Her maximum speed was about 103½ miles (166.5 kilometers) although she cruised at a lower figure.

Its floats were a very early design with no step to induce air under the float, allowing it to separate from the water. Fully loaded on a calm seaway, the III-D must have been very reluctant to take to the air. A fair amount of rocking, coaxing, and ripe comments may well have come from the pilot in the front cockpit before she took to the air. Nevertheless, the aircraft type—and there was a land plane version too— proved to be very successful and reliable, making several significant, long-distance flights before the Portuguese attempt.

(Coutinho's and Cabral's) feat is engraved in history as one of the heroic deeds of the Portuguese people.

FROM COUTINHO AND CABRAL'S SEAPLANE DISPLAY AT MUSEO DE MARINHA, LISBON

CLAIRMONT L. EGTVEDT

THE LEGEND WHO BUILT BOEING

William Boeing had learned to fly in 1915 at the Glenn Martin School. In 1917, working with a fellow aviator Conrad Westerveldt and using a boat repair yard in Seattle as a base, he designed and built a float plane, calling it the B&W 1. Boeing became the test pilot for the finished product and found it was well behaved and flew so sweetly that he thought he and Westerveldt might be able to sell some to the U.S. Navy. They failed, however, in that endeavor.

Westerveld left to join America's wartime forces so Boeing replaced him with Tsu Wong. Boeing and Wong designed and produced a handsome new float plane, which was designated as their model C biplane. This time it was a very successful venture. Boeing sold 50 Model Cs to the U.S. Navy alone. With that prestigious navy contract in his pocket, he felt more financially secure. He had started to make further plans when Wong resigned.

Boeing began to demonstrate his uncanny ability to pick people with outstanding talent. Unable to find any local replacement for Wong in Seattle, he cast a wider net. His search led him to the University of Washington where he

Clairmont Egtvedt

selected two graduates—Philip G. Johnson who proved to be an organizational genius and Clairmont L. Egtvedt, a mechanical engineering graduate who joined the newly established Boeing Company as a draftsman.

It was a masterly decision. Both of these men were to become powerful factors in the company's rapid growth. Johnson became President of the company at the age of 30 and Clairmont "Claire" Egtvedt was the creative dynamo who sparked Boeing's hugely successful research, experimental, and development policies. Egtvedt stayed with the company for 50 years, until his retirement in 1966, during which time he became President and Chairman of the most successful aviation company in the world.

In the 1920s and 1930s aviation manufacturing was a risky, cutthroat affair. The main source of financial stability was military orders. Although a designer was able to produce a winning design, the manufacturing company might still

Above: The Egtvedt-designed Boeing PW-9 pursuit plane of 1926 had a maximum speed of 163 miles (268 kilometers) per hour and a ceiling of 21,000 feet (6,468 meters). The U.S. Navy called their various models FB-1, 2, and 3.

not make money. The military often put the design to tender and awarded the manufacturing to the company that came in with the lowest quote.

Boeing's major breakthrough came in 1926 with Claire Egtvedt's Boeing PW-9 pursuit plane. Although the U.S. military had stated that it wasn't interested in another fighter, the PW-9 was so good that it changed its mind. The U.S. Navy came in with orders as well. A batch was ordered for the navy's new aircraft carriers. Little was new in the PW-9 design, however with this version Boeing had an ace in the hole. In building the new model, Boeing followed the lead of Dutch aircraft wizard, Anthony Fokker. The fuselage of the PW-9 was a strong, easy-to-maintain, metal-frame construction. Boeing made the competitive leap forward by using electric arc welding in manufacture. It was faster, more consistent, and more reliable than acetylene welding commonly used by other makers.

Military contracts kept aviation companies alive in the late 1920s and early 1930s. Within a few years the successful

Above: During his time as head of Boeing and its subsidiaries, Clairmont Egtvedt established a world-beating combination of engineering, production and design talents that gave the world some of the most advanced commercial and military aircraft of the day. With a management style and marketing expertise that would eventually overwhelm its competitors, Egtvedt allowed Boeing to become, as one company slogan proclaimed: "plane maker to the world."

Left: The Boeing Model C seaplane, 1917

Left: The Boeing F4B-4 or P-12 of 1928 was a nippy little pursuit plane, which became very popular, particularly in the U.S. Navy as a carrier-borne aircraft. Well over 90 craft served in the navy and marines. A Pratt & Whitney Wasp air-cooled radial engine of 450 horsepower gave a top speed of 178 miles (286 kilometers) per hour and a ceiling of 26,000 feet (7,924 meters).

Right: The Boeing P-26 of 1932 was a compromise between what military pilots wanted and what Boeing designer Claire Egtvedt knew to be a better design. The military preferred the known strengths of the biplane wing. So in the P-26 they got a monoplane—but with very visible and very strong wire stays.

She had an initial rate of climb of 2,500 feet (762 meters) and speed of 235 miles (378 kilometers) per hour. This colorful P-26 is typical of the day and was operated by the U.S. Army nineteenth Pursuit Group at Wheeler Field, Hawaii.

The Boeing P-26

The Boeing F4B-4

Boeing PW-9s were replaced by more Boeing models—by the popular F4B-4 biplane in 1929 and in 1932 by an all-metal monoplane, the fast and agile P-26. U.S. Army pilots nicknamed this model *The Peashooter*. Yet while Boeing was to hold its own in the battle for military contracts, Egtvedt and Johnson could see a large potential civilian market for passenger-carrying airliners. They were not alone. Rival companies Douglas and Curtiss were also looking to produce appealing planes by offering safety, comfort, and a reduction in noise—all factors that existing biplane airliners lacked. Boeing could also see that their own passenger-carrying models were not attracting sufficient new customers. The passenger market was in the doldrums. Then Claire Egtvedt's team at Boeing came up with the formula for success. In fact, the answers began to appear from a design for a mail plane. In the mid-1920s mail planes had emerged as specialized machines. They needed to be fast, reliable, and capable of carrying a great weight in mail. They also had to be very sturdy to cope with the unpredictable turbulence and violence of the weather across the United States. The mail had to get through! Typically, Boeing, under Egtvedt, took an aggressive, forward-looking stance. He designed a fast, single-engined

monoplane. It was the first American mail plane to feature a strong, unstayed metal wing in contrast to the usual construction of a strutted biplane. He called it the Monomail and it was built using a monocoque, stressed-skin, metal fuselage—a technique first developed by his rival, Northrop. The Monomail was bought in small numbers. She was ahead of her time. Operators and pilots remained distrustful of the unstayed monoplane wing.

But the Monomail had a positive spin. It provided the inspiration for a military bomber—the Model 214. The Boeing Model 214 became the B-9 bomber.

Below: The Boeing Monomail had a retractable undercarriage and also featured a two-position, variable-pitch propeller, which gave more efficient engine performance at takeoff and better fuel economy once in the air. With a wingspan of almost 60 feet (17.9 meters), she was a big airplane that carried her mail in the bins in front of the open cockpit. A 575-horsepower Pratt & Whitney Hornet enabled her to cruise at 135 miles (217 kilometers) per hour.

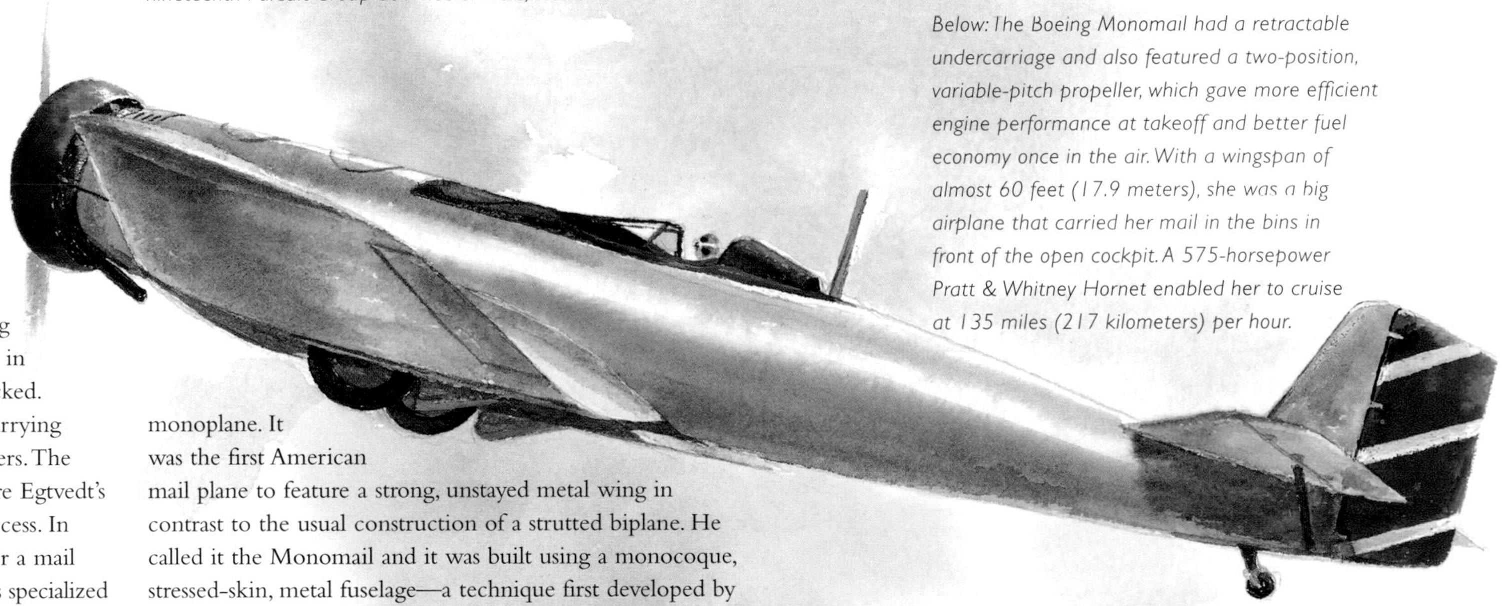

The Boeing Monomail, 1930

Introduced in 1931, the B-9 was a radical leap forward in design compared with the earlier biplane bomber. Even before the B-9 was complete and flying, Egtvedt, Johnson, and the Boeing engineering team realized that the bomber could be adapted to become a new commercial aircraft. They started working on Model 247, a proposed 10-seater airliner. Like the bomber, the 247 was planned as a fast streamlined monoplane—all-metal with supercharged engines faired smoothly into the wing. To reduce drag even further a retractable undercarriage was incorporated. Among other quite revolutionary ideas was the inclusion of small trim tabs placed on control surfaces. Control-column and rudder-bar loads were thus reduced resulting in less pilot fatigue and safer flying.

The passenger cabin was insulated against noise and was air-conditioned. These new performance and safety factors combined to have strong appeal for passengers and operators. Later 247s showed improved performance by being fitted with controllable-pitch airscrews designed by the Hamilton Standard Propeller Corporation. The 247 had loads of sales appeal. Airlines started ordering while the plane was still on the drawing board.

Superb and original as Model 247 was, its financial success was short-lived. The competition learned fast and the bigger Douglas DC-2s and DC-3s soon appeared. These Douglas models owed their success to the Boeing 247, which had so clearly mapped the way. Douglas leap-frogged Boeing in their design by providing greater passenger-carrying capacity, with some early variations offering sleeping accommodation.

The same fate overtook Boeing's trailblazing B-9 bomber. The Martin Company was quick to follow up with their version of a monoplane bomber. Though the U.S. Army ordered a few Boeings, Martin won the lion's share. Yet it was Boeing, with both the B-9 and the Model 247, that wrote the new aviation rule book by producing two of the greatest airplanes of the twentieth century.

In 1934 the American Government decided that Boeing had become monopolistic and, under anti-trust laws, the company was ordered to split up its empire—which then consisted of plane maker, engine maker, propeller maker, and airline operator—and was forced to sell off the wholly owned subsidiaries.

Left: Compared to the biplane bomber flying alongside, the Boeing B-9 displays its clean aerodynamic profile. Featuring a monocoque, low-drag fuselage and streamlined engine cowlings into which the retractable undercarriage fitted, the B-9 was faster than any contemporary fighter aircraft.

The Boeing B-9 bomber

Opposite page: Boeing's Model 247 airliner boasted such exceptional performance that it was entered in the England to Australia Air Race of 1934. It was to compete against a field of highly specialized racing machines. On the eve of the race the Boeing sat in a roomy hangar at Mildenhall aerodrome in England. Sponsors, dignitaries, and friends of the competitors were all there meeting the pilots, intoxicated by the heady atmosphere that the well-publicized contest had generated.

Roscoe Turner, a popular and flamboyant American racing pilot and wearing a military-style uniform of his own design, was skipper of the Boeing 247 and is shown in earnest conversation with a smart young lady of the day. Alongside the Boeing 247 was another American competitor—a Douglas DC-2 airliner in the livery of Royal Dutch Airlines (K.L.M.). The two all-metal passenger planes—large for their day—overshadowed the small, single-engined cabin monoplane sandwiched between them. This little De Havilland Puss Moth, owned and flown solo by Australian James Melrose, won third place in the race.

Boeing's Roscoe Turner and copilot Clyde Pangbourne were awarded second prize in the speed division. Significantly, in view of its subsequent commercial dominance, the DC-2 was to win the race on handicap.

As a result Bill Boeing resigned as Chairman in anger and disgust, and left the aviation industry permanently.

Clairmont Egtvedt stayed on as President of the scaled-down company. One of his early, uncomfortable tasks was to lay off staff as orders for B-9 bombers and the 247 airliners evaporated. In those harsh Depression years, the U.S. Army awarded a contract to Boeing for a new four-engined bomber, which saved the strapped Boeing business.

The new bomber was enormous for its time. Egtvedt labeled it the XB-15. The Russians had built larger machines for their army but they couldn't match the sophistication of the XB-15. Ultimately the XB-15 didn't go beyond prototype stage, mainly because there weren't engines powerful enough to deliver a competitive performance.

While the XB-15 was still on the drawing board, the U.S. Army asked Boeing to work on a slightly smaller bomber, destined to protect the eastern seaboard of the United States

from possible intrusion by enemy shipping. In mid-1934, Boeing started work on the new bomber, Model 299. It was destined to become the B-17—the fabled Flying Fortress of World War II.

Once production of the B-17 was under way, Egtvedt and Boeing designer Edward Wells started working on a concept that would launch another revolution in civil aviation— the first fully pressurized airliner. What emerged from the Seattle works was the radically new Boeing aircraft named Stratoliner. The aircraft provided unheard-of luxury

Above: The Boeing XB-15 prototype, under construction, had a wingspan of 149 feet (45.4 meters) and a top speed of 200 miles (321 kilometers) per hour and was first flown in October 1937 by test pilot Eddie Allen. On board was a galley with hotplate, coffee machine, and soup maker as well as an ice box—exceptional comfort for a military airplane. Two engines were installed just to drive generators for the complex electrical system. The four 850-horsepower Pratt & Whitney twin Wasp engines were not powerful enough to make this machine a practical proposition.

Boeing B-17G, Flying Fortress, 1944

Below: The prototype Boeing B-17 Flying Fortress, 1935

Right: The B-17G Flying Fortress was modified from the original production machines. Initially, it looked similar to the prototype (left). Modified versions, such as the ubiquitous B-17G models were used in European daylight raids during World War II.

The Boeing 314 flying boat, with a range of over 5,000 miles (8,145 kilometers), was a true intercontinental airliner. Engineers on the flight deck monitored the engines for best performance and could examine individual engines by climbing into the wing itself. The 74 passengers were cosseted on a separate deck and served gourmet meals prepared by chefs from the New Yorker Hotel—all to woo them away from booking flights with the competing Sikorsky and Martin flying boats which had been flying similar routes for some time.

and comfort in a large, high-flying, four-engined airliner. Passengers could be forgiven for believing that American commercial aviation had reached its peak. But then a war broke out, and the Stratoliner's big future was curtailed. Only 10 were made. They were sold to, and operated by, Pan American and Trans Western Airways before World War II started. The Stratoliner presaged the next wave of aircraft development.

Flying boats had long been seen as the ideal way of creating and flying long-distance air routes across continents and mighty oceans. Big land planes were faced with the lack of large airfields providing essential services. Boeing had produced flying boat designs for many years and finally, under the stewardship of Wellwood Beal, gave the world the last of the great intercontinental flying boats—the mighty Boeing 314. Her development, like that of the Stratoliner, was interrupted by World War II as she didn't enter service until 1939. Yet she had just enough time on the Pacific and Atlantic routes to give the world a sampling of what the future might hold.

The war shredded any future hopes for flying boats. World War II air operations caused such an incredible expansion of concrete runway construction in both the European and Pacific theaters that when the guns and bombs ceased their uproar, land planes as large as flying

boats had the facilities they needed. The gallant flying boat became an old-fashioned anachronism—a subject for the history books.

The United States strategic plans in the Pacific zone during World War II gave birth to a new heavy bomber—the Boeing B-29 Superfortress.

The B-29 was hugely successful and played a major role in the war by being able to bomb Japan from Pacific island bases. However, the enormous

Below: Despite her bulky-looking shape, the streamlined, fully pressurized Boeing Stratoliner had a cruising speed of 215 miles (346 kilometers) per hour at 23,000 feet (7,010 meters), carrying 33 passengers in sound-proofed comfort and separate rest rooms. Pressurization is taken for granted these days but in the late 1930s when the Stratoliner was conceived, it was an innovation of great significance.

The Boeing Stratoliner, 1940

problems encountered in designing the new Boeing B-29 Superfortress had never before been contemplated. Egtvedt's design team accomplished the impossible when the first B-29 flew in September 1942. The big bomber was fully pressurized allowing it to operate at high altitudes with three pressurized cells created for the crew. Drag had to be reduced to equal a plane of half its size! Even gun turrets of the computer-guided gunnery system needed to be designed with minimum aerodynamic profile—all rivets had to be flush with the aircraft's metal skin. The technical details in this alone were mind-boggling.

Toward the end of World War II, a new and very significant revolution had taken place in aviation: the arrival of the jet engine. This technological advance had already been blooded in later wartime fighters. The British moved first to

harness the new power source and leaped ahead in commercial airline design with the introduction of the De Havilland Comet. This sleek, high-flying, four-engined jetliner left American aircraft manufacturers flat-footed—they just weren't prepared for the postwar initiative of the British designers.

Dramatically, in the mid-1950s the British lead in jet liners was shackled when disastrous cabin pressure failures caused the grounding of all the Comet fleet. Spurred on by the dynamic Egtvedt, the Boeing Company—which had been making enormous strides in military jet bomber design—quickly wrested the lead in commercial jets with the introduction of the Boeing 707.

Among others, Boeing had benefited greatly from the

radical ideas revealed to the Allies with the fall of Nazi Germany. American, British, and Russian aviation industries had all learned from the astonishing advances and experiments conducted by the German aviation industry during the latter phases of the war. With the benefit of some of this information, Boeing created the radical and futuristic B-47 bomber. This brilliant machine became the backbone of the newly created U.S. Air Force and was a common sight in the skies over Europe during the tensions of the Cold War.

Just as the old Boeing B-9 bomber of the pre-war 1930s had spawned the Boeing 247 airliner so, once again, the Boeing B-47 bomber led to a commercial plane, the 707 jet liner. With De Havilland's Comet shoved to the sidelines, Boeing quickly signed up the world's leading airlines to the 707, and it became the most successful jet

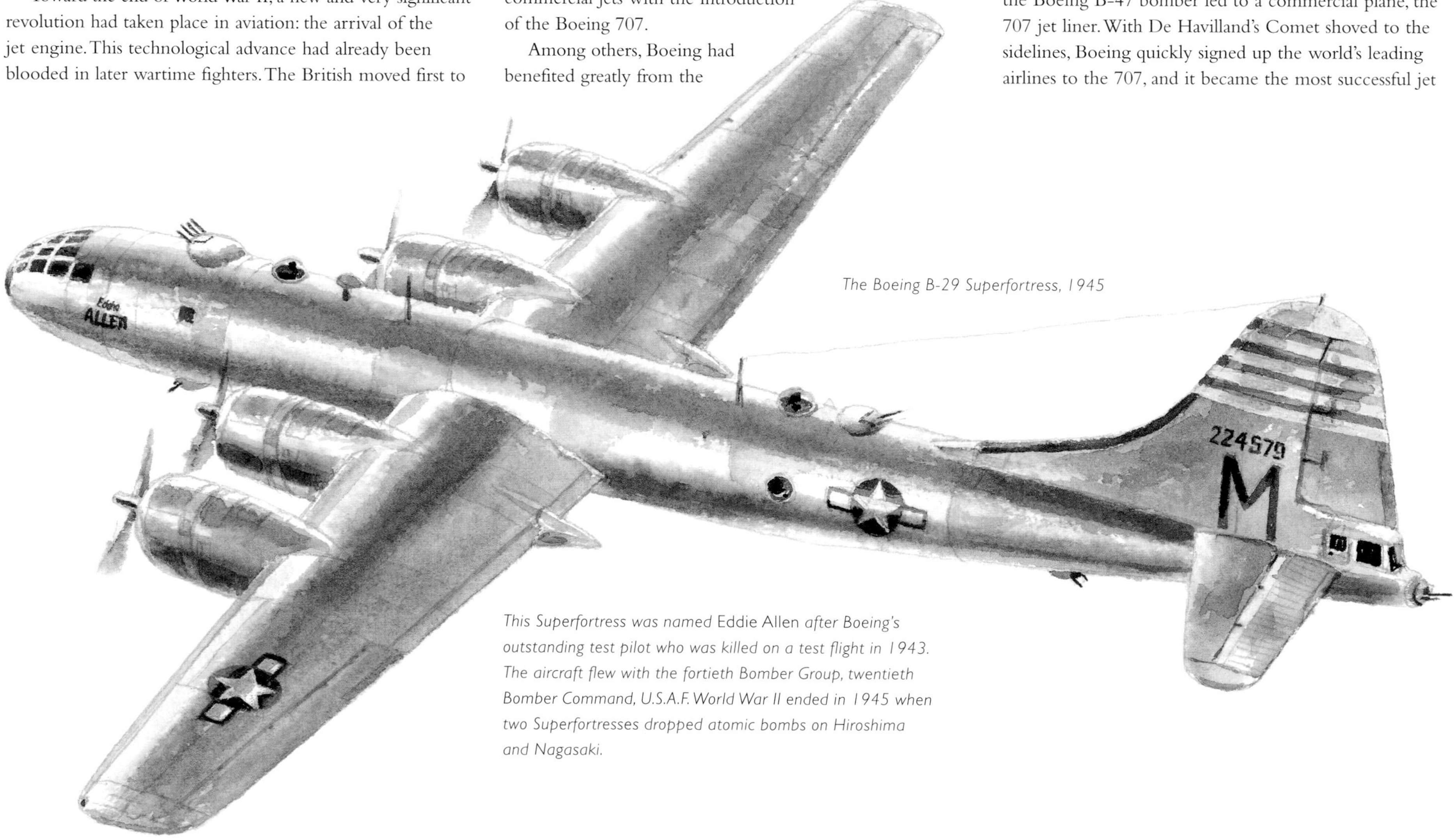

The Boeing B-29 Superfortress, 1945

This Superfortress was named Eddie Allen *after Boeing's outstanding test pilot who was killed on a test flight in 1943. The aircraft flew with the fortieth Bomber Group, twentieth Bomber Command, U.S.A.F. World War II ended in 1945 when two Superfortresses dropped atomic bombs on Hiroshima and Nagasaki.*

airliner the world had ever seen. Then, following Clairmont Egtvedt's pattern of aggressive, forward-looking activity early in the company's life, Boeing cemented its lead. It has continued pumping out remarkable and successful jets—the 727, 737, the mighty 747, 757, 767, and the 777—a range of aircraft that only Europe's Airbus Industrie is now beginning to match.

Though the name is Boeing, Clairmont Egtvedt was the dynamo who drove the company to become the most powerful force in the world of twenty-first century aviation. Despite the forced carve-up of the company in the 1930s, Boeing has emerged as the most dominant conglomerate, with ventures into aerospace, rocketry, helicopters, and hydrofoil development all now integral to the Boeing business in the twenty-first century.

Left & below: The Boeing B-47 Stratojet, with its radical 35-degree swept back, laminar flow wing, podded jet engines suspended on struts beneath the wing, and unique bicycle undercarriage, was a masterly display of aerodynamics. The B-47 really grew out of the extraordinary advances made by the end of World War II. Jet-engine technology was lagging behind aerodynamics. Under full operational load, the B-47 needed rocket-assisted takeoff as this dramatic photograph shows. Despite these shortcomings, this brilliant aircraft served the U.S.A.F. well. Production finished in 1957.

The Boeing XB-47 prototype, 1947

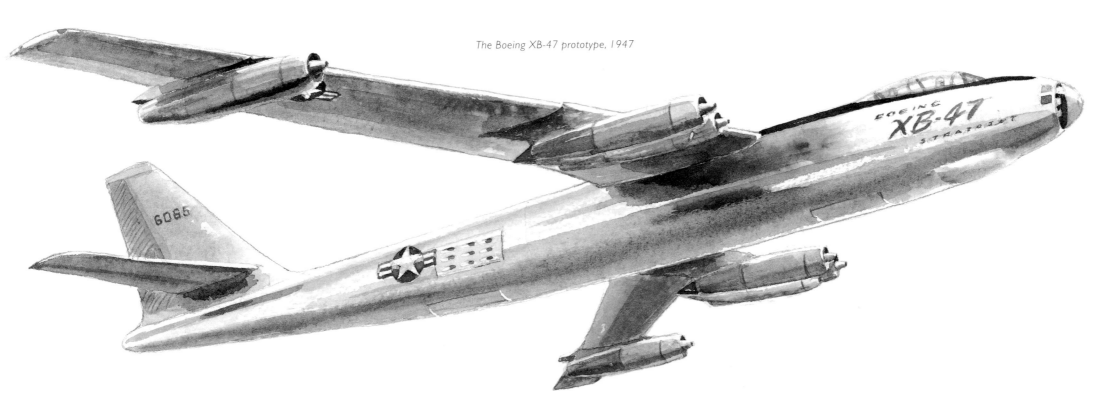

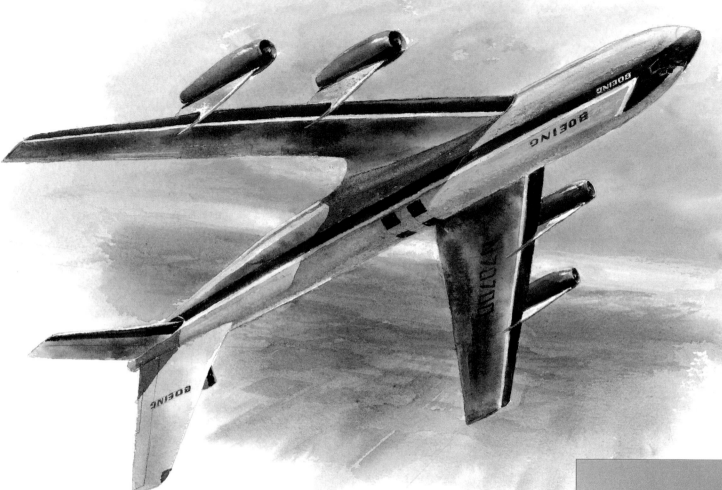

Opposite page: One of the many variations of the ubiquitous Boeing 747 is banking over the checkerboard marker on the final approach to Hong Kong's old Kai Tak Airport. This Jumbo is a 747-400 model, configured to Qantas Airways' specifications.

Left: The lessons learned from the Boeing B-47 bomber and the experience gained from the British Comet disasters were put to good use in the design of the famous Boeing 700 series of jet transport. The Boeing 707, the first of the breed and first known as the Boeing Dash-80, was barrel-rolled on a demonstration flight by test pilot Tex Johnson—a dramatic demonstration of its rugged design and a pointer to its future success as an airliner.

Below: The Boeing B-52 strategic bomber, first flown in 1952 and still in operation today, was a logical development of the B-47.

When we get moving, watch out! The momentum is tremendous.

"T" WILSON, PRESIDENT, BOEING AIRCRAFT, 1968

ARTHUR RAYMOND

DC-3—THE WAY TO GO!

In 1925 with the Douglas Aircraft business booming, Donald Douglas chose Arthur Raymond as the new recruit for his drawing office. Raymond was the supercharger the company needed to become a global high flier in aircraft production.

Donald W. (Wills) Douglas, the founder of the company, had become interested in the new business of aviation while still a student. He had been present at Fort Myer in 1909 when the Wright brothers staged a flying demonstration for the U. S. Army. Inspired, Douglas turned to the study of engineering and as a young civil engineer at the Massachusetts Institute of Technology, assisted Jerome Hunnaker to devise and build a wind tunnel. It was the first-ever wind tunnel made for testing aircraft models. Douglas then moved on to become chief engineer with Glenn L. Martin, an established aircraft manufacturer.

But Douglas was keen to build his own business and his own planes. In 1920 he designed and made one of the earliest aerodynamically streamlined aircraft, the Cloudster. In 1921, the U. S. Navy placed an order for three Cloudsters and, backed by financier Davis R. Davis, Donald Douglas started his own aircraft company.

The reaction of the U. S. Army to the success of a U. S. Navy Curtiss flying boat was what really drew attention to the infant company as this was the first airplane to fly across the Atlantic. Miffed, the army decided they needed to go one better. They organized to send four army planes—Douglas World Cruiser biplanes—to fly around the globe. On September 28, 1924, two of the Douglas planes completed the epic flight. It was the first time global circumnavigation by air had been achieved. That compelling demonstration of the reliability and performance of Douglas planes was a turning point for the company's future. So with expansion of the company firmly in mind, Douglas employed Arthur Raymond. It was his masterstroke.

By the early 1930s an intricate network of airfields, and radio and light beacons had been established for the planes carrying U.S. mail. Regular passenger air routes began to follow and use these facilities but the passenger airliners were technically little better than planes built for World War I. That changed overnight when, early in 1933, Boeing's all-metal 247 monoplane took to the air. Loaded with advanced features, providing air-conditioned comfort and relative quiet for passengers, the Boeing 247 carried passengers across the country at speeds faster than the latest military fighter planes. The success of this new airliner infuriated Jack Frye, president of the T.W.A. airline, as he watched his competitor, United Airlines, scoop the pool with the 247.

United was a Boeing-owned subsidiary, and the production of Boeing's 247s was being reserved for United.

Frye urged Donald Douglas and other manufacturers to pull out all stops to provide a competitive answer to the Boeing. His specifications: a three-engined machine similar to a Fokker triplane, able to compete in comfort and space with the 247, and able to fly fully laden over the highest part of the T.W.A. route—between Winslow, Arizona and Alberqerque in New Mexico. Jack Frye's last and most serious demand was safety—the aircraft would have to be able to maintain height on just one engine. Now there was a tough ask!

Douglas handed the assignment to Arthur Raymond. Working with characteristic concentration and energy, Raymond had his answer in short-haul. He decided against three engines, choosing to rely on twin motors. He designed an all-metal aircraft, bigger and faster than the Boeing, but with many similarities. It would carry 12 passengers against Boeing's 10-passenger capacity. Arthur tabled his blueprints

Left: The Douglas World Cruiser, Chicago, was one of two to complete the first aerial global circumnavigation in 1924. Pontoons replaced the wheeled undercarriages en route.

Left: Arthur Raymond in the 1960s

to T.W.A.'s top technical advisor, the American flying hero, Charles Lindbergh. Liking what he saw, Lindbergh recommended the Douglas solution to Frye. In a flurry of activity, the prototype, the self-styled DC-1, was up and flying for T.W.A. before the end of 1933. The next aircraft from the Douglas production line—also for T.W.A.—was modified to take two more passengers, and became the DC-2.

Raymond's resounding success soon showed up in the Douglas order book. In succeeding years, airlines all over the world bought DC-2s—over 200 were sold—while the trailblazing Boeing 247 faded into the sunset.

In 1935, Raymond was asked for another change to the basic design. American Airlines executive, C. R. Smith, suggested that the DC-2 be made larger to incorporate sleeping accommodation. Raymond's response was to modify the wing, install bigger engines, and fatten up the fuselage. The idea of sleeping accommodation didn't take on—but the new DC-3 surely did. Offering a 21-seat configuration, the DC-3 simply swept the competition away.

The DC-3 series made the company the most successful airline manufacturer of the era. On the back of the civilian airliners came orders for military adaptations of the DC-3.

Lady, you ask, "Is this old airplane safe to fly?"
Just how in the world do you think it got to
be this old?

DC-3 PILOT

Douglas DC-2, 1934

Above: The Swiss Air Lines Douglas DC-2 was one of the many DC aircraft exported to overseas airlines. The DC-2 was an improved production model of the original DC-1 and 220 were sold. The DC-2 first flew in 1934 and carried 14 passengers at 170 miles (274 kilometers) per hour. One of the Dutch K.L.M. DC-2s, a standard passenger airliner, took part in the Great Air Race from England to Australia in 1934. She was beaten only by a specially built British racing machine, the De H 88 Comet.

Left: T.W.A. flew the one and only Douglas DC-1 on-line which was quickly joined by the DC-2s.

Right: The splendid Douglas DC-7C airliner was the first airliner able to fly the tough but profitable North Atlantic route nonstop, both ways. Douglas dominated the four-engined airliner market at this time with over 1,000 of the DC-6 and DC-7 series being produced. This aircraft was a Scandinavian Airlines version that helped develop the transpolar route from the U.S.A. to Europe.

Once the U.S.A. entered World War II, many civil DC-3s were taken over by the military, and many thousands more were built as U.S. Army C-47 Skytrains and Dakotas. Rugged and reliable, they became troop transports, parachute-force droppers, tugs for gliders, supply and spy-droppers, and ambulances. They performed with distinction in Europe, North Africa, the Near and Far East, India, Burma (now Myanmar), and the Pacific. Besides the C-47 Skytrains, many other Douglas-designed aircraft were on operational service in every theatre of war: fighter-bombers, night fighters, torpedo bombers, low and medium altitude bombers, ground attack planes, and tank-busting aircraft.

Postwar, and with the arrival of the jet age, Donald Douglas produced a variety of jet aircraft with some early research into ogee-shaped delta-winged craft. The Skyray experimental fighter from the Douglas stable provided the first indicator of the advantage of this wing form, now common in many Mach 2 fighters and the famous Concorde supersonic plane.

With its wealth of experience in long-range, piston-engined aircraft—such as the first true intercontinental airliner, the DC-7—Douglas was expected to be a leader in jet-powered passenger airliners. But this was a time when the company started to falter. Old enemy Boeing was there first with the dramatic 707. The Douglas entrant, the DC-8, didn't fly until after the 707's high-profile introduction and acceptance. Douglas still achieved a good response and had orders for the DC-8 from international carriers but not in the numbers being posted for Boeing's 707s. The race to make the crucial deadline began to cripple the company. Financially, it was stretched too far to recover. Although by the 1980s other fine jetliners—the DC-9 and DC-10—were well advanced in concept and construction, the Douglas resources had been too thin, and the

company had already lost its individual identity. It had been forced to merge with rival, McDonnell Aircraft to become McDonnell Douglas.

Looking back over the years, it is easy to chart Douglas's finest hours. Arthur Raymond's brilliant solutions to T.W.A.'s dicta for a new passenger liner in 1933 launched the company into years of preeminence in commercial aircraft production. In wartime, Douglas produced 29,000 war planes—one-sixth of the total U.S. airborne fleet. The DC-3 has never been equaled as an individual transport aircraft. Even today, many Douglas DC-3s still operate around the world.

A number of the Douglas jet liners—the DC-9 and the DC-10—still fly today. They were all bought in considerable numbers and are still in production. Although badged as Douglas, the sad truth is that McDonnell Douglas—the company that swallowed the original Douglas concern in 1967—has, since 2000, been owned by that implacable Douglas enemy of the 1930s, the mighty Boeing Aircraft Corporation.

Above: The 150-seat Douglas DC-8 jet airliner first entered service in 1959 and was Douglas's entrant in the race to be the first to produce a jet airliner. A stretched version with a new wing and longer body carried over 350 passengers.

Opposite page: The first Douglas DC-3 was designed for sleeper accommodation and was first flown in 1934 by American Airlines. She could fly faster than the best fighter aircraft of the day. The DC-3's wing construction was so strong that it resisted metal fatigue for about 60,000 hours—or 60 times longer than contemporary expectations. It became the world's most famous transport aircraft and is still in service in the new millennium. Well over 10,000 were built in the U.S.A. and 2,000 more, under license in Russia. Over 10,000 C-47 military versions were built in World War II. At the end of the war, this exceptional aircraft also spawned a big family of larger four-engined Douglas transports.

Left: Many Douglas military aircraft took part in operations in World War II, the Korean conflict, and Vietnam. The DC-4 Skymaster, Devastator, Dauntless, A26 Boston, Invader, Skyraider, Globemaster, and Skyhawk to name a few, will bring back memories of heroic actions fought in World War II, Korea, Vietnam, and The Falklands. The Skyhawk (left) is just one of designer Ed Heinemann's brilliant creations—it proved to be one of the most popular jet fighter-bombers of all time. This particular one, an A4G, still flew in 2001 with the Royal New Zealand Air Force.

PROF. WILHELM EMIL MESSERSCHMITT

A GIANT AMONG HIS PEERS

"The world will never see another designer like Willi Messerschmitt." These words, written by his English biographer after Messerschmitt's death, have been borne out by so many: Field Marshal Göring admired him; Erhard Milch, Hitler's Secretary of State, disliked him and fought him; Rudolf Hess was an old friend and flew his planes; Ernst Heinkel detested him; and Allied bomber crews feared his fighters.

Wilhelm, known as "Willi," was born on June 26, 1898, at Frankfurt am Main, Germany, the son of Johan Baptist Ferdinand Messerschmitt, a well-off wine merchant, and Anna Maria Schaller. Ferdinand had left his first wife and was living with Anna. Wilhelm was their second child and was baptized Catholic. When he was seven years old, his parents married by which time the family was managing and living in the hotel Weinhouse at Bamburg in Bavaria. Messerschmitts had been established in Bamburg for centuries—there is an ancient Messerschmitt coat of arms to prove it.

But the past didn't attract Willi. Two events focused his mind on the future, making an everlasting impression on him in 1909 when he was just nine years old. He visited Friedrickshafen and was staggered when he saw Zeppelin's giant, roaring dirigible airship flying overhead from its base. Then, in the same year, he was taken to the International Aviation Exhibition at Frankfurt where the Wright brothers were demonstrating their brilliant new flying machines.

Though he never worked as an engineer, his father Ferdinand Messerschmitt had as a youth been an engineering student at the Technishe Hochschule in Zurich and he continued to be interested in things mechanical. No doubt some of his father's interest rubbed off on Willi. When still a schoolboy Willi was introduced to the state architect, Frederich Harth who spent all his spare time thinking about, drawing, and constructing gliders. The young Messerschmitt was entranced and joined Harth in his experiments. He later wrote, "Every free minute that the school allowed me, I devoted to further development of sailplanes." By 1913, at 15, Willi was Harth's main unpaid assistant, helping to design and construct Frederich's fourth glider. Harth decided that they should complete the glider closer to where they could fly it—in Bad Kissinger, 62 miles

Willi Messerschmitt
started his career in aviation as a designer of gliders. It is fitting that one of his last designs to see service with the Luftwaffe in World War II was the huge Me. 323 Gigant (1842), a six-engined transport plane with a wingspan of 180 feet (55 meters). Originally it was designed as the Me. 321 transport glider, to be towed by powered aircraft—first flown in 1941. The 323 could carry over 20 tons (20.3 tonnes) of cargo, loaded through huge clamshell doors that made up the nose of the aircraft. The Me. 323 was successfully used as a supply aircraft on the Russian front.

Above left: Willi Messerschmitt in the 1960s

(100 kilometers) northwest of Bamburg. Frederich Harth built a hangar on a mountainous ridge and they completed the construction there. The test flight was successful—the glider flew 984 feet (300 meters) or so at an altitude of 66 feet (20 meters). Shortly after this Willi went off to study at the Munich Institute of Technology. Then the war stopped everything. Years later when at last it was over, construction of aircraft was forbidden in Germany, however gliders were allowed to be built. Willi and Harth started again and before long Messerschmitt was seen as one of the foremost designers of gliders in the country.

Left: Willi Messerschmitt's enormous Me. 321 glider was towed aloft by three Me. 110 twin-engined fighters.

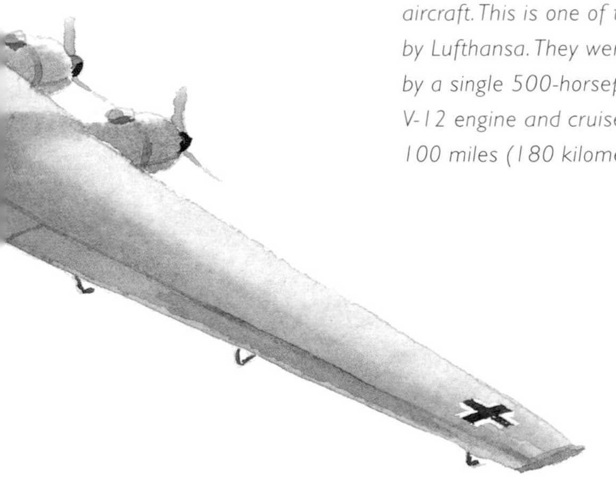

Above: Messerschmitt's M20A airliner was his first commercially viable aircraft. This is one of the two operated by Lufthansa. They were each powered by a single 500-horsepower B.M.W. V-12 engine and cruised at about 100 miles (180 kilometers) per hour.

Below right: Conceived in 1933 and first flown in 1934, Messerschmitt's Me. 108 Taifun was a speedy, fully aerobatic, four-seat, all-metal, stressed-skin cabin monoplane, which could climb to nearly 30,000 feet (9,144 meters). It was the finest machine of its type.

In 1923 Willi set up his own company. In 1924 he started building powered gliders with 500cc Douglas motor cycle engines, and then gliders with larger engines—like the S-16b Betti, named after his sister, a two seater with a 21-horsepower engine that would fly about two miles (three kilometers) on one and three-quarter pints (one liter) of petrol at speeds of up to 70 miles (112 kilometers) per hour.

In 1927 with the partial ban on German aircraft production lifted, Messerschmitt merged his company with Bayerische Flugzeugwerke A.G. and produced a series of all-metal 10-seat airliners. Lufthansa immediately ordered two of the most advanced design, the M-20. This was a very successful machine but a subsequent Lufthansa order to bring the number up to 14 was cancelled because two M-20s had crashed elsewhere. Having to refund the deposits Lufthansa had placed on these machines forced Bayerische Flugzeugwerke (B.F.W.) into bankruptcy.

Willi was saved by the surge of activity that came with the sudden rise of Hitler and the Nazi party the following year. He was commissioned to build and supply powered gliders for the training of Luftwaffe pilots. The financial injection and the rapid build-up of the German armed forces over the next decade saw the Messerschmitt name soar.

With each new design Willi created, his reputation increased. His first outstanding aircraft was the Me. 108, produced in 1934 when he was the designer for the B.F.W. company. It was a single-engined, low-winged monoplane— a remarkable advance over the sports planes of the day. It was to become a training and communications aircraft for Luftwaffe pilots.

Left: This machine was built to create a new world speed record for Nazi Germany in 1939. It was publicized as an Me. 109R for propaganda purposes so that Europe would believe that the Me. 109 fighter version would be capable of the speeds this racing machine attained. In fact, this hazardous little machine was a purpose-built Me. 209 VI, a dangerous machine to fly—of the three machines built, two crashed. It had a Daimler Benz engine that would normally deliver 1,400 horsepower and could be boosted to give 2,300 horsepower for about one minute. The engine was cooled by evaporative cooling via radiators in the wings and it gulped two gallons (9.1 liters) of its 100 gallons (455 liters) of coolant every minute.

At high speed it could flick lethally onto its back if the pilot turned a little too tightly and it tended to pitch up violently at high speed. The pilot, Flug Kapitan Fritz Wendel, who crashed in it once, was a courageous and skillful operator. He certainly earned the personal congratulations and handshake he got from Willi Messerschmitt (left) when a new world record of 469 1/4 miles (750.75 kilometers) per hour over a 1 4/5-mile (2.9-kilometer) course at 300 feet (91.5 meters) was achieved— a record that remained unbeaten for 20 years.

Messerschmitt's next design was to build a reputation as the most famous German aircraft ever built—the Messerschmitt Me. 109. It was a low-wing monoplane, with metal monocoque fuselage with a cantilevered wing, and a single engine— the prototype fitted with a Rolls-Royce 695-horsepower Kestrel engine. Later the Kestrel was replaced with a more powerful Junkers Jumo engine, and the Me. 109 was eventually fitted with a muscular Daimler-Benz power plant producing 1,300 horsepower. The first Me. 109 flew in September 1935, competing with prototypes from other German makers including one from Ernst Heinkel, who loudly denigrated the Messerschmitt entry to all who would listen. After testing, when Heinkel's plane lost to Willi's 109, the two became implacable enemies.

Messerschmitt 109s were flown by the controversial Condor Squadron for Generalissimo Francisco Franco in the Spanish Civil War (1936–39), a proving ground which demonstrated the plane's superiority as a maneuverable and powerful fighter. When World War II started, improved versions of the 109s were to become the scourge of the skies and one of the most dangerous German weapons against Allied bombers. They were destined to become the backbone of the Luftwaffe, with an amazing 35,000 produced during the war.

Left: The Me. 109 was one of the greatest fighter aircraft in aviation history. It was the direct descendant of the Me. 108. Many variations were developed as World War II progressed. It was highly maneuverable, had a high rate of climb, and was only bettered by the rate of turn of the British Spitfire, its principal adversary. German pilots could escape this disadvantage in a dogfight by diving vertically at uncatchable speeds. The Me. 109E model shown here was shot down over the English Channel during the Battle of Britain.

In 1938, Willi was already working on what was to become the pinnacle of his designing genius, the Me. 262—the world's first fighter designed to be powered by turbo jets. When the initial twin-engined prototype was ready, the power plant was not sufficiently reliable to install, so conventional piston engines were used. That allowed arch competitor Heinkel to beat Messerschmitt to the punch by flying his prototype He. 208 with twin turbo-jet engines in March 1941. It was a hollow victory for Heinkel. His plane never went into production as he was stymied when the decision was made to halt the development of his Heinkel He. S8A gas turbine engines.

The Me. 262, with Junkers Jumo turbo jets installed, flew just over one year later in July 1942. With problems still to be overcome in the power plant, the 262 didn't become operational until two years later, in July 1944. Adolf Hitler, a frequent visitor to Messerschmitt's Oberammergau factory, didn't help the delay when he decided that he wanted a fighter-bomber version of the 262. The old World War I fighter ace and commander of the Air Force, Herman Göring, desperately wanted fighters but Hitler had his way and production was slowed to allow for the development and building of the Sturmvogel or Stormbird fighter-bomber version.

Time was running out for the Third Reich, and although the 262 was a superb aircraft—with many saying that had it become available earlier in the war, it may have changed the course of history—it was too little, too late. In 1945, peace was imposed on Germany as the Allies swarmed over Europe and took the stronghold, Berlin. The Oberammergau factories had been destroyed and Willi was imprisoned as a war criminal. In 1948, he was tried by a German de-Nazification court, which found he had been a "reluctant beneficiary" of Hitler's regime.

Some years later, he started a new factory making sewing machines, motor scooters, and cars, including a strange,

Just like being pushed by an angel...

ADOLF GALLAND, LUFTWAFFE TEST PILOT, AFTER TESTING THE NEW
MESSERSCHMIDT ME. 262 JET FIGHTER

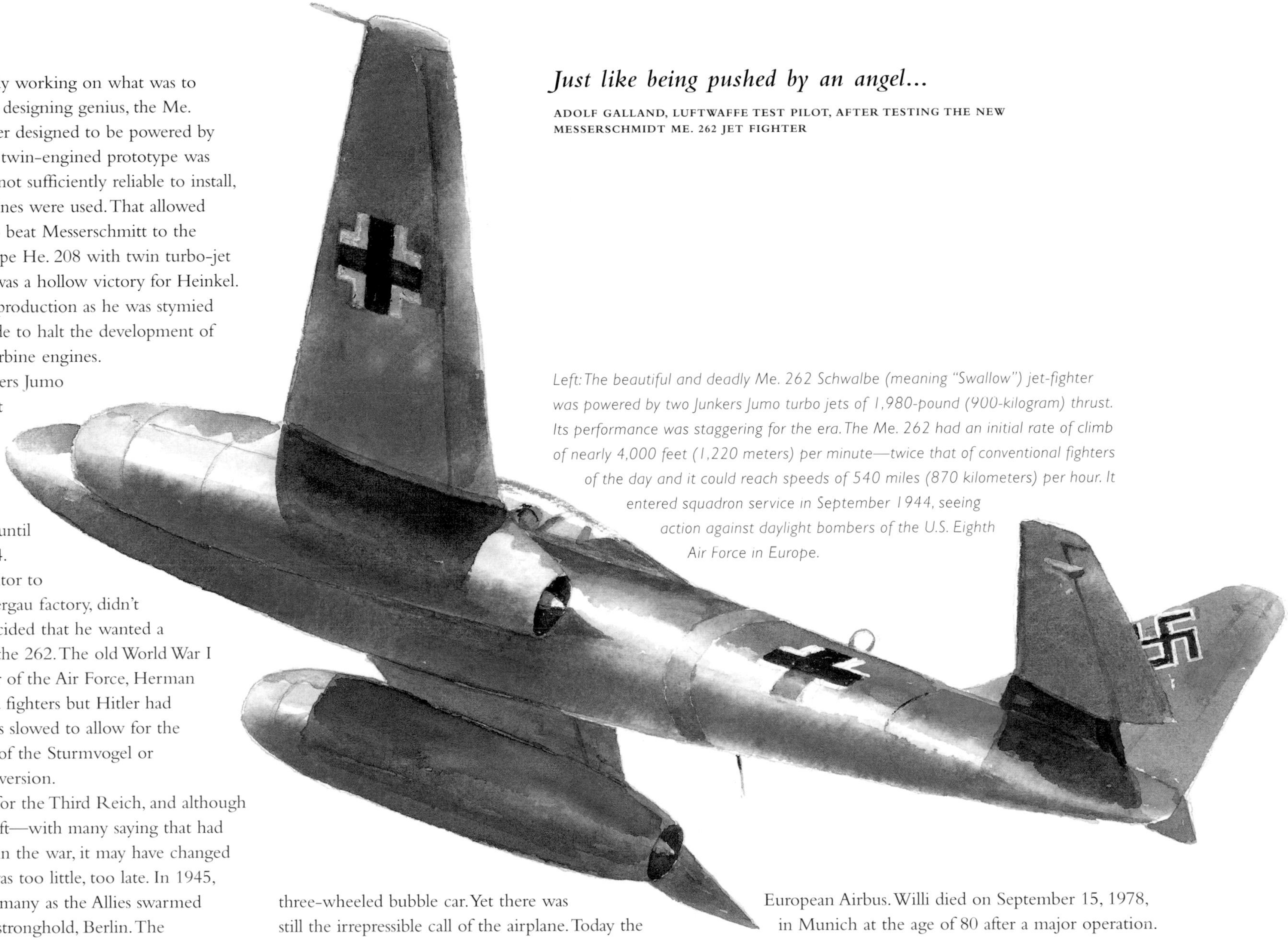

Left: The beautiful and deadly Me. 262 Schwalbe (meaning "Swallow") jet-fighter was powered by two Junkers Jumo turbo jets of 1,980-pound (900-kilogram) thrust. Its performance was staggering for the era. The Me. 262 had an initial rate of climb of nearly 4,000 feet (1,220 meters) per minute—twice that of conventional fighters of the day and it could reach speeds of 540 miles (870 kilometers) per hour. It entered squadron service in September 1944, seeing action against daylight bombers of the U.S. Eighth Air Force in Europe.

three-wheeled bubble car. Yet there was still the irrepressible call of the airplane. Today the German aerospace company, Messerschmitt-Bolkow-Blohm, with headquarters in Munich, keeps the designer's name alive. He was an active partner in the enterprise from the start until his retirement and was involved in the planning for the production of the N.A.T.O. all-purpose, American-designed Lockheed Starfighter supersonic aircraft and the

European Airbus. Willi died on September 15, 1978, in Munich at the age of 80 after a major operation.

The world will never see another designer like Willi Messerschmitt because aircraft design is now a team effort, heavily reliant on computers and computer science. For future developments, the day of the inspired, creative individual has passed but while it lasted, Willi was a giant among his peers.

SIR HUDSON FYSH

THE SECRET ORDER OF THE DOUBLE SUNRISE

Hudson Fysh, 1919

In February 1942, Japanese troops overran Singapore, capturing British and Australian army and navy forces. The unstoppable Japanese headed south to Indonesia and began a rapid drive through New Guinea with Australia as their target. In what was then the Dutch colony of Java, five Royal Netherlands Naval Air Force flying boats escaped ahead of the Japanese advance. They reached Australia, later flying on to Ceylon (now Sri Lanka) to join other members of their naval unit.

That flight pointed the way to a quite unique air service which was to provide an aerial and information lifeline to the island continent. With the Japanese controlling both sea and air, Australia was being cordoned off from the rest of the world. Because of the war the flying-boat service from Britain to Australia provided by Britain's Imperial Airways and Qantas Empire Airways had broken down.

Sir Hudson Fysh D.F.C.—the pioneering airman who helped start Qantas in the 1930s—was then Managing Director and Chairman of the airline. In his book *Qantas at War* he wrote, "...in May 1943, when the R.A.F. Catalina

Squadron at Trincomalee were ready to carry out their survey flights to Australia preparatory to Qantas taking over, a Catalina commanded by Wing Comdr. J. E. Scott of the Royal Canadian Air Force set out from Ceylon and landed in Perth the next morning after a nonstop run." A number of test flights were made before civilian Qantas pilots were flown into Ceylon from Australia and a remarkable and regular "secret service" began.

Imperial Airways pilots had ferried out four Catalinas from Britain to Ceylon. A fifth came later. Qantas Capt. W. H. Crowther was put in charge of the operation. The aircraft were named after the stars that were useful for celestial navigation over the long night section of flights across the Indian Ocean: *Altair Star, Vega Star, Rigel Star, Antares Star,* and *Spica Star.* These five unarmed aircraft ran a regular shuttle service, starting once a week but building up to three flights every two weeks. The Catalinas carried vital mail and special supplies, and ferried V.I.P. military and diplomatic personnel to Australia and back. The aircrafts' maximum speed was 130 miles (209 kilometers) per hour. They always traveled in absolute radio silence because the Japanese were conducting a comprehensive air and sea blockade.

Yet not once did the Qantas flights fail to get through in two years of operation. The flying boats used Lake Koggala

in Ceylon and the Swan River in Perth, Western Australia, as landing and takeoff points. The Pratt & Whitney engines were overhauled by the R.A.A.F. in Western Australia and new replacement engines for the Catalinas were built in Australia.

Because passengers on these flights flew for over 24 hours nonstop they watched the sun rise twice. As a memento of the event, Hudson Fysh produced a gift for all who flew with them—the Secret Order of the Double Sunrise, which was an ornate certificate presented to each passenger with their name on it. He also produced a Long Range Operations Gold Star that was proudly worn by the Qantas air crews who earned them.

Two years after the first crossing, the Catalinas were signed off, the last officially alighting in Perth on July 18, 1945. The remainder of the fleet flew in on July 24. Together they had flown 271 crossings of the Indian Ocean. They had carried 858 passengers, 90,793 pounds (41,182 kilograms) of war priority cargo, and 207, 260 pounds (94,038 kilograms) of mail. In two years they had flown 1,380,119 miles (2,220,610 kilometers).

For those splendid flying boats that had performed so well, it is sad to contemplate their miserable fate. In late 1945 they were towed out to sea from Fremantle—Perth's seaport— and scuttled in the very ocean they had so valiantly traversed.

Left: After flying in World War I, W. H. Fysh went home to Australia and surveyed the wild "top end" during 1919 for a future air route to link the capital cities of the eastern states of Australia.

Hudson Fysh greets Ross Smith after Smith had just made the first-ever crossing of the world in his Vickers Vimy in 1919. Smith was to follow the route south that Fysh helped to survey.

Hudson Fysh and his wartime friend, P. J. McGinness, went on to found what is now Qantas Airways Ltd. McGinness left the company but Fysh rose to become its Chairman and Managing Director.

Opposite page: Altair Star leaves Perth, Western Australia, at sunrise. This catalina was one of five used on secret "double sunrise" flights of up to 27 hours duration nonstop across the Indian Ocean from Australia to Ceylon (now Sri Lanka) during the Japanese blockade of Australia in World War II. These Qantas "specials" operated with an enormous overload of 6,000 pounds (2,720 kilograms). An average of 400 to 600 pounds (181 to 227 kilograms) of this overweight was hand mail—diplomatic, armed forces, and P.O.W. mail. Over time, the mail was stored in microfilm form so that more could be carried.

MARCEL DASSAULT

The Bloch MB-152, 1938

FROM CONCENTRATION CAMP TO SUPERSONIC MIRAGE

In the last days of World War II, Frenchman Marcel Bloch was among the skeletal figures who were still alive in the notorious Buchenwald concentration camp when American troops arrived to relieve them. Bloch was reprieved from certain death in the gas chambers by just hours.

The sick, emaciated Bloch—who changed his family name to Dassault after the war—had been a giant figure in the early, heady days of aviation when the French were building a reputation as pioneers and innovators in the new science of aircraft design and construction. Marcel's survival at war's end found him still passionate, with ambitions and creative ideas that would trigger a rejuvenation of French aviation in the modern era.

Nearly 40 years earlier, as a wide-eyed schoolboy in Paris, Marcel Bloch watched as a Wright biplane owned by le comte de Lambert made an exhibition flight around the Eiffel Tower in October 1909. It was the key event that sparked and dictated the future course of his life. Those were exciting, volatile days when the French wrenched the lead from the Americans in the wonderful new world of powered flight.

Inspired by the Wright example, Marcel studied at the École Nationale Supérieure d'Aéronautique,

where he gained his diploma. By 1914 he was well placed to assist in the designing of military aircraft, and quickly demonstrated his creative abilities. He helped produce the original drawings for the airframe of the Caudron G-3, a single-engined reconnaissance and training plane. The young engineer dreamed up a new propeller that increased the plane's performance enough to prompt the military to order it. Bloch's propeller was named Eclair and it improved other French planes including the legendary Spad. Encouraged by his success, Marcel formed a partnership with Henri Potez, and their company, Société d'Études Aéronautiques, produced the SEA IV, a twin-engined fighter reconnaissance aircraft. Of the 1,000 aircraft ordered, over 100 had been built before World War I ended in 1918, by which time Marcel was just 25 years old.

Following the armistice in 1918, there was a glut of aircraft in all the ex-combatant nations. A lack of new orders for military aircraft saw the French aviation industry close to bankruptcy. Marcel Bloch had to turn his talents to real estate and building construction.

But by the 1930s he was back working in the aviation

Above: Marcel Bloch's sharp-looking little fighter plane, the Bloch MB-152, was somehow symbolic of the French aviation industry immediately prior to World War II. When these craft arrived at operational stations, some were minus vital equipment such as gun sights and even propellers. The 152 was no match for the German frontline fighters of World War II, though many captured machines were used by the pro-Nazi Vichy government after the fall of France—which would not have pleased Marcel Bloch.

Left: Marcel Dassault in the 1960s

industry again, creating his own research department, which included the skills of Benno Claude Valliéres and Henri Desplante, two engineers who remained with Dassault for the rest of their careers. Marcel was in the business he loved best—aviation.

Courageous French aviators made exceptional, record-breaking flights in the 1930s, yet the aircraft industry in France clung to traditional and often outmoded designs compared to significant developments being made by an increasingly belligerent Germany. The French government made belated efforts to catch up and, as a result, nationalized Marcel Bloch and other French manufacturers. However the reality of the situation became tragically obvious in World War II with the devastating effectiveness of the part played by the Luftwaffe in the German Blitzkrieg.

In 1940, the French authorities rounded up the Jewish Marcel Bloch and placed him under house arrest. Four years later, after stubbornly refusing to work for the Germans, Marcel was transported to the concentration camp at Buchenwald in Germany, destined for the gas chambers.

In 1933 Avions Marcel Bloch produced the twin-engined Bloch 200 bomber with a wingspan of just over 73 feet (22.4 meters) and a speed of 143 miles (230 kilometers) per hour. It was obsolete by the time the bomber made squadron service in 1934.

The Bloch 200, 1936

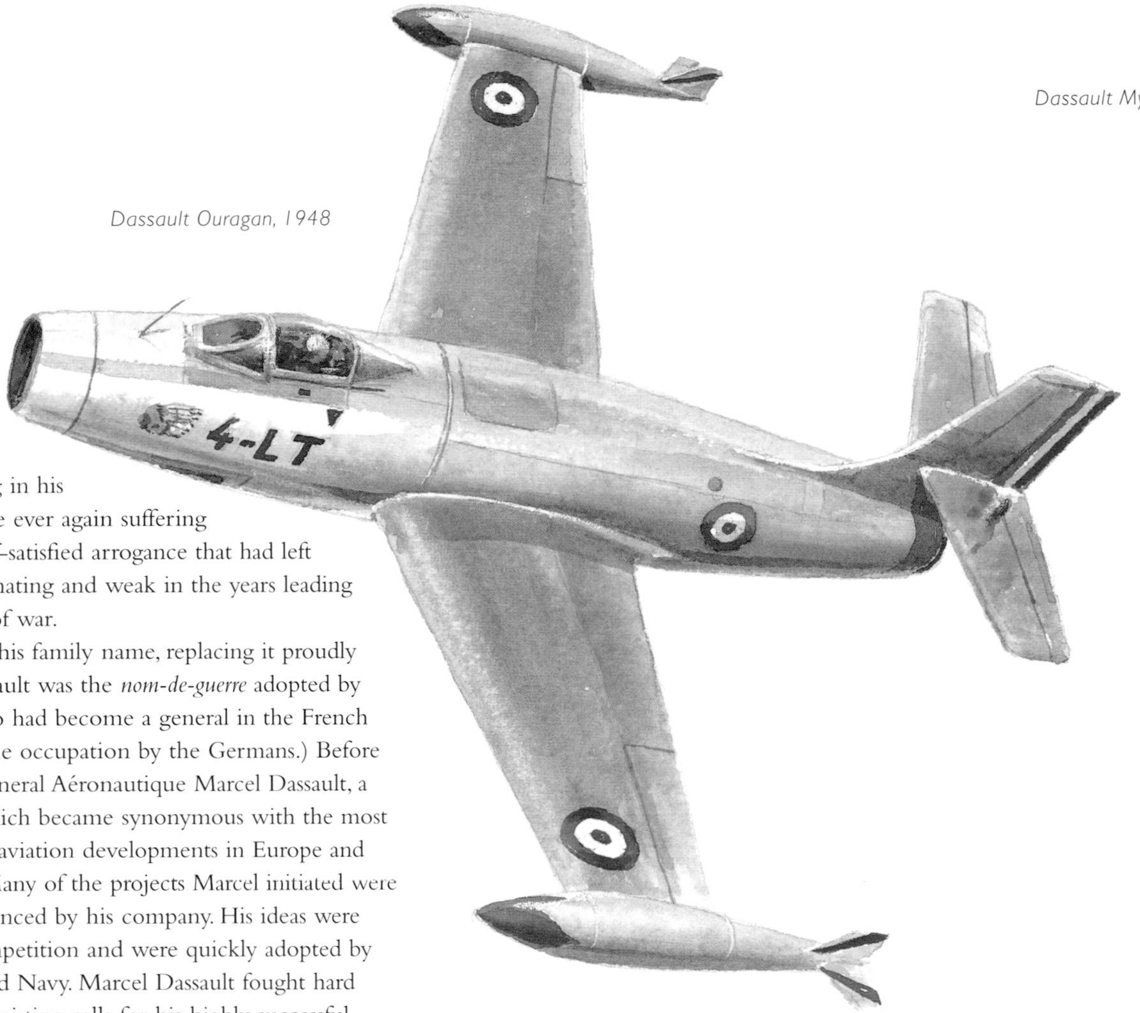

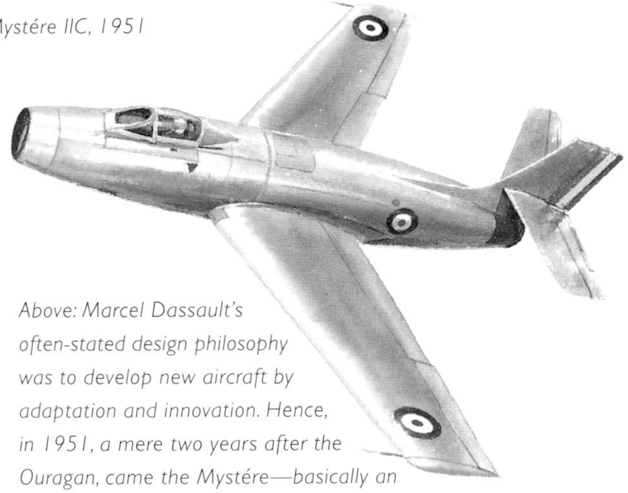

Dassault Mystére IIC, 1951

Dassault Ouragan, 1948

Once freed by the American Army, Bloch returned to France in 1945 vowing he would do everything in his power to stop France ever again suffering the results of the self-satisfied arrogance that had left French aviation stagnating and weak in the years leading up to the outbreak of war.

He first dropped his family name, replacing it proudly with Dassault (d'Assault was the *nom-de-guerre* adopted by his brother Paul who had become a general in the French Resistance during the occupation by the Germans.) Before long he founded General Aéronautique Marcel Dassault, a private company, which became synonymous with the most advanced jet fighter aviation developments in Europe and indeed, the world. Many of the projects Marcel initiated were dreamed up and financed by his company. His ideas were far ahead of the competition and were quickly adopted by the French Army and Navy. Marcel Dassault fought hard and successfully in resisting calls for his highly successful organization to be nationalized.

The famous Ouragan, Mystére, Mirage, and Étendard delta wing and swept-wing jets quickly earned their places at the leading edge of the French military forces.

It was Dassault's intention to see his planes provide the means to make his beloved France the force majeure in European affairs, but so advanced and desirable were his designs that they became key models in the fleets of many countries' air forces. The first of the Dassault highly successful Mirage series of delta-wing jets flew in 1956. The arrival of the Mirage cemented Dassault's leading position in world aviation as the Mach 2 version proved to be a winner and was ordered not only by the French Armée de l'Air during the 1960s but by many foreign air forces.

Above: Marcel Dassault's often-stated design philosophy was to develop new aircraft by adaptation and innovation. Hence, in 1951, a mere two years after the Ouragan, came the Mystére—basically an Ouragan with swept wings. The Mystére IIC is preserved in the Museé de l'Air et de l'Éspace in Paris.

Left: The Dassault Ouragan was a private venture by Dassault and was the first French-designed and produced jet fighter. The Ouragon was first flown in February, 1949. Armed with four 3/4-inch (20-millimeter) cannons, the jet fighter's maximum speed at sea level was 584 miles (940 kilometers) per hour and she was powered by a Rolls-Royce-designed Nene jet engine of 5,070 pounds (2,300 kilograms) thrust.

Dassault Super Mystére B-2, 1956

Above: The Super Mystére B-2 single-seat fighter-bomber was a direct development of the Mystére IV. This fine aircraft was so successful it remained in frontline service until 1965.

Right: The Mirage concept was a highly successful private venture, which quickly proved its worth in 1958 by becoming the first European aircraft to exceed Mach 2. Among the many records captured by the Mirage series was that of the famous French airwoman, Jacueline Auriol, who flew a Mirage III to create a world speed record of 1,148 miles (1,850 kilometers) per hour within the 62-mile (100-kilometer) closed circuit.

   The arrival of the Mirage series cemented Dassault's leading position in world aviation. There were many variants of this famous aircraft.

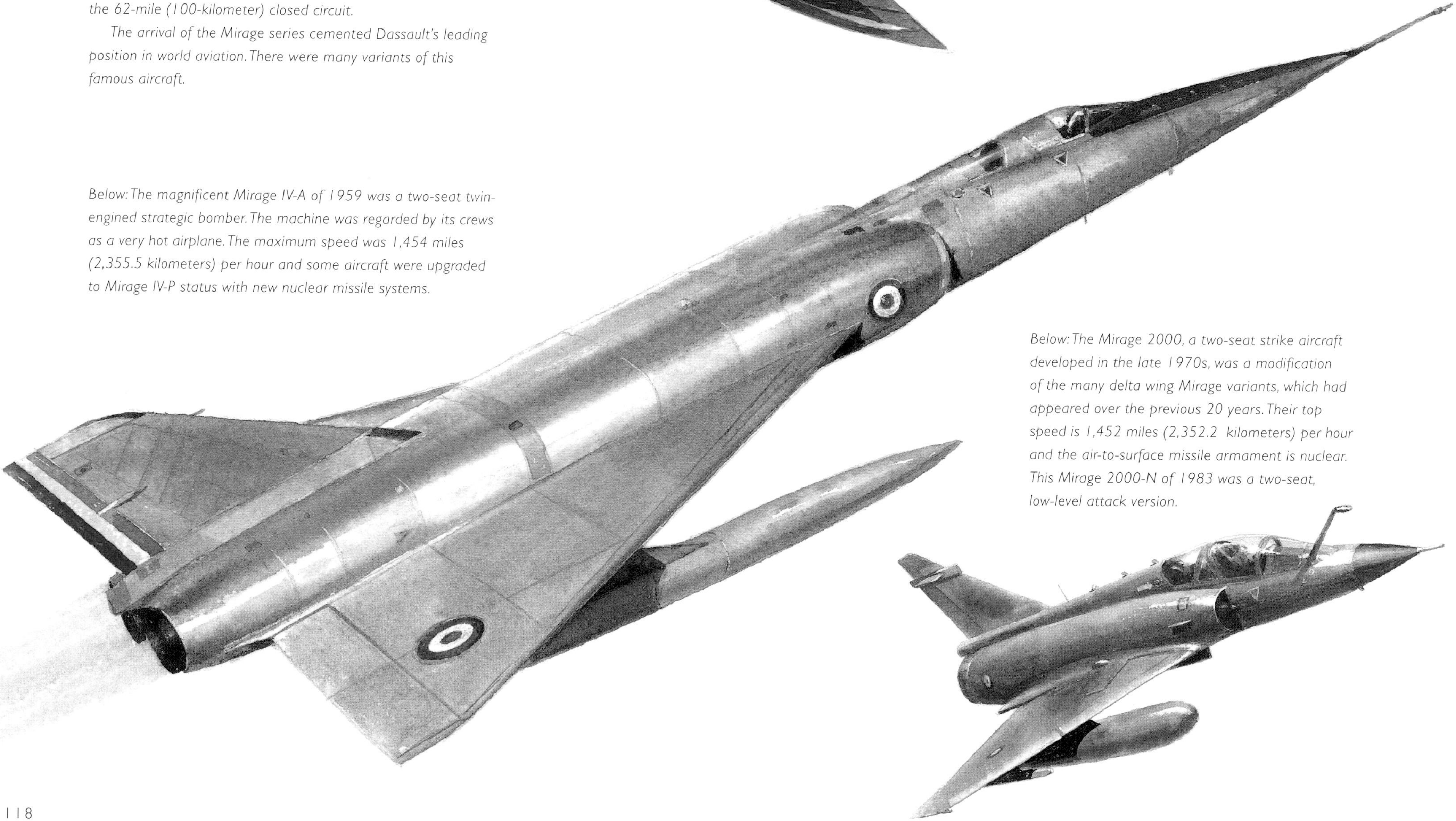

Below: The magnificent Mirage IV-A of 1959 was a two-seat twin-engined strategic bomber. The machine was regarded by its crews as a very hot airplane. The maximum speed was 1,454 miles (2,355.5 kilometers) per hour and some aircraft were upgraded to Mirage IV-P status with new nuclear missile systems.

Below: The Mirage 2000, a two-seat strike aircraft developed in the late 1970s, was a modification of the many delta wing Mirage variants, which had appeared over the previous 20 years. Their top speed is 1,452 miles (2,352.2 kilometers) per hour and the air-to-surface missile armament is nuclear. This Mirage 2000-N of 1983 was a two-seat, low-level attack version.

In the latter years of the twentieth century, production of advanced weaponry such as military aircraft became so horrendously expensive that a number of European nations combined skills and resources to produce a European Fighter Aircraft (EFA). It was a highly sophisticated airplane. However Marcel Dassault, at the request of the French government, worked at producing his preferred version of a European fighter—the deadly supersonic Rafale.

Rafale, a Mach 2 interceptor, is the most recent aircraft to bear the Dassault name. Made with composite materials and featuring fly-by-wire and voice-activated control systems, it is a complete flying machine of the new age. It is also an awesome tribute to the man who suffered grievously, yet devoted so much of his spirit and inventiveness to his country. Marcel wasn't there to see it fly. In April 1986, only three months before the Rafale took off for its maiden flight, Dassault died in Paris—the city he loved—where, as Marcel Bloch, he was born 94 years before.

The success of the Dassault organization was due to Marcel Dassault himself, not just to his creative drive but to his business acumen and political awareness. His step-by-step method of developing new designs and close cooperation with the armed forces saved millions of dollars. For instance, an American study of his success during the "Mirage" years found that the cost of a development program was about 40 percent less than the American equivalent; his design and administration teams were smaller and produced results faster and more economically. And his aircraft were not all the result of good housekeeping. Marcel Dassault is quoted as saying that an aircraft which is beautiful is one that flies well, and one "what pleases me is to be able to invent and produce."

In post-war France he was a follower of General Charles de Gaulle and was elected to Parliament as a deputy. In that role he would have been fully aware of the significance and power of political influence—no small factor when fighting off those who wished to nationalize his business. Marcel Dassault emerged as a giant among Frenchmen and was one of the great contributors to world aviation.

The aircraft I created bear the names I chose specially ... names that make people dream.
MARCEL DASSAULT, PARIS, 1969

Dassault Rafale prototype, 1986

Below: The Caudron G-3 was Marcel Bloch's introduction to aircraft design. Thirty years before changing his name to Dassault at the end of World War II, Bloch worked on the drawings for the two-seat Caudron G-3 reconnaissance aircraft of 1914. The G-3 pushed the air aside at a stately 82 miles (132 kilometers) per hour, powered by a rotary engine of less than 100 horsepower. This model is wonderfully preserved in the Musée de l'Air et de l'Éspace in Paris. That the same man oversaw the extraordinary lines of the Dassault Rafale prototype of 1986 (above) speaks volumes for his contribution to modern aviation in Europe. The Rafale reflects state-of-the-art thinking in the final decades of the twentieth century. It's maximum speed is quoted at 1,320 miles (2,123 kilometers) per hour at 55,000 feet (16,764 meters). The sleek, space-age fighter is capable of delivering nuclear missiles and was the last development in which Marcel Dassault was involved.

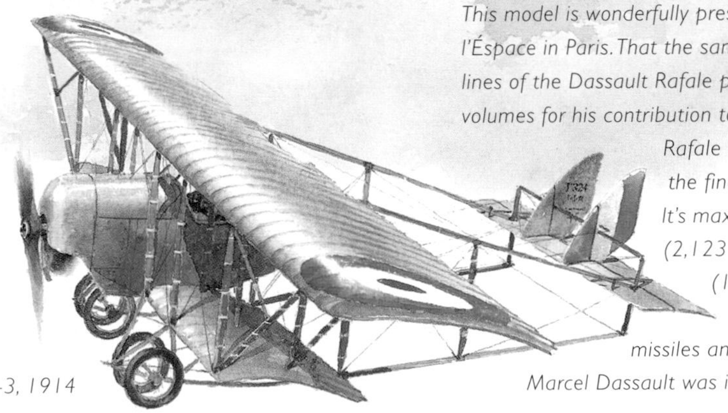

The Caudron G-3, 1914

Percival Mew Gull, 1939

EDGAR PERCIVAL

HANG ONTO YOUR HAT—WE'RE RACING!

Edgar Percival was an air-racing man who loved to compete and wanted to win so he designed a plane to win air races. The premier race in England that he ached to conquer was the King's Cup. Captain Percival often had the fastest plane flying at the fastest speeds and although he was always among the leaders, the handicappers somehow ensured that he never came first. Yet the publicity he gained helped sell many of his Percival Gulls to famous fliers who admired the performance characteristics of his machines. One of the most publicized and effective demonstrations of the qualities of the Percival Gull was in October 1933 when Sir Charles Kingsford Smith mounted a 60-gallon (273-liter) long-range fuel tank in the rear of the cabin and flew from England to Australia in 7 days, 4 hours, and 44 minutes—a new world record then. It was just one of many records to be broken. The list

of pilots flying smart, speedy, and reliable Vega Gulls or the smaller racing Mew Gull included Amy Johnson, Jimmy Broadbent, Alex Henshaw, Jean Batten, C. J. Melrose, and Beryl Markham—all long-distance, record-breaking fliers of the 1930s. Their achievements were covered in newspapers, on radio, and in cinema newsreels, creating a surging demand for Percival's creations. In 1936 the strain on manufacturing caused Percival's company to move production from Gravesend to a new, larger factory at Luton.

Edgar Percival had been a captain in the Royal Flying Corps in World War I. He transferred from the Australian Light Horse to train as a pilot, first in the Middle East then in England. After training he joined No. 111 Squadron in the Middle East for the remainder of the war. In the intermediate post-war years, he took up air racing in Australia, finishing fourth in the 1924 Australian Derby. In 1928 he was back in England to fly in the King's Cup race at Brooklands, and in September of that year, came second in the French light airplane trials at Orly near Paris. In 1931, Percival worked with Saunders Roe Ltd. on the design of a three-engined plane, but later switched to designing his own two-seater craft which he named Gull.

Evidence suggests that Percival's new plane owed much to the Hendy 302—a two-seater machine designed by Basil B. Henderson. Percival had been test pilot for Henderson's earlier plane, the Hobo. He had raced the Hendy 302 in the 1930 King's Cup and in the Heston to Newcastle race in 1931 when he achieved a top speed of 145 miles (232 kilometers) per hour. The Gull had many similarities to the Hendy 302 and was built, tested, and officially certified in time for Percival to race it in the 1932 King's Cup where it flew at an average speed of $142\frac{1}{4}$ miles (228.5 kilometers) per hour—the marque was on its way.

Photographs of Percival taken over the years rarely showed him without his hat. He seemed to prefer trilbies and, even sitting in a cabin ready to take off, his hat was always jammed firmly on his head. In those days pilots were

often superstitious—perhaps his hat was his good-luck charm.

In World War II Percival Aircraft Ltd. adapted the Vega Gull for the Royal Air Force. Called the Proctor it was supplied in a number of versions and was generally used for communications and in the training of wireless operators. Other aircraft were built under contract for the R.A.F. including the twin-engined Airspeed Oxford trainer and the high speed Mosquito bomber. Edgar Percival left the company in 1940 but continued to be involved in aircraft business and design. His major achievement in the history of flight was the Gull. It advanced the cause of aviation by its speed, air-worthiness, and the admiration it aroused in the famous pilots that flew it to write new records.

In his book *The Flight of the Mew Gull* English test pilot Alex Henshaw paints a wonderful picture of the competitive racing scene of the 1930s in England, in which Edgar Percival was a prominent entrant. Henshaw flew himself and Percival into aviation history with an astonishing 12,754-mile (20,406.4-kilometer) flight from London to Capetown and return, over desert and jungle, in the tiny Percival Mew Gull.

This Mew Gull is still flying in England's famous Shuttleworth Collection of veteran flying machines. Only six were made. The beautiful record-breaker was much modified by Henshaw and flew at a top speed of 240 miles (384 kilometers) per hour—even the Hawker Hurricane fighter could not have caught it at sea level.

Opposite page: One of the first Percival Gull 4 series of monoplanes was seen over Sydney Harbour Bridge after the pilot, Charles Kingsford Smith, set a new England to Australia world record for light aircraft of 7 days, 4 hours, and 44 minutes. The aircraft carried a large extra fuel tank in the rear of the cabin.

Far left: Edgar Percival with his Mew Gull racer

ROY CHADWICK

20,000 RIVETS FLYING IN CLOSE FORMATION

Roy Chadwick showed precocious interest in the new field of aviation in the early 1900s. He started building and flying model planes from the age of ten. Later, he attended the College of Technology in Manchester before taking up an apprenticeship in engineering with British Westinghouse. His overwhelming desire was to be involved in aviation. In Manchester at that time, Alliot Verdon Roe, the man dubbed in 1909 as the first to design and fly a British airplane, had a small factory for building planes. Once he had finished his apprenticeship, Roy Chadwick applied to Roe for a job. Roe was so impressed with the young Chadwick that he engaged him on the spot as his personal assistant. It was to be a very productive partnership. The two men became firm friends while producing great innovative aircraft.

The company was called Avro, and Chadwick assisted Roe in production and design. From 1914, at the start of World War I and in the period immediately after the war, Chadwick's first success was the famous Avro 504 aircraft. After the war he designed the Baby and the Avian, both of which made amazing long-distance flights at the hands of Bert Hinkler, Charles Kingsford Smith, Lady Heath, and others. He also designed the *Antarctica*—an Avro Avian adapted to land on water with folding wings, which enabled the plane to be winched on board ship. The aircraft was built for Sir Ernest Shackleton who took it on his final expedition to the Antarctic in 1921.

Left: A.V. Roe's triplane, the first English-designed powered airplane, flew at Lea Marshes, London, in 1909.

Above: In 1914, at the outbreak of World War I, Roy Chadwick was 21 and involved in the design of the famous Avro 504, which made Britain's first strategic air raid by attacking German airship sheds at Friedrickshafen in November of that year. Over 8,000 of the 504s, of various marques, were built, and were mostly used as training aircraft. Hundreds of R.A.F. pilots learned to fly in them.

Opposite page: One of Roy Chadwick's most popular airplanes—the Avian. Australian aviator Bert Hinkler flew in an Avian over the desolate and forbidding country between Jask and Karachi during his epic solo flight from England to Australia in February, 1928.

This historic flight made Hinkler an international hero. His meticulous preparation, navigational skills, and mechanical aptitude, along with the rugged and reliable design of the Avian, produced a trouble-free, though arduous, 15-day flight across the world.

Roy Chadwick's ill-fated Avro Manchester

When Sir Alliot Verdon Roe decided to bow out in the late 1920s, the company was sold to the Saunders Group, headed by Roy Dobson. The new owners continued to use the Avro name and kept Chadwick on as an executive and chief designer.

In the late 1930s the air ministry in Britain encouraged the company to develop warplanes because the international situation was deteriorating. Roy Chadwick quickly had a twin-engined bomber, the Manchester, on the drawing board. Shortly after the start of war in 1939 the first prototype was in the air and, due to the pressures of war, was urgently commissioned. It was not a success, more being lost to engine trouble than through enemy action.

Chadwick set about modifying the Manchester. He added 12 feet (3.7 meters) to the wingspan and gave the aircraft four 1,460-horsepower Rolls-Royce Merlin engines in place

Opposite page: Avro Lancaster "We Dood It Too" of 550 Sqdn. R.A.F. corkscrews violently away from a German Me. 110 night-fighter, which had approached from the shadowy side of their flight path.

Enemy action was not the only hazard on bombing missions— the Avro Lancaster had front, rear, and mid-upper hydraulically oper-ated gun turrets. Once in their turrets, the air gunners usually stayed in their cramped spaces for the complete bombing missions of seven hours or more. Navigator Bill Mann, who briefed the artist on this painting, said that some gunners had to put their boots in position on the floor first and then squeeze themselves into the confined space of their turrets.

At the operating height of about 20,000 feet (6,096 meters) at -40°Fahrenheit (-71°Celsius), many crew suffered frostbite and had to be helped out of their turrets at the end of a mission.

Crews who took part in the massive R.A.F. night raids on German targets during World War II suffered very high losses. All crew members of this Lancaster survived and were still in touch with each other at the turn of the century.

of the two troublesome 1,800-horsepower Vultures. As a result of these modifications he had created the Lancaster bomber. The Lancaster first flew in January 1941 and commenced flying operationally in 1942. It quickly became a favorite of Allied pilots and aircrew. In all, 7,377 Lancasters were built and they flew 156,000 sorties.

The "Lanc," as it became affectionately known, could carry almost its own weight in bombs and fuel. One immense bomb, the Grand Slam bomb weighing 22,000 pounds (9,988 kilograms), was designed to penetrate concrete and explode beneath the surface. It could be delivered only by the Lancaster, thanks in part to its 33 feet (10.1 meters) of uninterrupted bomb bay. Sir Arthur Harris, Marshal of the Royal Air Force and wartime chief of Bomber Command wrote, in part, "The finest bomber of the war! Its efficiency was incredible ... the Lancaster far surpassed all other types of heavy bombers. Not only could it take heavier loads, not only was it easier to handle, and not only were there fewer accidents than any other types, the casualty rate was also consistently below those of other types."

One of the reasons for its design success was the fact that its airframe, influenced by pioneer Jack Northrop's stressed skin construction, could be riveted together by a nonskilled workforce—vital in wartime with manpower shortages. Also,

Above: From the moment the first prototype of the Lancaster took its maiden flight, its performance looked good. Commenting on the way Chadwick transformed the Manchester into the Lancaster, a colleague stated: "Chadwick showed himself to be a most resourceful and courageous designer, ultimately snatching success from failure in the most ingenious way with a superlatively successful operational aircraft."

engine replacement, repair, and maintenance was made easier using a "power-egg" principle, where all engine accessories were installed as a unit; control lines going in and electrical, hydraulic, and pneumatic power lines feeding out. Unlike U.S. bombers of this size, the Lancaster dispensed with a copilot and was used operationally with only one pilot in the cockpit.

Shortly after the end of World War II, Roy Chadwick, by then aged 54, designed a large passenger airliner known as the Avro Tudor. Anxious to know how the prototype Tudor II would perform, he joined the pilots on a test flight. Due to an inadvertent reversing of the aileron controls by a technician, the aircraft crashed. Chadwick, probably standing behind the pilots, was hurled 60 feet (18.3 meters) into the air. His skull was fractured and he died within minutes on August 23, 1947.

P. G. TAYLOR

TAKING A NEW TACK

P.G. Taylor

Fighter pilot, navigator, yachtsman, author, and entrepreneur—Patrick Gordon Taylor was a man of extraordinary abilities. He was the kind of practical, hands-on visionary needed to command a key role in the development of human flight.

Although Australian-born, Taylor, popularly known as P. G., was a true citizen of the world. He flew with the Royal Flying Corps, winning the Military Cross in World War I. He then stayed in England in the 1920s to work with the De Havilland aircraft company and in the 1930s was selected as a senior pilot for Australian National Airways. After he had joined Charles Kingsford Smith in a record flight from Australia across the Pacific to the United States he propounded the view that wide oceans should support regular air routes operated by flying boats. Financed by the British and Australian governments, he made his proving flights across the Indian Ocean in *Guba*, an American Catalina flying boat. The day after he lodged his report, World War II began. In 1944, he persuaded the Royal Australian Forces and the United States authorities to allow him to make a survey flight from Bermuda across the Pacific to Australia. Again, in 1951, this time with the backing of the Australian government, he set out on a new aerial survey.

P. G. never did things by halves. The flight was impeccably planned. Easter Island was a tiny dot at the end of a long, demanding flight over the world's largest expanse of water. In his consolidated Catalina flying boat named *Frigate Bird II* Taylor alighted in the sea off the rocky coast of Easter Island bang on schedule. He chose a small bay at the southern tip of the island as a landing place. Taylor planned to taxi back around the rocky tip should the wind change while they were there. The island had no facilities or protection, just rocky inlets open to dangerous and huge Southern Ocean swells.

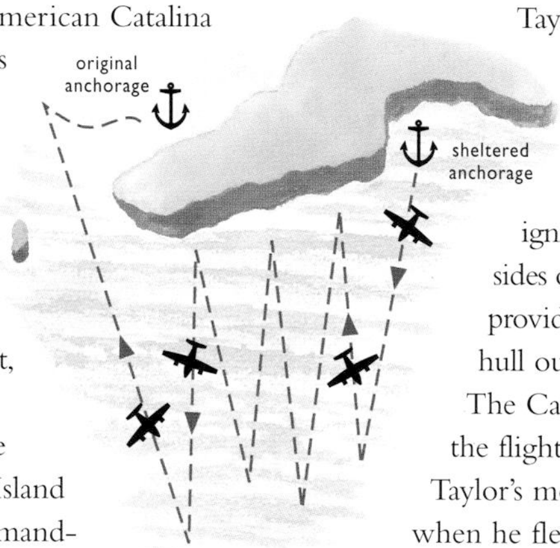

The worst happened. Suddenly the wind changed and *Frigate Bird II*'s anchor line parted while half the crew was ashore. They were rounded-up and brought back to the plane, clambering aboard and trying to negotiate the *Frigate Bird II* to shelter around the point. The plane still needed to be refueled and required safe anchorage but the crew knew they couldn't just taxi against the onshore wind and swell or the Catalina's hull would be broken in two.

Showing great ingenuity, P. G started a series of tacks, just as he would use with a yacht facing a strong head wind. Using engines, ailerons, and rudder, he made a series of long, narrow tacks gradually creeping across the large and sometimes breaking swells. After an extraordinary display of seamanship Taylor finally sailed round the point to safety.

Next morning, heavy with fuel, *Frigate Bird II* had a hazardous run through rough seas before she could take off. As she approached lifting speed, Taylor had to ignite rockets installed on the port and starboard sides of the cat's fuselage for just such an emergency, providing the extra thrust necessary to raise her hull out of the turbulent water and into the air.

The Catalina rose splendidly to the occasion and the flight went on to conclude successfully. One of Taylor's most heroic exploits must have been in 1935 when he flew from Sydney to New Zealand with Kingsford Smith in the famous *Southern Cross* to deliver the King George V Silver Jubilee mail. Half way across the Tasman Sea, the propeller shattered on the starboard engine of the Fokker trimotor. Smithy turned back, flying on two engines. They noticed that the oil pressure in the port engine was rapidly falling. Taylor climbed out on the wing strut into the slipstream, collected oil in a thermos from the stationary starboard motor and handed it to John Stannage

who was with Smithy in the cockpit. He did this several times, with Stannage eventually saving about a gallon (4.5 liters) of oil in a leather suitcase. Taylor returned to the cockpit and climbed out the other side then transferred the oil to the port engine. While he slowly poured in the oil Smithy had to shut down this engine and fly only on the central engine.

Southern Cross, powered by only one engine, lost height before they could restart the port engine. Climbing again to a passable height Taylor had to repeat the process twice more before they nursed the *Southern Cross* back to Sydney. In 1954 Taylor was knighted for his pioneering services to aviation.

In December 1966 he died quietly in Honolulu.

Left: In Taylor's system of tacking he ran the left engine, applying the right rudder and putting the right-hand aileron down to create drag on that wing, then put the left-hand float in the water. One tack covered about a mile (1.6 kilometers). At the end of the tack, he turned off the engine, sailing backward with the left aileron down and with full left rudder. This kept the nose pointing out to sea, just enough off the wind to keep control and to enable the flying boat to slide back in toward the coast (and along it a little) in the direction of the point around which they wished to sail.

Opposite page: Frigate Bird II made one of its final tacks to seaward off the dangerous lee shore of the southern tip of Easter Island. Taylor sat calmly on the cabin roof steadying the control column with his foot. A broken anchor warp dangled from the bow—Taylor fell overboard attempting to retrieve it and was pulled back on board by the crew. Eventually the Catalina sailed backward through a gap between the mainland and the pinnacle of rock seen at the left. Above them, the crew saw what they regarded as a symbol of good luck—a frigate bird soaring on the wind.

original anchorage

sheltered anchorage

"KELLY" JOHNSON AND THE SKUNK WORKS

IT TAKES A LOCKHEED TO BEAT A LOCKHEED

Johnson named them, Lockheed made them—the Electra, Hudson, P-38 Lightning, Constellation and Super Constellation, Shooting Star, Starfighter, Star Lifter, Hercules, U-2 spy plane, Galaxy, Blackbird, and the *Columbia* space shuttle.

Right from the production of the first Lockheed Vega, designed by Jack Northrop in the hell-raising, air-racing 1920s, Lockheed planes were something special, not just in America but around the world. The Lockheed brothers were the first manufacturers to mass-produce strong mono-coque bodies, building fast, reliable planes whose reputation reinforced the company's catch phrase among pilots: "It takes a Lockheed to beat a Lockheed."

When America became involved in World War II, the twin-engined P-38—known as the Lockheed Lightning—quickly became a highly respected ground attack fighter. After teething problems that burnt out supercharged engines, over 40,000 of the P-38-1s were produced according to the designs of Clarence Leonard "Kelly" Johnson. From the mid-1930s, over 40 of the Lockheed aircraft owed much to the design genius of Johnson. His first major commercial success was the Lockheed 14 with its many innovative features. In

1939 his famous 40-seat, four-engined, tricycle undercarriage design for T.W.A., the Constellation, followed. The *Connie* cruised at 298 miles (480 kilometers) per hour over a 3,000-mile (4,828-kilometer) range. Later models carried up to 95 passengers and flew them farther and faster. Today this airplane has a near-cult following, being regarded as one of the most beautiful aircraft of its type ever flown. Fellow designer Howard Hughes was a consultant in the early design stage.

In 1943 Johnson sketched out fresh, new concepts planned by his team with utmost secrecy in the surrounds of the Skunk Works at Burbank, California. Originally, this venue was designated Area 51 or Paradise Ranch. But those who went to work there quickly labeled it Skunk Works because of the awful odors that wafted in from a plastics factory near the circus-tent "offices" which initially housed the team. Chief engineer Kelly Johnson dreamed up the idea of working in this space to enable designers and engineers to work quickly and efficiently with little management oversight, avoiding being bogged down by office beaurocracy. He said: "The Skunk Works is a concentration of a few good people solving problems in advance—and at a fraction of the cost—by applying the simplest, most straightforward methods possible to develop and produce new products."

One of Kelly Johnson's early trademarks before he initiated the Skunk Works was the twin fin concept. He first employed

Howard Hughes' record-breaking Lockheed 14, designed by Kelly Johnson

it on the Lockheed 10 Electra. The larger Lockheed 14 was a very fast airliner, also with twin fins. It first flew in 1937 and was powered by two Wright Cyclone radial engines, which gave it a 230-mile (370-kilometer) per hour cruising speed. The Lockheed 14 featured integrated fuel tanks, fully feathering propellers, two-speed superchargers, under-floor freight storage, and large, extending Fowler flaps, the guides for which protrude from the trailing edge of the wing.

Howard Hughes owned the Johnson-designed Lockheed 14 in 1938. In this aircraft he created a round-the-world record of 3 days, 19 hours, and 17 minutes. At the opening of hostilities in World War II the Lockheed 14 was modified to become the Hudson reconnaissance bomber.

Left: Howard Hughes (left), a consultant during the development of the Constellation, on the Connie's flight deck.

Opposite page: Twin Constellations show the world. On January 14, 1958, two Qantas Lockheed Super Constellations took off from Kingsford Smith Airport and flew toward Sydney Harbour Bridge where they headed off in different directions. One turned west, the other headed east. Each plane circumnavigated the globe, arriving back at the same time, 6 days later. The round-the-world service was one of those firsts for which Qantas is famous.

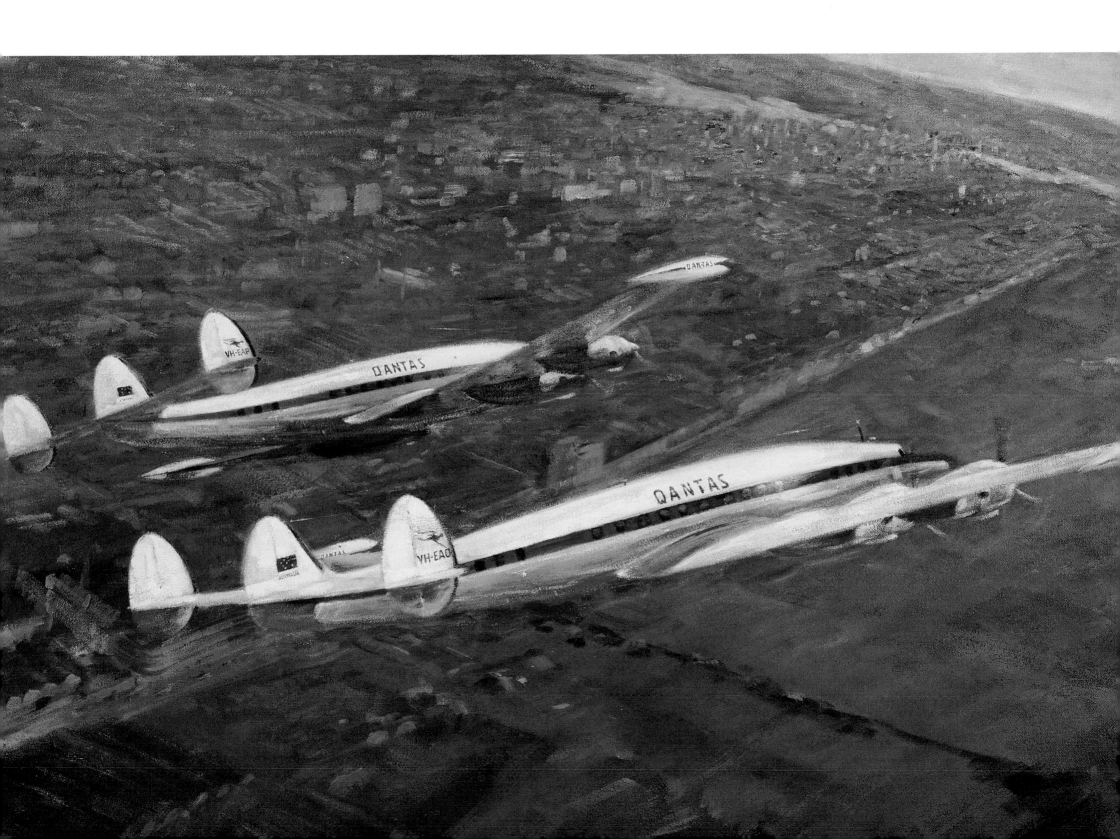

The Lockheed Shooting Star, 1948

Engineers should always work within a stone's throw of the airplane being built.

A KELLY JOHNSON RULE AT THE SKUNK WORKS

Kelly Johnson in his fifties

Below: The amazing Lockheed Starfighter was another spectacular offspring of the Skunk Works. It was developed as the result of Korean War experience. In 1952 Kelly Johnson had to devise a machine with outstanding dogfight performance at greater speeds and higher operating altitudes. The Starfighter was an astonishing aircraft with a tiny, thin, razor-edged wing of pronounced anhedral and capable of flying 1,150 miles (1,850 kilometers) per hour at 50,000 feet (15,240 meters).

It was, said pilots, more like a missile than an airplane "with as nice a cockpit as you'd find anywhere." It proved

very demanding of its pilots, with very small margins for error. If a pilot was caught out with no power, he landed at 240 miles (388.8 kilometers) per hour! At one time, Starfighters in Germany were killing 4 out of every 10 of its pilots. The U.S.A.F. operated a few squadrons and some Starfighters were used, not with great success, in the Vietnam War during 1967. Starfighters were bought by Canada, Japan, and European nations for use in N.A.T.O. Each was armed with a single $\frac{3}{4}$-inch (20-millimeter) cannon, and could carry Sidewinder missiles, and conventional and nuclear bombs. One of the German-operated machines is shown.

The Lockheed Starfighter, 1958

Opposite page: The Lockheed Shooting Star was the first fighter jet to be designed by Kelly Johnson's team. It was a response to the progress made by Britain late in World War II. Britain, like Germany, had invented the jet engine and had flown jet airplanes. Using a British De Havilland Goblin engine, the prototype Shooting Star was first flown on January 8, 1944—a mere six months after leaving the drawing board—by Milo Burcham. After a few disastrous setbacks it was produced for the U.S.A.F. using American Allison jet engines of 5,400-pound (2,449-kilogram) thrust. World War II finished before it could see active service but Shooting Stars flew nearly 100,000 operational sorties in the Korean conflict of 1950-53.

Right: The Lockheed F-104 Starfighter gained an awesome, dangerous reputation among German pilots, but that didn't faze one of the greatest women pilots, Jackie Cochran. She was coached and checked out on the F-104 by Chuck Yeager—the famous American pilot who first broke the sound barrier in the SX-1 experimental jet. In 1964, in an F-104, Jackie Cochran created the women's world speed record of 1,429 $\frac{1}{3}$ miles (2,300.2 kilometers) per hour.

The Lockheed U-2, 1955

Left: Kelly Johnson poses beside his masterpiece.

Opposite page: A Lockheed SR-71 Blackbird climbs to its operating height of up to 80,000 feet (24,384 meters). Its crew of two wear flying suits similar to those worn by astronauts. The SR-71's fuel system occupies virtually the whole of the wings and fuselage and, with air-to-air refueling, the Blackbird can stay airborne for as long as the crew can endure it.

The brave man who took this highly unorthodox product of the Skunk Works on its first flight in 1962 was project chief test pilot, Lou Schalk. It was a flight he completed despite dangerous control problems. In 1976, a 10-year-old SR-71 Blackbird set a new world speed record for powered aircraft of 2,193$\frac{1}{5}$ miles (3,528.8 kilometers) per hour. While spy satellites have now taken on their strategic reconnaissance duties, the SR-71s did sterling work with the U.S. Air Force for 25 years until their retirement in the early 1990s.

The Skunk Works (its official name is Lockheed Martin Advanced Development Program), became an inspiring success, producing highly secret but startlingly innovative results. Another of the aircraft designed in this way was the U-2 spy plane requested by the C.I.A. The U-2 was a fragile-looking, jet-powered sailplane which could sustain subsonic flight at an altitude of 60,000 feet (18,288 meters) and which could photograph areas of interest to the U.S. Defense Forces and military strategists. The U-2 was designed to fly at a height out of range of conventional weapons.

After first flying in 1955, it did its job well until May 1960 when a U-2 piloted by Francis Gary Powers, was shot out of the sky over Russian territory. Powers, who parachuted to safety, was captured and imprisoned for spying. In February 1962 he was released and exchanged for captured Soviet spy, Rudolf Abel.

It was a U-2 which, later in that same year, detected that the U.S.S.R. was establishing missile bases in Cuba. This caused a diplomatic crisis between President John F. Kennedy of the U.S.A. and Nikita S. Krushchev of the Soviet Union, resulting in an embarrassing back down and removal of the missiles by the Soviet Union.

Today, satellites do the surveillance job much more efficiently, but for its time, the U-2 was outstanding and unique.

The other memorable aircraft Kelly and his team developed was the SR-71 Blackbird. It remains the fastest and highest-flying aircraft in the world today, 36 years after it first took flight in 1964. Johnson built the Blackbird of titanium alloy to enable the aircraft to withstand its excessive heat build-up to 800°Fahrenheit (427°Celsius)—at which heat it glows cherry red—when flying at over 2,000 miles (3,200 kilometers) per hour and at altitudes exceeding 85,000 feet (26,000 meters). When flying at Mach 3, the Blackbird moves faster than the speed a bullet moves as it leaves a rifle barrel. Blackbird could photographically survey 100,000 square miles (160,000 square kilometers) from its operating altitude.

Though he retired as senior vice president of Lockheed Martin in 1975, Kelly remained a director until 1980, and was senior adviser until his death at the age of 80 in 1990. A legacy of his design innovations is the space shuttle with the first of them, the *Columbia*, developed at Kelly Johnson's Skunk Works.

Right: U-2 Pilot Gary Powers, seen in full flying gear, made world headlines when he survived his U-2 being shot down by a Russian missile.

ANDRÉ TURCAT

CONCORDE—VIVE LA DIFFERENCE!

André Turcat's place in the honor roll of aviation had been assured—he was the first man to pilot the Anglo-French Concorde SST and was also the first to break the sound barrier in Concorde.

Turcat, born in 1921, is a graduate of the prestigious École Polytechnique. He commenced his flying tuition in 1945 after Germany withdrew from France at the end of World War II. He started training in Moranes at Chateauroux and followed up with further training in British Tiger Moths at La Rochelle and Cognac. As a graduate pilot of the French Armée de l'Air, he first flew Ju 52 military transports. By 1948, at the age of 27, he was a squadron leader flying Dakotas in the Indochina war in Vietnam.

In 1951 he joined E.P.N.E.R.—the famed school for test pilots in France—as professor of flight mechanics and was appointed director of the school a year later. In 1952, he was one of the first French aviators to break the sound barrier in a Mystére II fighter. After his time at E.P.N.E.R., André flew as test pilot, first in a new delta-winged Gerfaut, and then in the Griffon built by Nord Aviation. In 1959, he recorded a world speed record for a closed circuit flight in the supersonic Griffon before joining Sud Aviation as a test pilot.

Once Sud Aviation was awarded the contract to work toward a new supersonic transport aircraft, Turcat was named as test director. From 1964 to 1976, when André Turcat retired from the company now called Aerospatiale France, he lived, worked on, and believed in the Concorde—the unique airliner that flies faster then sound.

Right: André Turcat brings in the Concorde prototype to make its first touchdown at Toulouse after its historic first test flight in 1969.

Left: André Turcat in the 1970s

Turcat was more than simply a splendid airman and a fearless pilot. Between 1971 and 1977 he served as joint Mayor of the city of Toulouse and has achieved recognition in several institutions. He is a Doctor of Letters from the University of Toulouse in France, was a director and professor of flight mechanics at l'École du Personnel Navigant d'Essais—E.P.N.E.R.—a special school for test pilots, and was the founder and first president of the National Academy of Air and Space at Toulouse. His decorations include Commander of the Legion of Honor, Grand Officer of Merit, Commander of the British Empire, Croix de Guerre, Médaille de l'Aéronautique, and in 1972, the Harmon International Aviation Trophy, awarded to him by President Richard Nixon. Now in his late seventies, André Turcat is retired and living quietly in Aix-en-Provence.

When André Turcat trained to fly in the French Air Force on a "rag-and-stick" De Havilland Tiger Moth similar to this one, he would never have dreamed he would be the first man to fly Concorde.

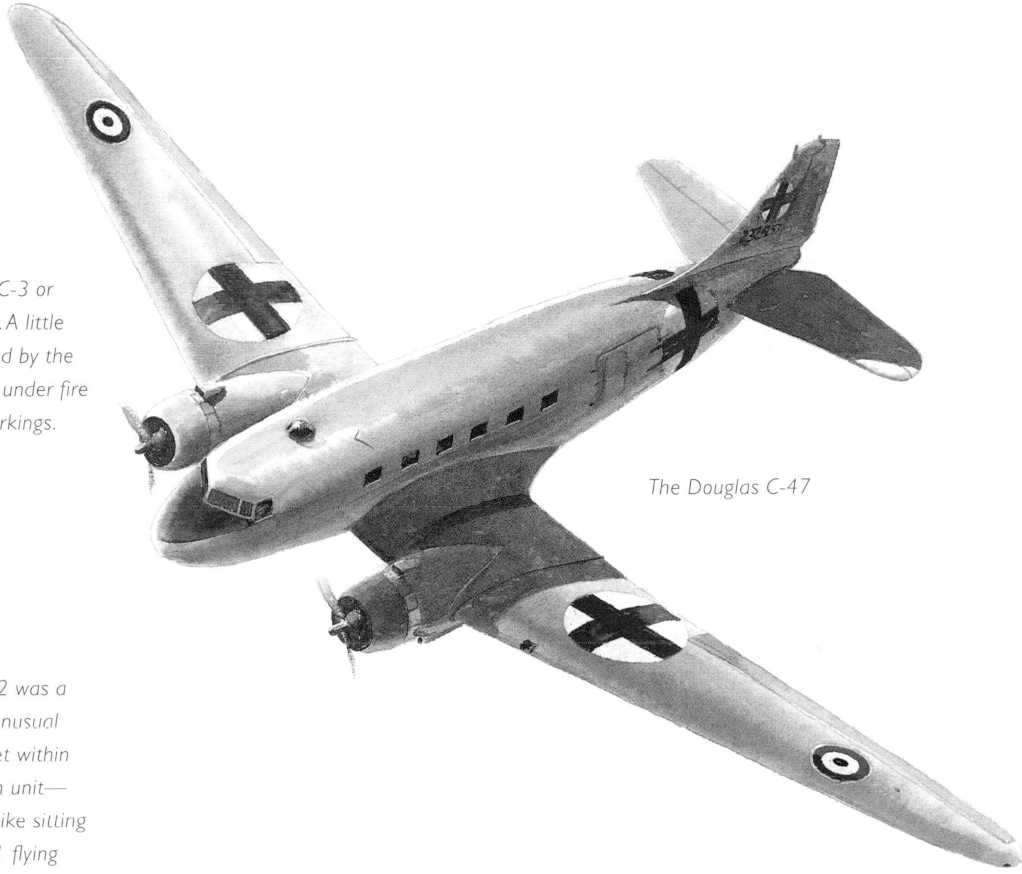

Right: André Turcat flew the famous Douglas DC-3 or C-47 troop-carrier in the 1950s Indochina war. A little known ambulance version of the C-47 was used by the French Air Force in Indochina. They often came under fire despite their large, international Red Cross markings.

The Douglas C-47

Below: The extraordinary Nord 1500 Griffon 02 was a dangerous and very fast machine. It owed its unusual appearance to its engines: It had a turbo jet set within the housing as a starter for its main propulsion unit— a ram jet. For Turcat it must have been rather like sitting on a roaring flying bomb—Hitler's notorious V1 flying bomb was powered by a ram jet.

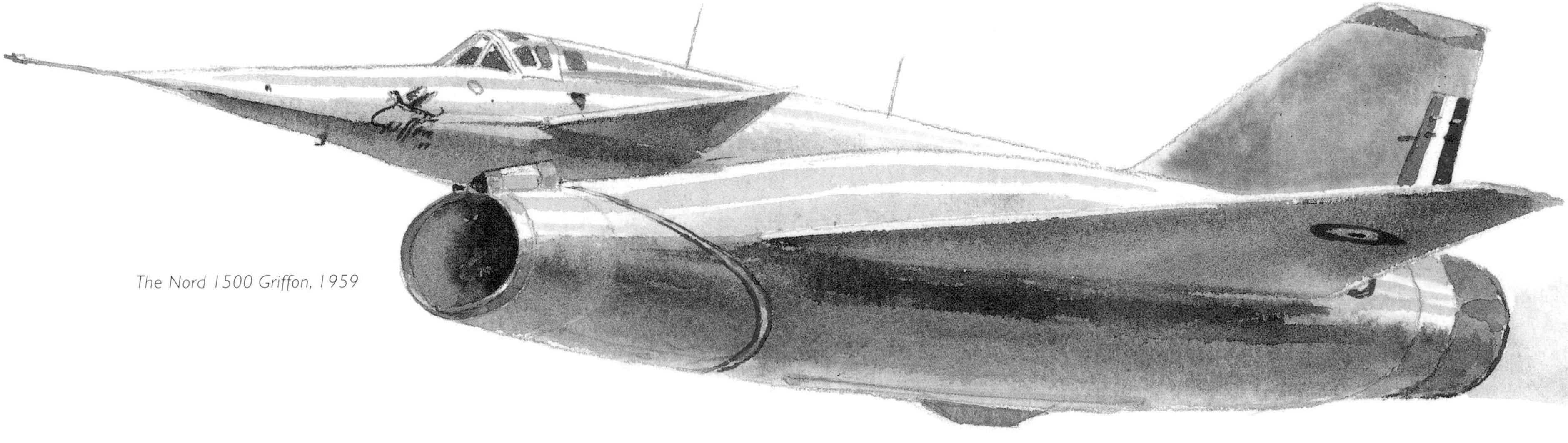

The Nord 1500 Griffon, 1959

The Handley Page HP-115

Many experimental aircraft were employed both in Britain and France as research vehicles into the problems associated with supersonic flight. These two airplanes were employed to find the most efficient wing shape. While the delta wing shape was preferred there were many types of delta to explore, an extreme example being the Handley. The Fairey Delta FD II was another aircraft originally designed to find out the effects of accelerating from sub to supersonic flight. This model achieved a world speed record of 1,131¾ miles (1,821.34 kilometers) per hour at the hands of Peter Twiss . It also featured a movable "droop snoot" nose, which was incorporated into Concorde to allow the pilot to see forward on takeoff and landing.

By the early 1960s the French and the British began considering start-up programs to build SSTs. They started swapping views on how they should embark on the project. On November 14, 1962, a council of ministers of the French and British governments signed an agreement to share the burden of the huge scientific, engineering, and economic tasks involved. The Russians, fearing they might be left behind and anxious to prove technical superiority, handed the task of building a Soviet SST to André N. Tupolev's manufacturing collective in 1963.

By the mid-1960s four of the world's major economic powers had teams working on this most challenging of commercial flying projects.

The Anglo-French effort was aptly named Concorde. In Toulouse in France and Filton in England, two identical prototype aircraft, 001 and 002, were being built. The designers and engineers faced monumental challenges.

Though the SST aircraft would be flying at a height of 55,000–62,000 feet (16,775–18,910 meters), where the thin, frigid air would be as cold as -70° Fahrenheit (-56° Celsius), the plane would "fly faster than a speeding bullet." The buildup of a wave of air pressure ahead of it and the friction

The Fairey Delta FD II

of compressed air rushing over the aircraft would mean the plane's skin would have to dissipate heat of more than 400° Fahrenheit (205° Celsius)—hot enough to boil water. That same heat would require special fuel treatment to stop a buildup of tarry "coked" residues caused by long soaking at high temperatures.

The center of gravity for the plane had to be finely calculated, compensated, and tuned because of different angles of flight from takeoff at relatively low speeds, climbing to cruising altitudes, accelerating to break the sound barrier and differing passenger loads. This would require fuel to be constantly pumped from one part of the aircraft to another during flight. Many parts of the aircraft had to be cut from solid blanks of light alloy, a process called hogging, which required specially designed machine tools to do the job. This would avoid many joints and welds, greatly reducing the problem of metal fatigue. So during supersonic flight, the Concorde's fuselage would—through heat expansion and pressurization in the cabin—increase by nearly a foot (30.5 centimeters) in length.

A hinged "droop" nose was evolved to enable the pilots to see from the cockpit during takeoff and landing. This nose then straightened out to a smooth needle-sharp shape for supersonic speeds. To overcome shock waves, which built up in speeds over 1,000 miles (1,600 kilometers) per hour, the aircraft needed thin, strong wings with a high degree of sweepback. The resulting delta wing configuration drew heavily on several experimental aircraft from Britain and from General Aeronautique Marcel Dassault, the company that had developed the superb delta-winged supersonic fighters, Mirage III and IV.

New problems were faced and overcome along the way, such as the development of heat-resistant graphite brakes now used on jumbo jets, airbuses, and other aircraft. The air intake at Mach 2 (twice the speed of sound) had to deal with air pressures eight times the normal atmospheric pressure. This force, effectively utilized by the four Rolls-Royce Olympus turbo jet engines and combined with French S.N.E.C.M.A. afterburners, provided Concorde's mighty thrust. The intakes had to be designed to slow the air to a subsonic speed acceptable to the engines. This needed to be done without inducing a drag penalty.

On August 20, 1968, four months before the Russian's first flight, André Turcat climbed into Concorde 001 at the Toulouse-Blagnac airfield to spend most of the day on runway tests. On 2 March, 1969, he took 001 down the runway once more, this time taking off for the first test flight of the Concorde. Then a month later, from the airfield at Filton in England, British test pilot Brian Trubshaw took Concorde 002 aloft for the first successful SST test flight in the United Kingdom. The combined care of the French and British engineers was paying dividends.

On October 1 that year, Turcat took Concorde 001 through the sound barrier, to Mach 1.05 at a height of 36,000 feet (10,980 meters), but the Tupolev had already entered the record books on June 5, 1968, as the first supersonic commercial airliner to break the sound barrier. Interestingly, an American Douglas DC-8, though not designed for supersonic flight, had flown at Mach 1 speeds in a shallow dive on August 2, 1961—nearly eight years earlier.

Careful testing and checking of Concorde continued. On December 13, 1969, Turcat exceeded 1,000 miles (1,600 kilometers) per hour for the first time, in a 2-hour, 10-minute flight, when he flew 001 supersonic for a total of 57 minutes. Almost a year later, on November 4, 1970, in the same model, he flew through Mach 2 for the first time.

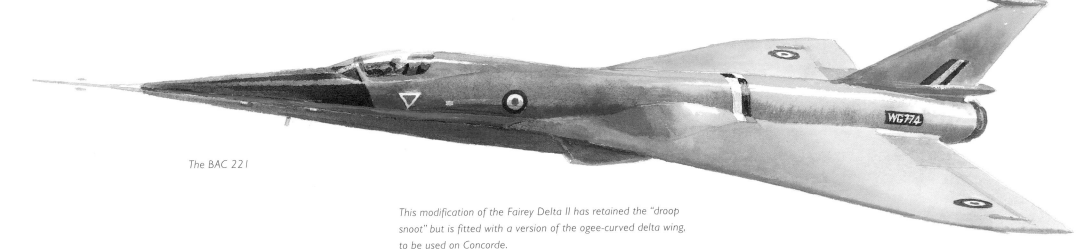

The BAC 221

This modification of the Fairey Delta II has retained the "droop snoot" but is fitted with a version of the ogee-curved delta wing, to be used on Concorde.

The Tupolev Tu144

The Russians first displayed their SST design as a model in 1965 at the Paris Air Show in France. Three years later, on the last day of December 1968, the Russians won the race. Their Tupolev Tu144 prototype, with a double-delta-shaped wing made its first demonstration flight. It was another six months before the plane broke the sound barrier, but Tu144 was the first SST to be up and flying.

In September 1972, an updated and refined Tu144 SST airliner flew a demonstration flight from Moscow to Tashkent, a distance of 1,700 miles (2,720 kilometers) in 1 hour, 50 minutes. Now the world's press were satirically calling the aircraft the *Koncordski* because of its startling similarity to the Anglo-French SST. Then, at the Paris Air Show in June 1973, on a demonstration flight from Le Bourget, the Tu144 crashed into the village of Groussainville, killing the pilot Mikhail Koslov, all five of his crew, and seven people on the ground. Twenty-eight villagers were injured. No official reports or reasons for the disaster were ever released in the West.

From December 1975, the Tu144 commenced flying regular mail and cargo flights from Moscow to Alma-Ata in Kazakhstan. Then in November 1977, scheduled passenger services to Alma-Ata were announced, but five of the first six flights were cancelled. In total, 13 Tu144s were flown, 4 of them for passenger flights. In June 1978, after a second crash, the Tupolevs were withdrawn from any further flight with no reasons given. Of all the supersonic contenders, only Concorde remained.

The Concordes had continued on their rigorous testing programs. With Brian Trubshaw in England and André Turcat in France piloting the two prototypes, 102 test flights were conducted. In January 1976 with modified, lengthened, and refined models, Air France and British Airways offered seats for their inaugural flights. On January 21 they commenced commercial flights, British Airways from London to Johannesburg, Air France from Paris to Rio de Janeiro. It was the culmination of the longest and most thorough testing of any aircraft in the history of aviation. Altogether, 2 prototypes were built, followed by 2 pre-production models, then 16 production aircraft. British Airways and Air France bought seven Concordes each. The first Concorde flew to America in response to being invited to the opening of what was then to be the world's largest airport—the Dallas Fort Worth complex. Test pilots Trubshaw and Turcat shared the roles of pilot of Concorde 002, which they flew in for the airport opening on September 21, 1973. While in the U.S.A., they were invited to join President Richard Nixon in Washington, where he presented them with prestigious Harman International Aviation Awards. In the following years, Air France and British Airways Concordes flew daily to Washington and New York while both airlines ran charter flights and lavish world-circling adventure tours for the rich and famous. The Concordes were running at a profit, and held the world record as the safest airliners ever built, until July 25, 2000, when an Air France Concorde crashed in flames at the village of Gonesse shortly after takeoff from Paris's Charles de Gaulle airport. The aircraft plowed into a small tourist hotel, Le Relais Bleu. Later evidence showed that a sharp strip of metal, which had fallen onto the runway from an earlier plane, had ripped into a tire. An explosive blowout followed that slammed a heavy lump of rubber into the underside of the Concorde, fracturing a fuel cell in the wing. The resulting fire engulfed both port engines, leaving the pilot unable to control the aircraft. It stalled and crashed, killing 7 crew, 100 passengers, and 4 people trapped in the hotel. Until that fateful flight, no Concorde had crashed in the 31 years the aircraft had flown (25 of them commercially).

As a result of the crash Britain and France grounded the planes to allow for air-safety investigations. No faults could be found in either the airframe or controls. British Airways engineers decided to strengthen the landing gear and change the fuel cells in the wings to ensure that a leakage of fuel could not happen should a similar freak accident ever recur. Millions of pounds were spent in lining the fuel compartments with specially molded Kevlar, a self-sealing plastic. In 2001, following grueling test flights, the U.K.'s Civil Aircraft Authority reinstated the Concorde's Certificate of Airworthiness. The reconfigured Concordes were again flying commercially and were thought to have a working life of up to 14 years. However by June 2003 scheduled flights were cancelled by British Airways and Air France. The reasons given were the slow turn-down in world air travel following the terrorist attack on the World Trade Center and the Iraq war, together with increasing maintenance and fuel costs. While further flights of Concorde are not ruled out, regular scheduled flights have ceased.

André Turcat reported that on one of his test flights in the Prototype Concorde 001, when being observed by two chase planes, one of the pilots radioed to him a message he'll never forget. The pilot said: "You cannot imagine how beautiful you look!"

Concorde—a glorious tribute to Anglo-French accord.

Opposite page: Surely there has been no more beautiful aircraft than this—a Concorde supersonic airliner flying over Paris. The elegant ogee-curved delta wing is featured. Its profile is complex and the airfoils vary in section throughout its span, twisting down at the wing tips. Its subtlety is in stark contrast to the angular double delta of the ill-fated Russian supersonic transport. The Concorde wing cannot be stalled and the aircraft carries no flaps to assist landing. The pilot rotates the airliner to a nose-up attitude of precisely 10.5 degrees to create drag and slow the aircraft as she goes over the threshold of the runway at a speed of 187 miles (301 kilometers) per hour to land. The aircraft is at full capacity with 100 passengers and three crew.

THE DAREDEVILS

Daredevils were the outrageous, the brave, the excitable, the egotistical—often those with a mixture of all of these traits. They became flying aces in two world wars. They flew flimsy planes high in the sky performing gutsy and hair-raising aerobatics and took unbelievable risks, challenging fate to pioneer and chart air routes over land and sea. This fearless breed diced with the devil in do-or-die air races and drove government bureaucrats to distraction by ignoring national borders and air space. They also demanded more of themselves than they did of others. But while onlookers gasped or swore, the daredevils were proving and testing airplanes and the flying potential and limits of aviators.

GLENN CURTISS

A SPEED-CRAZED BIKER WHO BECAME AIRBORNE

Glenn Curtiss was motorbike mad. He started designing and building motorbike engines in the 1890s and went on to build his own complete motorcycles which, of course, he had to try out. Then he yearned for more power and he built bigger engines. That's how Glenn Curtiss came to set an unofficial world record when in 1907 he drove an eight-cylinder motorcycle at Ormond Beach, Florida, at the record speed of 136⅓ miles (219.3 kilometers) per hour. It was a speed not equaled by any land vehicle until 1911, and by no motorbike until the beginning of the 1930s.

Curtiss was impressed by the Wright brothers' flights at Kitty Hawk. In 1906 he visited them to try to sell them one of his engine designs. He had no success. Two years later he was part of a group that designed an aircraft powered by one of his engines. It was called the *June Bug* and with Curtiss at the controls it won the *Scientific American* trophy for the first plane in the U.S.A. to fly a distance of ⅗ mile (one kilometer). Curtiss forgot motorbikes and became just as enthusiastic about aviation. He designed some spectacularly successful biplanes built around his own engines. His designs resembled the Wrights' *Flyer* but with one very important difference. He guessed that the Wrights' invention of wing warping would impose severe future limitations to the integrity of large wings on a big airplane so he fitted ailerons to the wings.

He headed for the city of Reims in France where the city was hosting the first-ever international air show—the Great Week of Aviation. Curtiss decided he would try to win the coveted Coupe Gordon Bennett Trophy for the fastest airplane. He bunkered down in a hangar alongside other contestants on the site at Bethany. In atrocious weather he watched as a succession of incidents, accidents and hair-raising flying from machines barely under control, whittled away at the competition. Glenn conserved his energy, flying only when necessary.

His strategy was faultless. He and his *Golden Flyer* made it through to the final day. Amid enormous excitement and crowd hysteria, Curtiss dueled with Louis Blériot flying his latest and most powerful model, the No. XII airplane. Blériot crashed spectacularly before the race was over. With the victor's crown, Glenn Curtiss had impressed all who were in attendance at the world's first air show.

For Curtiss, the Great Week of Aviation at Reims was the launch pad for a highly successful aircraft and engine manufacturing business. He surged ahead to become the world's most successful flying-boat designer, creating a machine for the U.S. Navy that was the first to cross the Atlantic, as well as many other planes for military and private use—some achievement for a man from Hammondsport, New York State, who started off by tinkering with basic one- and two-cylinder motorbike engines in the 1890s.

Above: In 1924, Lieutenant Maugham of the U.S. Army Air Force flew a Curtiss fighter with a 435-horsepower Curtiss engine, 2,698 miles (4,342 kilometers) from New York to San Francisco from dawn to dusk on the same day, in 21 hours, 44 minutes.

Curtiss's expertise with powerful engines inspired a strong reputation for his company. His flair for streamlining cowlings around them set the example for the rest of the world—and provided inspiration for R. J. Mitchell, designer of the legendary Spitfire fighter of World War II.

Even the great Rolls-Royce company in England bought and examined one of Curtiss's liquid-cooled V-12s that he used to win the Schneider Trophy Races. This engine, in turn, inspired the development of the Rolls-Royce Merlin engine that was to power the famous Spitfire fighter.

Left: Glenn Curtiss outside his hangar at Reims. Glenn eventually lost interest in his business. By the mid-1920s he was following other pursuits. His company, however, as Curtiss-Wright, continued to build airplanes. Curtiss would have been delighted to see how his beloved internal combustion engines matured into a wide range of reliable, powerful air engines, from the Wright Whirlwinds that carried flight pioneers across the world to the multi-row radial engines of post-World War II that powered airliners and military aircraft.

Below: Glenn Curtiss practices with his Golden Flyer during the Great Week of Aviation at Reims, France, during 1909. He won the coveted Coupe Gordon Bennett Trophy (left) with this machine. Curtiss had been the first to use ailerons successfully. He set them between the tips of the biplane wings.

The Wright brothers were furious. They accused Curtiss of infringing their wing-warping patents and came out fighting. What followed were literally years of fierce recriminations and litigation. The strain of his dogged anger, and the years of court battles and emotion, is thought to have driven Wilbur Wright into an early grave. Curtiss simply continued his energetic love affair with flying.

It satisfied my craving for speed.

GLENN CURTISS, AFTER SETTING AN UNOFFICIAL WORLD SPEED RECORD OF 136 MILES (261 KILOMETERS) PER HOUR ON HIS MOTORBIKE, 1907

LOUIS BLÉRIOT

THE CHANNEL? IT IS NOTHING!

Louis Blériot

In 1908, near the little town of Le Mans west of Paris, Louis Blériot—who manufactured acetylene lamps for motor cars but who had an overwhelming desire to fly—stood with fellow members of the Aero Club of France. They formed a crowd—most highly skeptical—watching a dour American slowly and meticulously check rigging wires, propellers, struts, drive chains, and control levers of a flying machine that was supposed to demonstrate its first flight outside of America. Blériot and the other members of the club doubted the claims made by the taciturn Wilbur Wright and the press about its remarkable sustained flight at Kitty Hawk. They were looking at a Flyer, a machine similar to the one the Wrights had flown in America. But—like many other attempts made before—the cynical club members expected this to be just another debacle.

Finally, with all his checks made, Wilbur climbed through the wires and struts and settled himself onto the pilot's seat. The propellers were swung and the engine warmed up. When he was satisfied that everything was ready, Wright gave his signal. A counterweight, designed to shorten his takeoff run, was released from a tripod. As it fell, a wire connecting it with the front of the Flyer, whipped the plane along a prepared track—and the machine was airborne. After climbing to about 30 feet (9.1 meters), Wilbur, with consummate ease, banked the Flyer into a smooth turn, and for close on two minutes, demonstrated through his assured handling the coordinated control and responsiveness of the craft. The crowd needed no further convincing. The moment of truth had come. After he had brought the aircraft in to land, Wilbur had the by now enthusiastic Frenchmen at his feet. "Il n'est pas un bluffeur!" They were generous in their praise and fascinated by the plane.

Louis Blériot, who had previously been caught up in the fevered activity before and after Santos-Dumont's famous flight in the *14 bis*, now threw himself into designing his own aircraft with dedicated energy, so much so that he nearly bankrupted his acetylene lamp business. His early attempts were unsuccessful. Then—after attending a school set up and conducted by Wilbur Wright at Pau, near France's border with Spain—he built his Blériot No. XI, a machine that incorporated the Wright brothers' wing-warping principle as well as a carved, aerodynamic propeller. Blériot's No. XI became his first effective airplane. Not only did it successfully fly but it catapulted him into the history books.

The British media magnate Lord Northcliffe, through his *Daily Mail* newspaper, offered a prize of £1,000 for the first crossing of the English Channel by air. In the early morning of July 25, 1909, Louis Blériot, sitting proudly upright in his new monoplane, flew from France to England. He landed to much applause, but nothing compared to the accolades heaped on him in the weeks that followed. The praise was based mainly on the perceived technical achievement—even though Blériot's plane showed no great technical advances. Longer distances had already been flown. What Blériot had demonstrated with his daring flight across the Channel was that national barriers had been smashed. For the first time the world was given notice that geographical protection would, in future, be highly vulnerable. Nations could no longer hide safely behind oceans or mountains.

Opposite page: Louis Blériot leaves the French coast on his way into the history books as the man who first crossed the English Channel by airplane. Notice the wing-warping wires attached to the central pylon in front of Blériot's cockpit.

The only baggage Blériot took with him was a pair of wooden crutches—he needed them as a result of an injury sustained in one of his many earlier crashes.

After his Channel flight Blériot was a hero, feted and rewarded for his spectacular feat. This was quite timely because it bailed him out of his financial troubles and set him up as a successful aircraft manufacturer.

Just a few years later, Blériot was involved in creating the S.P.A.D. company, which would become famous for developing Spad fighter planes incorporating some of the features of the Blériot XI.

Left: Wilbur Wright demonstrates the Flyer in 1908 at Pau, France, where he established a flying school. Louis Blériot was one of his pupils at the school.

ADOLPHE PÉGOUD

DESCRIBE A LOOP IF YOU PLEASE, MONSIEUR!

Adolphe Pégoud

Adolphe Pégoud left the French army after many years of military service and took to the air, obtaining a civilian pilot's certificate in February 1913. He loved to fly and to attempt unusual things. In August of 1913, Adolphe took off in a Blériot monoplane, jumped out and then descended by parachute—leaving his machine to display some amazing antics before it hit the ground. He was the first man in Europe to float safely down from the sky in that way.

Also in 1913 Louis Blériot wanted to demonstrate to potential buyers of his airplanes that the stability offered by his competitors' box kites was not the only factor that mattered. He claimed that his aircraft were very maneuverable and this made them safer to fly—because they could be extricated from the unusual positions in which pilots of the day often found themselves. So he employed Adolphe Pégoud as his test pilot to prove the point and Adolphe flew his yellow-painted Blériot XI up in the sky to show

the world the amazing things he could achieve in an airplane.

He was, in truth, the inventor of aerial acrobatics. Admiring crowds came to watch Adolphe do the most astounding things in the sky. He did flick-rolls, tail-slides, flew inverted, and looped the loop. No one before him had tried such breathtaking tricks. This was at a time when a gently banked turn could spell disaster for pilots less accomplished than Pégoud.

After impressing his countrymen, he went to Brooklands in England and held crowds in awe at his mastery. He flew upside down, he looped the loop eight times in succession and carried out an astonishing maneuver, an outside loop— later called "the bunt" by the Royal Air Force. He was soon training and teaching other pilots the skills he had perfected.

Exactly 12 months after his first parachute demonstration, the fury of World War I began. Adolphe was an adjutant

reservist in an aviation group. It was not long before he was involved in air combat, earning himself a Médaille Militaire for downing two enemy aircraft and forcing a third to surrender. In 1915, he was made a Chevalier de la Légion d'Honneur—the citation stated: "He has attacked heavily armed enemy planes alone countless times. On August 25, 1915, during the course of an aerial duel, his plane was riddled with bullets and he was forced to land and immediately took every means available to save his plane in spite of intense German fire."

Pégoud had used his aerobatic skills to good effect and early became a famous French fighter ace. He was, sadly, the first Allied ace to be killed in aerial combat. Ironically, he was shot down and killed by a German two-seater piloted by one of his former pupils, Unteroffizer Kandulski. He died only a few days after the action that won him his Légion d'Honneur award.

Left: In August 1915, Pégoud was shot down by a German adversary. His body is seen here being carried by his comrades from the wreckage of his aircraft.

Opposite page: In 1913, Frenchman Adolphe Pégoud in this yellow-painted Blériot XI, enthralled the crowds with breathtaking flick-rolls, loops, inverted flying, tail-slides, and spins. This was at a time when virtually any attitude other than a gently banked turn could spell disaster for most pilots. This courageous airman gave the public and professionals of the day greater confidence in the airplane by showing that a properly equipped airplane, flown by a correctly trained pilot, could maneuver itself out of difficulties with safety.

The optimist invents the airplane,
the pessimist, the parachute.
GEORGE BERNARD SHAW

HARRY HAWKER

DRAMATIC RENDEZVOUS IN THE ATLANTIC

Harry Hawker was born in Australia, in Moorabbin, Victoria. His aeronautical career began in 1911, when, aged 21, he traveled to Britain and began working with a young airplane manufacturer called Tom Sopwith. Hawker learnt to fly at this time and proved to be a natural, exuberant pilot. Teaming his flying skills and talents as a first-class mechanic, he soon became chief pilot and a valuable partner in the Sopwith Aviation Company. Between 1913 and 1916, Hawker established several endurance and altitude records in Britain, demonstrating his mettle and that of the company's planes. One of his most memorable achievements was in 1913 when, along with copilot Harry Kauper, he attempted a competitive circumnavigation of the British Isles. The duo crashed after 1,043 miles (1,670 kilometers) but the record stood as they had traveled 843 miles (1,357 kilometers) more than their nearest rivals. In that same year, Hawker continued his success and together with Sopwith designed a very successful fighter plane, the Sopwith Tabloid.

Following the outbreak of World War I, Harry Hawker embarked on a dangerous and arduous four years of flight-testing new aircraft. The British War Office considered him too valuable to take part in operational flying and instead he made valuable and practical contributions to the production of the Sopwith Aviation Company. Hawker was able to improve the design, performance, and handling characteristics of Sopwith's famous and successful fighters.

In 1919, once the war was over, it was not surprising to find the still young Hawker among a group of competitive aviators in Newfoundland. The British newspaper baron, Lord Northcliffe, offered a £10,000 prize to the team that could complete the first nonstop crossing of the North Atlantic. Hawker and his Scottish navigator, Lt. Comdr. Kenneth McKenzie-Grieve R.N., came to fly the Sopwith Company's Atlantic airplane—especially prepared for the flight. The competitors, from England, France, Germany, and Australia, gathered in the frosty cold of Newfoundland, all working doggedly to ensure their machines were in the right shape to tackle an historic flight over the daunting and dangerous Atlantic.

Powered by a single Rolls-Royce Eagle engine, and carrying a rescue dinghy faired into the rear fuselage in case of a forced ocean landing, the Sopwith Atlantic was first away. The aircraft staggered off the airstrip on May 18, 1919,

Harry Hawker, with his irrepressibly cheerful dispositon, won the hearts of the Australian public when he visited Australia in 1914 to demonstrate the brilliant little Sopwith Tabloid fighter.

heavily burdened by the weight of the fuel needed for the flight. Once airborne, Hawker jettisoned the specially designed, detachable undercarriage in order to reduce drag.

These brave aviators needed all the help they could muster. The unconquered North Atlantic crossing was 1,900 miles (3,058 kilometers) of savage ocean, strung with a succession of warm and cold fronts stirring up strong winds, fog, and freezing temperatures. There was only one advantage—the winds were behind them which would accelerate their flight.

After several hours flying through squalls, fog, and generally atrocious weather, their Eagle engine started to overheat. Hawker, one of the best pilots in the business, tried everything he knew from years of testing airplanes to correct the problem. Nothing worked. He realized he would have to ditch in the Atlantic or risk catching fire.

Hawker's navigator for the North Atlantic attempt was Lt. Comdr. Kenneth McKenzie-Grieve, a Royal Navy navigator who had served in World War I. Hawker described him as "a cool customer."

Opposite page: The Sopwith Camel was the most effective in a long line of fine fighting aircraft to come from Tom Sopwith and Harry Hawker. This fighter came into operation on the Western Front during 1917 in World War I, and soon proved a popular, if tricky, machine to fly. It shot down more enemy airplanes than any other aircraft and remained in service until the end of the war. Tom Sopwith of the Sopwith Aviation Company said, "There was a lot of Harry Hawker in the Camel." These two Camels on patrol are from No. 4 Squadron, Australian Flying Corps.

Left: Harry Hawker had to be rescued by mounted police from an enthusiastic crowd of well-wishers in London, following his return to Britain after his unsuccessful flight across the Atlantic.

Hawker and McKenzie-Grieve had flown 1,250 miles (2,012 kilometers). Accurate navigation had been near impossible. McKenzie-Grieve warned they were well south of their intended route and would have little hope of finding a ship, as they were away from normal shipping lanes. Hawker descended to sea level, breaking through the cloud low over the water. They began radioing distress calls. In the forlorn hope of finding a ship, Hawker zigzagged over the 12-foot (3.7-meter) waves that were building up on large swells driven by near gale-force winds.

Then, at the edge of their restricted visibility, a ship crept out of the murk. It was the *Mary*, a tiny tramp steamer flying the Danish flag. They circled her, firing distress flares to alert the crew. Hawker flew ahead of the 1,800-ton (1,836-tonne) vessel, and ditched successfully in her path. Working fast, Hawker and McKenzie-Grieve released and boarded the dinghy, their plane breaking up quickly in the heavy seas. It took the *Mary*'s crew an hour and a half to reach and secure the cold, weary, and seasick airmen and haul them on board.

The little ship had no radio, and it took eight days for her to reach the north of Scotland. During that time Hawker and McKenzie-Grieve were assumed to have perished. When close enough to land, the *Mary* was able to signal with flags that the two airmen were on board. They were transferred to

a Royal Navy destroyer and brought ashore to a hero's welcome. Lord Northcliffe was so proud of the combined efforts of the Australian pilot and the Royal Navy commander that he awarded them a consolation prize of £5,000.

Not long afterward, Harry Hawker set up the Hawker Engineering Company to take over the Sopwith Aviation Company when Sopwith's company went into voluntary liquidation.

On July 12, 1921, Harry Hawker was piloting a racing biplane—a Nieuport Goshawk in an aerial Derby in Britain. During a test flight, the plane caught fire at 15,000 feet (4,572 meters), went into a dive and slammed into the ground. Hawker did not survive the crash. It is believed that a hidden illness and a previously undetected abscess on Hawker's spine may have contributed to the tragedy, resulting in sudden paralysis, as some believe he could have parachuted to safety.

Aged only 31, his untimely death was mourned, but Hawker's name is remembered and honored. Internationally famous aircraft bearing his name include the Hawker Hurricane, which shot down the largest number of enemy aircraft in the Battle of Britain during World War II, and in more recent times, the unique Hawker Harrier jump jet, which saw combat in the Falklands and Gulf Wars.

Harry Hawker died in Britain on July 12, 1921, testing a Nieuport Goshawk (above) before a planned race in an aerial derby. At a height of about 15,000 feet (4,572 meters), observers saw fire in the nose of the aircraft. The Goshawk turned suddenly, dived toward the ground, flattened out, and crashed at high speed, throwing Hawker clear, but badly injured. He died at the scene.

For reasons still not clear, the Air Ministry's subsequent accident report was classified "Secret: Not to be released for 50 years". In 1972, when it became available, the report revealed that one of the radial engine's three screw-topped carburetors had come loose and sprayed burning fuel over Hawker's legs and shoes. His spectacular dive had doused the flames but he was unable to effect a successful crash-landing. A post-mortem revealed that Hawker was suffering from an extensive tubercular disease, as well as a spinal abscess. This could have resulted in a sudden paralysis affecting Hawker's ability to control the machine in an effort to avoid the crash.

Right: The battered remains of the Atlantic found by the S.S. Charlotte two weeks after the rescue of Hawker and McKenzie-Grieve.

Far right: The two airmen are transferred from the Mary to a British destroyer off the coast of Scotland.

Opposite page: The Mary appears out of the murk as the doomed Sopwith Atlantic prepares to ditch in the North Atlantic. It was later discovered that the engine trouble which forced Hawker and McKenzie-Grieve down was caused by a faulty linkage in the cooling mechanism.

A day before Hawker and McKenzie-Grieve started on their unsuccessful crossing of the North Atlantic, the United States Navy sent three of its flying boats, designed by Glenn Curtiss, on what they hoped would be the first crossing of the Atlantic by air. The aircraft were NC class patrol boats built towards the end of World War I and they were commanded by Lieutenant Commander Read. They left Newfoundland on May 16, 1919, with a support team of about 100 naval vessels scattered along the route.

Lieutenant Commander Read

The organization of the crossing was superb. The flying boats were equipped with long-range radio navigation aids. Even so, two of the aircraft came down in the sea near the Azores and had to be rescued. *NC 4*, dubbed "Nancy Four", reached Plymouth on May 31, 1919 after staging at Horta, Punta Delgarda, El Ferrol, and Lisbon. The flying boat took a more southerly route than the one the contestants in Newfoundland were to take and, while the trip was broken into several stages, *NC 4* rightly claims the honor of being the first aircraft to link the U.S.A. with Europe.

Left: Lieutenant Commander "Putty" Read, of the United States Navy captained the crew of six airmen aboard the successful Naval Curtiss No 4 flying boat. Read and his crew, the first to complete an air crossing of the Atlantic were given an enthusiastic reception on their return to the United States.

Above: In 1919 the United States Navy flying boat, NC 4, was the first aircraft to cross the Atlantic Ocean. The flight was completed in several stages. The flying boat was designed by Glenn Curtiss and, unlike the other two flying boats selected by the Navy to accompany it on the Atlantic flight, it featured an extra engine mounted at the rear of the centrally mounted nacelle.

Right: In a Vickers Vimy, Englishmen John
Alcock and Arthur Whitten Brown were the
pilot and navigator who won the prize
offered by Lord Northcliffe. In 1919 they
were the first to fly nonstop across the
Atlantic Ocean. They were rugged
up in heavy flying gear—clothing
that was essential to keep
out the cold as the airmen
were exposed in the open
cockpit of their aircraft.
There was a radio
on the aircraft but it
failed when the generator
propeller parted company
with the aircraft. There were
no blind-flying instruments, so
flying in cloud was dangerous.

Vickers Vimy, 1919

Left: Harry Hawker was not the only
one to fail in the Atlantic attempt.
Fred Raynham in his Martinsyde
biplane crashed on takeoff.

PARER AND MCINTOSH

LET'S DRINK TO A GREAT EFFORT

Ray Parer

John McIntosh

They joined the great England to Australia Air Race in an ex-World War I, single-engined, two-seater reconnaissance plane—a battered De Havilland De H 9. They were late starting, and very nearly didn't start at all. Ray Parer, a wartime test pilot for the Royal Flying Corps was planning to go home to Australia anyway. His friend, John McIntosh was anxious to do the same. When Australian Prime Minister, "Billy" Hughes, announced a £10,000 prize for the first Australian aircrew to fly back to Darwin, it sounded like a great idea to them. All they needed was a plane and some financial backing.

Parer found a backer—the millionaire Scotch whisky distiller, Peter Dawson. They bought the plane for £900 and had Dawson's initials P. D. painted boldly on the fuselage. They also tucked a bottle of Peter Dawson Scotch Whisky in a safe place in their flying machine.

They couldn't start on time—in fact, the winning team of Ross and Keith Smith had already landed in Darwin in their Vickers Vimy before the intrepid pair were airborne. Unfazed, in January 1920 they began an extraordinary flight of hair-raising adventures, accidents, and engine failures that would have quickly brought any ordinary

human to a shuddering halt. But these were not ordinary men.

As their Armstrong-Siddeley engine proved to be cranky and unpredictable, stopping sometimes without warning, they became used to forced landings. Parer was one of those amazing characters who never gave up, even in the face of what seemed to be complete disaster. One particular incident is indicative. They were flying over Burma's (now Myanmar) Irrawaddy River on the way to Rangoon. The weary airmen were looking down at dense jungle—with not a sign of air-fields or landing places. They had also been warned about the dangers posed by uncivilized and hostile tribes in the area. True to form, the Armstrong-Siddeley Puma engine coughed and spluttered. It caught again, backfired then stopped altogether.

Having been well skilled because of a number of similar experiences, Ray Parer executed a copybook dead-stick landing on the tiny sand bar shown in the painting on the facing page.

Not only did he land safely, he then (and what followed, in detail, is a story in itself and well told in John Godwin's book *Battling Parer*), repaired the engine and took off again. With the help of the local tribe—with whom they communicated through desperate hand signals—the two were able to move the aircraft to the other side of the river where the tribe cleared a strip for them. From there, Parer was able to make a perilous takeoff and then fly safely on to Rangoon.

They struggled to reach Darwin, months after their departure from England. In spite of all the troubles and alarm, it was the first-ever flight of a single-engined aircraft from England to Australia. They were the only fliers other than the team on the Vimy to complete the journey. For their courageous effort, the Australian

Government awarded them £500 each, and both were invested with the Air Force Cross. In turn, the aviators presented the Prime Minister, "Billy" Hughes, with the sponsor's bottle of Peter Dawson Scotch Whisky that they had kept safe all the way from England.

One would imagine that the events of such an adventurous flight would be enough for any man to endure, but not for the indefatigable Parer. With Geoff Hemsworth as copilot, he entered the second England to Australia Air Race, held in 1934. He flew an ex-R.A.F. Fairey Fox. As one would expect, he made an eventful flight—it included a near head-on collision with another aircraft while flying low over a railway track to keep on course in a desert dust storm.

Opposite page: The tired ex-World War I De H 9 again gives up the ghost as its engine fails over the inhospitable jungle of Burma (now Myanmar). This was but one in a chapter of incidents that befell the dogged aviators, Parer and McIntosh, on what eventually proved to be the first-ever flight of a single-engined aircraft from England to Australia. Note the prominent P. D. (for sponsor Peter Dawson Scotch Whisky).

Left: Parer and McIntosh are welcomed at an Australian country town after their epic flight across the world from England. The long trip south from Darwin to Melbourne was the last straw for their battered biplane. With its incurable addiction to engine failure and forced landings, and with the rips in its fabric patched with brown paper, their De H 9 staged yet one more forced landing two days short of their destination. This time it was the last. The De H 9 made the depressing final stage to Melbourne on a railway truck.

BERT HINKLER

YOU'VE COME A LONG WAY, BABY

Bert Hinkler, 1921

In 1920, in a tiny plane called the Baby by the British Avro company that made it, a previously unknown pilot, Bert Hinkler, made a record-breaking flight from Britain across Europe and back. Hinkler purchased the plane from his employer, A.V. Roe and Co. Early the next year he had intended to fly solo all the way to Australia in the same little biplane, but a war then being fought in Syria blocked his way. Having reached Italy, he turned around and flew back to the U.K. From there he shipped the Avro Baby to Sydney, New South Wales, Australia. On April 11, 1921, Bert Hinkler added to his growing list of records by flying nonstop from Sydney to Bundaberg in Queensland—the town where, on December 8, 1892, he had been born. That flight created a new long-distance record for a light plane. Hinkler also created a local sensation in Bundaberg by taxiing the Baby on roads through the town and parking it outside the Hinkler family home.

Bert Hinkler had all the requirements to be a magnificent airman. He was a natural pilot who simply loved flying. He was a brilliant navigator, a practical mechanic and an inventive engineer. His highly developed sense of adventure was challenged by distant horizons. Before he was through, people would write poetry about him, compose and sing songs in his praise and, particularly in Australia, idolize him. The press would label him "Hustling Hinkler"—which in those days was positive praise!

Below: At the age of 19 years in far-off Queensland, Australia, Bert Hinkler was already showing the talent of a natural flier and innovative engineer when he designed and built his own glider. The machine is shown here in a family photograph taken near his hometown of Bundaberg.

Right: In one of his sparkling aerobatic displays, Bert Hinkler flew his diminutive Avro Baby beneath the road bridge in his hometown of Bundaberg, Queensland. Record-breaking flights and public displays such as this were welcomed and sometimes backed by the plane's makers. (Although he owned the Baby, Hinkler was Avro's test pilot). This little plane's exploits were followed with interest by Avro in Britain because the company was aware that it had produced a new class of airplane—small, cheap to run and maintain, and easy to fly— just right for a new type of pilot who flew for pleasure: the private owner. The Avro Baby is the progenitor of the thousands of light aircraft flying today.

Opposite page: *If ever there was a man who loved flying for its own sake, it was pioneer aviator, Bert Hinkler. He later recalled that one of the happiest days of his solo flight across the world from England to Australia in an Avro Avian was on February 17, 1928. He was near exhaustion after eight days of grueling flying and weary from lack of sleep, yet he simply couldn't resist zooming and climbing among huge cumulo-nimbus clouds, soaring into the sky above the coast and forests of Burma (now Myanmar). After some magical moments enjoying the thrills of freewheeling in and around the clouds, he turned back on course and headed for Rangoon.*

Right: After the first solo flight from England to Australia in 1928, Bert Hinkler was the idol of the age. Here, he is greeted in Brisbane, Queensland, after landing on the racecourse in his Avro Avian.

Hustling Hinkler, up in the sky.

LYRICS TO A TIN PAN ALLEY SONG, WRITTEN WHILE BERT HINKLER WAS FLYING FROM ENGLAND TO AUSTRALIA IN 1928

He returned to his job as a test pilot with the Avro company in England before setting off again, in 1928, to fulfill his dream of flying solo from England to Australia—this time in a larger biplane, an Avro Avian. Once again, he achieved a Hinkler record—the first solo flight halfway around the world.

Three years later, in 1931, he flew nonstop in a De Havilland Puss Moth from New York to Jamaica, Venezuela, and Trinidad. Then he chalked up a new record, flying solo from Brazil west to east across the South Atlantic to British Gambia, and on to London. Again, it was a triumph of courage and determination. Hinkler's meticulous preparation, disciplined working methods, and attention to detail paid dividends. On his long and arduous flights, his aircraft rarely suffered from any mechanical problems.

It was not a failure of skill, of his aircraft, or his engines that abruptly halted his enviable successes. On January 7, 1933,

attempting to once more break the England to Australia record for a solo flight, Bert Hinkler again took off in his trusted De Havilland Puss Moth. Only hours later he became trapped in low storm clouds and crashed to his death in the Italian Alps. It was four months before his body was recovered and he was solemnly buried with full military honors in the beautiful medieval city of Florence.

He was such an Australian icon that his English home in Southampton was carefully taken apart, brick by brick, and shipped to Bundaberg, Queensland, to be reerected as a permanent Hinkler Museum. The record-breaking Avro Avian is on display in the Brisbane Museum. Alongside it, Hinkler's Avro Baby, powered by an engine of a mere 35 horsepower, is preserved as a reminder of the days when Bert was an Avro test pilot, a record-breaking aviator, and Queensland's hometown hero.

LAWRENCE BURST SPERRY

AN AMAZING BALANCING ACT FOR AIRCRAFT

Lawrence Sperry, 1913

In 1893, to celebrate the four-hundredth anniversary of the discovery of America, Chicago presented the world's Columbian Exposition. It was lit at night by lamps produced by Chicago's Sperry Lighting Company. The arc lamps, only recently perfected, "turned night into day." On May 1, when the exposition opened, inventor and head of his company, Elmer Sperry, took his family along—wife Zula, daughter Helen, five, Edward, two years, and four-months-old Lawrence, cradled in Zula's arms.

Zula and the children were most interested in going aloft on the 300-foot (91.4-meter) high wheel invented by Gale Ferris and lit by 2,500 lights supplied by the Sperry Company. But when she tried to leave her Ferris wheel car after the ride, Zula had a problem on her hands. The baby Lawrence screamed when she tried to leave. He kept screaming until Elmer relented and they all went up for a second turn. Lawrence's screams turned to squawks of joy— until they got back to earth, when he screamed for more— but this time Lawrence was bundled out and taken home. It has been suggested that those two Ferris wheel

rides may have triggered Lawrence Burst Sperry's lifelong zest for flight, height, and danger.

There were to be three Sperry sons, Edward, Lawrence, and Elmer Junior. But the one who was gifted with the same inventive genius as his father was Lawrence. He started early and was fascinated with all things mechanical, particularly the newest development—the flying machine. He decided that, after finishing school, he wouldn't go on to college, but showed a driving urge to be involved with airplanes. Father Sperry, in 1913, arranged for Lawrence to work and learn to fly with famed pioneer and holder of Pilot's License No. 1 from the Aero Club of America, Glenn Curtiss. Lawrence had expressed an interest in developing a gyroscopic stabilizer for a plane, like the gyroscopic stabilizers Elmer Sperry's company had perfected for ships. So father Sperry gave him a threefold challenge: firstly to experiment with a gyroscopic stabilizer; secondly to develop and demonstrate it; and thirdly to learn to fly.

At the Curtiss Flying School at the edge of Lake Keuka, New York State, with the backing of the U.S. Navy, Lawrence Sperry achieved all three of Elmer's specifications. In less than a year and before his twenty-first birthday, Lawrence had produced what would prove to be the most important and revolutionary aircraft control and navigation tools in the history of aviation. He also gained Pilot's License No. 11 from the Aero Club of America. That's when Curtiss urged him to demonstrate his gyroscopic stabilizer invention in Paris and supplied him with a brand new Curtiss C2 flying boat for the purpose. Curtiss had heard of the French Concours de Securité planned for June 1914, offering a prize of 50,000 francs (U.S. $10,000) for the best safety device demonstrated to a judging panel of 20 distinguished jurors. Demonstrations would be held near Paris, at Bezons, alongside the Seine.

Left: Lawrence Sperry's auto-pilot, seen from the front of his Curtiss flying boat. Sperry demonstrated this machine in Paris during 1914. The gyroscopic stabilizer, a feature of the model, is seen in the foreground in front of the compass. A landing light and drift indicator are mounted close to the port wing root.

Left: At the age of 18 Lawrence Sperry and his ever-willing brother Elmer Junior, designed and built a glider, at home, indoors. Unfortunately, the wings were too large to fit through the doors, so the boys demolished a bay window in their parents' bedroom in order to assemble the glider in the garden. Mr. and Mrs. Sperry were away at the time. Lawrence crashed the glider on his first flight but later flew it with an engine.

Opposite page: Lawrence Sperry in his Curtiss C2 demonstrates his remarkable gyroscopic autopilot, starting his final run to Bezons over the bridge at Argenteuil—a bridge made famous by the Impressionist painter, Claude Monet. He flew up and down the River Seine, over bridges and buildings, while his invention automatically operated the flying boat's controls.

To drive his message home, Lawrence and his French mechanic, Emil Cachin, both climbed out on the wings to stream their national flags. Despite this, the autopilot kept the little flying boat under perfect control. Sperry romped in to win a 50,000 francs (U.S. $10,000) prize over 50 other competitors, including the famed Louis Blériot.

Lawrence's gyroscopic stabilizer used two gyroscopes in gimbals, one to control yaw in the vertical axis, the other to regulate pitch and roll in the horizontal axes. Electrical contacts operated servo motors which, in turn, controlled and adjusted ailerons, elevators, and rudders of the airplane as a pilot would. On June 18, at Bezons, Lawrence staged a dramatic event no one would forget. For the French judges sitting in specially constructed grandstands and the thousands of spectators lining the river, he flew up and down the Seine, over bridges, and over buildings—flying high, flying low— while the Sperry invention automatically operated all of the

flying boat's controls. To drive the message home even more theatrically, Lawrence stood up in the cockpit, holding his hands high above his head while his French mechanic climbed out on one of the wings. In spite of the mechanic's weight, the controls compensated, and the aircraft kept perfect balance. Sperry romped in to win the prize over 50 other competitors, including the famed French designer/pilot Blériot.

War broke out in August of 1914—only two months after Sperry's prizewinning display at Bezons. Sperry's ideal of assured, balanced flying was forgotten as the pattern of aerial warfare developed over the battlefields. In the dogfights of World War I, it was the ability of the pilots to hurl their planes around the sky that made them either aces or a sad statistic. Fast reflexes, combined with aerobatics and a devil-may-care attitude, were what kept pilots alive and famous. Automatic controls were ignored—but not for long. Sperry instruments were beginning to show up in cockpits. The Sperry synchronized drift sight became part of the standard equipment for the U.S. Army Air Corps. It enabled navigators to compensate for both the speed and direction of air currents. The Sperry incidence indicator warned pilots of potential stalls, and helped in avoiding dangerous climbing or diving angles. The Sperry turn and bank indicator was another vital instrument to keep the plane on an even keel and for the pilot to avoid skidding or slipping sideways in a turn, which could lead to a spin. For the development of all these instruments Sperry

was not only part of the innovation, he insisted on testing the products of his imagination in the air in actual flight conditions. It's no surprise that his nickname among the flying fraternity became "Gyro" Sperry.

Among his other inventions, Lawrence developed the seat pack parachute, retractable landing gear, and the aerial torpedo (today's "guided missile" is a direct descendant of Sperry's original concept). He also started what is now a major aerial sport. He was the first to make parachute jumps "just for fun"—thrilling crowds at the Dayton Air Show in 1918 with the first, bold parachute jumping display.

General Mitchell of the U.S. Army encouraged him to produce a small training plane. Lawrence named it the Messenger and found many ways, including daring stunts and aerobatics, to popularize flying. He flew his own version, demonstrating its versatility by landing on streets and fields all over America. He booked himself and his Messenger a passage to Britain on the *Mauretania* sailing on October 30, 1923—causing a commotion by flying down West 53rd Street in New York and landing on the Cunard Line pier to load the plane aboard. He flew his plane over many parts of Britain in the next few months. Both the French and Dutch issued invitations for him to demonstrate the Messenger. Lawrence decided to fly the English Channel to Amsterdam in Holland, taking off from Croydon aerodrome on a cold day in December.

He flew south over the historic battlefield of Hastings, then turned eastward above the Sussex Downs and out over the Channel. About 3 miles (4.8 kilometers) out, flying at about 1,000 feet (304.8 meters) above the water, the engine

Above: The Sperry Messenger, 1923. It was designed by Alfred Verville and built by the Lawrence Sperry Aircraft Co.

Left: Anything to popularize flying! Lawrence Sperry lands his Messenger biplane in front of the Capitol Building, Washington.

Sperry's Aerial Torpedo, 1915–1919. This pilotless bomb, stressed to 9 G, was designed to be catapulted off the ground to fly at about 90 miles (144 kilometers) per hour (on a predetermined course and altitude) to strike its target up to 90 miles (144 kilometers) away from its departure point. In order to monitor the autopilot during test flights, the fearless Lawrence Sperry strapped himself to the fuselage of this machine. By 1918 it was radio controlled.

sputtered and died. A member of the coastguard saw the Messenger descend until it landed on the water. Mist was rolling in and a lifeboat and launch went looking for the plane but couldn't locate it. Finally, about two hours after the forced landing, the plane was found, low in the water but in perfect condition. Lawrence was not aboard.

The sea was freezing. It is believed that Lawrence, in an effort to swim ashore, was overcome by hypothermia and drowned. His body was found over three weeks later. For the superstitious the day was December 13. Lawrence Sperry, daredevil, inventor, popular legend, and pioneer aviator, was just 31 years old.

Lawrence's brother, Elmer Ambrose Sperry Junior, always a willing helper from the days of building his glider, was to further Lawrence's work with gyros by introducing the artificial horizon to the instrument panel. In turn, this led to the first blind-flying test conducted in September 1929 by Lt. James H. Doolittle—Chief of the Guggenheim Full Flight Laboratory at Mitchell Field, Long Island. Doolittle had recruited the Sperry Company along with the Kollsman Instrument Company to provide him with instruments needed for his test. While a most important innovation was the use of a radio compass and radio beacon to guide him on a glide path to a safe landing, the Sperrys provided a direction-finding gyroscope and a gyroscopic artificial horizon, which Elmer developed just two weeks prior to Doolittle's test flight. This was to become an essential aircraft instrument, along with many other Sperry inventions.

By 1919 Sperry had successfully demonstrated his Messenger Aerial Torpedo, guided to its target by a combination of radio and Sperry's autopilot. He couldn't have known where his inventiveness would lead.

In 1998, 70 years later, the RQ-4 Global Hawk Unmanned Air Vehicle (U.A.V.) was first flown by its makers, Grumman Northrop, and later went into operation in Europe. It could stay in the air for 24 hours, fly 15,530 miles (24,993 kilometers) and report back information from visible and infrared imaging. Its flight was controlled from a U.S. Air Force base at Eglin, U.S.A.

By 2002, the RQ-1 Predator Unmanned Air Combat Vehicle (U.A.C.V.) was flying as a weapons carrier on active service in Afghanistan, equipped with electro-optical and infrared sensors. Built in the U.S.A. by General Atomics, it is able to perform in all weather conditions, controlled with deadly accuracy from a remote base a long distance away from any action. Fitted with air-to-surface missiles, the Predator was also used as a frighteningly accurate weapons platform, able to fire precision, laser-guided bombs. In November of 2002, operators in a control room hundreds of miles (kilometers) away were able to guide a Predator to locate and follow al-Qaeda terrorists driving on a remote road in Yemen. The Predator's weapons system was activated to destroy the terrorists and their four-wheel drive vehicle in an unprecedented operation. Powered by a small 80-horsepower Rotax engine (as used in Ultralights) the Predator has an eight-hour range, flying to a height of 20,000 feet (6,096 meters) with a virtually invisible radar signature. U.A.C.V.s such as Predator cost about one-third the price of a manned aircraft and about one-quarter of the cost to operate. But the remote control of the U.A.C.V. depends on modern equivalents of Sperry's instruments. James H. Doolittle, General of the U.S. Army Air Force in World War II, said of Sperry: "He conceived and invented the automatic pilot, turn indicator, rate-of-climb indicator, bank indicator, and an improved radio compass, and he tested and demonstrated them himself." The Predator and other U.A.C.V.s mark the beginning of a revolution in aerial warfare that was initiated so many years ago by the remarkable Lawrence Burst Sperry. It is just the beginning of a revolution in aerial warfare initiated so many years ago by the remarkable Lawrence Burst Sperry.

Above: A General Atomics RQ 1 Predator Unmanned Air Combat Vehicle, controlled by sedentary pilots in a mobile office hundreds of miles (kilometers) away, fires a Hellfire missile. Air-to-surface missiles such as the Hellfire can be fired with pin-point accuracy from high in the sky to hit a target as small as a single vehicle. Unmanned Air Combat machines, used in a variety of roles are direct descendants of Sperry's Flying Torpedo.

CHARLES LINDBERGH

I LOVE PARIS IN THE SPRINGTIME

Almost unknown at the time, Charles Lindbergh roared out of the West and, while the world held its breath, took 33½ hours to fly from New York across the Atlantic to Paris. It was 1927 and he was 25 years old. In completing the flight, he soared into the Pantheon of fantastic fliers. He was one of those dashing, young American pilots who, in a latter-day equivalent of the early West's Pony Express, flew the mail—rain, hail, or shine—between American cities. His run was St. Louis, Missouri to Chicago, Illinois.

Brought up on his parents' farm at Little Falls, Minnesota, Lindbergh grew into an unusually self-reliant and strong-willed young man with an exceptional aptitude for engines and mechanical things. He didn't smoke or drink alcohol, yet this seemingly straight-laced individual burned with an adventurous spirit that relished dangerous challenges. Charles surprised his parents when, in 1922, he forsook his impressive practical knowledge of farming and his university studies for the risky occupation of airplane pilot. As he later

said, "I knew the farming days I loved so much were over. I had made my choice. I loved to fly still more."

His first job was barnstorming as "Daredevil Lindbergh"—a parachutist and wing-walker. His first solo flight was in 1923, on the very day he bought his first airplane, a Curtiss Jenny. He soon found that barnstorming was not the best way to make a living. Business inevitably went flat so Charles joined the U.S. Army, buckled down to study as a fully fledged fighter pilot and topped his course.

Later, while remaining an officer in the Army Reserve, Lindbergh became a chief pilot for a company that operated a mail run from St. Louis to Chicago. He flew single-seater mail planes similar to a De H 4 in all kinds of weather, and twice had to "hit the silk"—parachute to safety from his plane because of appalling weather conditions.

While battling the weather and all that it threw at him, Lindbergh still had time to ponder his own future in flying. One day in a newsreel theatre in Chicago he saw a story on a Sikorsky airplane being tested in preparation for a bid for the Orteig Prize. Lindbergh knew he had discovered his challenge.

Raymond Orteig, a Frenchman who owned hotels in New York City, had offered a prize of $25,000 to the first aviator who could fly non-stop from New York to Paris or the reverse. The trip would be a distance of 3,400 miles (5,470 kilometers)—farther than any plane had

Left: In September 1926, unpredicted fog was one of the problems that forced Lindbergh to parachute from a De H 4 mail plane. These World War I bombers were designed by Britain's de Havilland and built under license in the United States of America. De Havilland lost the contract once specifically designed mail planes were introduced.

previously flown in one leg. With the Orteig Prize still on offer, Lindbergh figured: "I have more than four years of aviation behind me, and close to 2,000 hours in the air. I've barnstormed in over half the 48 states. Am I not qualified for such a flight?"

With the backing of the St. Louis Flying Club, the St. Louis Chamber of Commerce, and some city businessmen, Lindbergh set about finding the right plane for the flight. No manufacturer was prepared to build a plane for this unknown pilot, except one—the Ryan Aircraft Company of San Diego, California. In February 1927, knowing that there were others planning an early attempt at the prize, Lindbergh pressured Donald Hall, Ryan's engineer and chief designer, to build a plane to his own specifications in just two months.

Lindbergh's plane began to take shape. A 220-horsepower, air-cooled, Wright Whirlwind radial engine was fitted with a special greasing mechanism that would operate during the long transatlantic flight. For safety reasons, the fuel tank of the high-winged monoplane was placed forward of the cockpit, blocking the view ahead. A periscope was mounted in the left side of the plane, which Lindbergh could use if he wanted to see in front of him.

To achieve a maximum distance range of 4,000 miles (6,440 kilometers), items considered too heavy were omitted. Consequently, the plane had no radio, parachute, fuel gauges, or navigation lights, and was installed with a light wicker chair instead of a leather pilot's seat. Lindbergh designed special lightweight boots to wear, and took only maps bearing the reference points he would need.

Lindbergh dubbed the silver plane *Spirit of St. Louis*, named after the French King Louis IX, the patron saint

The Curtiss Jenny, 1920s

Above: The Stearman C3MB of 1927 is in trouble over Portland, with mist closing in to blanket the landing ground. In the early 1920s, the beginnings of what would become a vast network of radio and light beacons across the United States with entire landing fields dedicated to mail planes, had just kicked off. Meteorological forecasting was in its infancy. In those days, aircraft couldn't climb above bad weather so mail pilots often became the tragic victims of violent weather, or more insidiously, of fog.

Left: Lindbergh arrives in London after his nonstop flight from New York to Paris.

We didn't carry any astronomical instruments, and I don't know how to use a sextant.

CHARLES LINDBERGH, AFTER CROSSING
THE ATLANTIC SOLO, 1927

Charles Lindbergh, 1927

of the Missouri city of the same name. He flew 1,600 miles (2,575 kilometers) from San Diego to St. Louis, where he showed his new plane to his supporters. He then re-fueled and flew on to New York. Without trying, Lindbergh had created a new transcontinental record.

On May 20, 1927, at Roosevelt Field, New York—although the flying conditions could have been more favorable—Lindbergh climbed into his cockpit and started the engine. He took four sandwiches and a bottle of drinking water with him. While carrying out his warm-up checks he discovered that the engine would not deliver full power, yet he decided to make a start as he figured there was still enough power in the engine to get the plane airborne. Lindbergh pressed on, determined to complete his mission. With two of the competing airplanes sitting in front of their hangars, he lined up his plane and opened the throttle wide. The *Spirit of St. Louis* moved sluggishly forward on the muddy runway to start its epic flight. As archival film of the takeoff shows, the aircraft, overweight by 1,000 pounds (454 kilograms), bounced a couple of times before staggering into the air. It then disappeared into the mist.

Lindbergh stayed low and headed north on a great circle track that required 40 course changes en route. He needed all his courage and all his flying skills. He flew through frontal storms, thick cloud, ice, hail, and rain until, after 28 demanding hours and fighting to stay awake, he crossed the coast of Ireland at Valencia and Dingle Bay.

Finally on May 21, 33 hours and 29 minutes after leaving New York, he was landing the *Spirit of St. Louis* in darkness at Le Bourget, outside Paris. As he taxied in, a welcoming throng of over 100,000 French people was hysterical with joy and praise for his success. When he could be heard over the crowd, Charles Lindbergh was able to claim: "I am the first man in Paris to say 'I was in New York yesterday!'".

Two rival airplanes had let Lindbergh slip away from New York in the early morning on a day they thought unsuitable for flying. He was over the Atlantic, headed for Paris and the Orteig Prize, while the two planes, ready to fly for the same prize money, sat immobilized on the tarmac at Roosevelt airfield. One was a Fokker trimotor, emblazoned with the name *America*. The other was a single-engined Bellanca called *Columbia*. They soon made their own headlines.

After leaving New York, Charles Lindbergh had been flying alone over the Atlantic for 27 hours in shocking weather. He had not slept for 48 hours and he had had to fly the Spirit every second of the way because she wouldn't fly "hands off." Lindbergh had needed to focus not just on his flying but on navigation, changing course, checking his compass, and watching his instruments. In his noisy cockpit Charles started to hallucinate.

At about 3:00 P.M. local time, he descended through a cloud layer and found himself flying over a group of what appeared to be a few fishing vessels making their way through the oily swells of the Atlantic. Lindbergh descended, flying his Ryan monoplane low over the water to pass the first vessel. She was "all shipshape" with sails furled and ropes neatly coiled but, like the Marie Celeste, not a soul was to be seen. Was the vessel just a fevered phantom of his imagination?

He flew low alongside a second vessel and noticed a pale face peering up at him from a porthole. He cut back the throttle, leaned out his side window and yelled, "Which way to Ireland?" But there was no response, just a startled, unbelieving look. Lindbergh gunned the engine and climbed away into the sky again, dispirited, wondering whether the whole episode was another eerie hallucination.

An hour later, around 4:00 P.M., he sighted the coast of Ireland, and at 9:24 P.M. saw the Eiffel Tower. He knew that was no dream. Shortly after, he landed to an unbelievably tumultuous reception. He had left New York almost unknown, flown 3,400 miles (5,470 kilometers) to Paris and had come out of the sky to land as an international hero, a world celebrity to be feted and adored. For Charles Lindbergh, nothing could be the same again.

Above: Only weeks before Lindbergh's flight, Clarence Chamberlin with copilot Bert Acosta had broken the world record for continuous flight in the Bellanca Columbia over New York's skies. On June 4, just two weeks after Lindbergh's flight, Chamberlin, with Charles Levine as a passenger, took off from the same runway in the same plane and flew nonstop to Eisleben near Berlin, Germany. He outdid Lindbergh by flying farther—close to 3,800 miles (6,114 kilometers)—but his fine achievement did not receive anywhere near the acclaim lavished on Lindbergh.

Chamberlin and Levine arrive in Berlin at the end of their pioneering flight.

Right: Comdr. Byrd was the leader for the America's transatlantic attempt. In May 1926 Byrd reportedly made the first airplane flight to the North Pole and he was both navigator and leader of this expedition. His pilots were Bert Acosta and Berndt Balchen with Lt. George Norville as his wireless operator. Again from Roosevelt Field, they took off at dawn on June 29, aiming for Paris.

Forty hours later in a pitch-black night, fighting dreadful weather, radioing distress messages, and running out of fuel, they crashed into the seas near a lighthouse, coming to rest on the beach near the tiny town of Vers sur Mer. At least they had made it to France. The beach— just outside the town—would be written into history, not because of the America's crash landing, but because 17 years later in World War II, on June 6, 1944, it would become "Gold" beach in the Normandy Invasion landings of the Allied Forces.

The Lockheed Sirius, 1931

Charles Lindbergh taught his wife, Anne Morrow, to fly. She became his enthusiastic copilot and navigator on many of the pioneering flights commissioned by Juan Trippe, the charismatic, farsighted head of Pan American Airways. In 1929, Charles had pioneered the route to South America and flown a new Sikorsky flying boat on its inaugural run. But Anne and Charles Lindbergh are best remembered for world-girdling flights in their colorful Lockheed *Sirius* floatplane. *Sirius* was a distinctive black and orange color, later repainted fire-red and black. In 1931, together they flew *Sirius* over the Arctic on the great circle route to Tokyo. Anne Morrow always credited the brilliant Australian aerial navigator Harold Gatty, for helping her become an expert navigator. She was a keen exponent of Gatty's innovative methods.

During World War II, although a civilian, Lindbergh was attached to the Pacific Theater of War to teach combat pilots how to conserve fuel. Dogfights consumed a lot of fuel and many pilots were lost because the fuel ran out before they could return to base. By adopting Lindbergh's fuel-efficient engine handling techniques the P-38's effective radius of action was increased from a distance of 500 to 700 miles (805 to 1,127 kilometers). This improvement allowed for longer flights and saved many lives.

Anne Morrow Lindbergh

The Lockheed P-38 Lightning, 1945

CHARLES KINGSFORD SMITH

AN ODYSSEY OF HEROIC DIMENSIONS

Kingsford Smith was one of those young, daring Australians who fought in World War I as a pilot in the Royal Flying Corps. An audacious and courageous flier, his wartime exploits earned him the Military Cross. His achievements in peacetime were to be equally daring, and in a little over a decade, Charles Kingsford Smith became a hero to his fellow Australians as he challenged distance and broke records in his airplanes. He was talked about and his adventures followed with all the attention and adulation granted to top sporting heroes. With affection and pride, they called him "Smithy."

In 1927, Kingsford Smith made a record-breaking flight around Australia. Then in 1928, as captain of the crew of four, he tackled "the big one"—possibly the most hazardous long-distance flight of all—across the planet's biggest area of water, the Pacific Ocean.

The flight would start from Oakland, California, and finish in Brisbane, Australia. This would take them a distance of over 7,600 miles (12,231 kilometers) and require 83 hours of flying time. Smithy's achievement was to set the example to future airlines by showing them how to link the prosperous North American continent with the burgeoning economies and communities of the South Pacific.

The aircraft chosen for the flight was a Fokker Trimotor, a monoplane with an open-sided cockpit. He named it *Southern Cross* after the star formation that also features on Australia's

PACIFIC CROSSING, 1928

national flag. Smithy was the pilot, with another Australian, Charles Ulm, who organized the event, as second pilot. Harry Lyon, the navigator, and Jim Warner, the radio operator, were Americans.

Laden with extra fuel, they lumbered into the air from Oakland, and in cramped and freezing conditions flew for 27 hours to Honolulu. With the cockpit open on the sides, the crew were deafened by the noise of the motors and the slipstream. Even though jammed in side by side, Ulm and Smithy could communicate only by writing notes to each other. Often, during the flight, they were drenched with icy rain.

After Honolulu, they flew the longest leg of the flight—to Suva, Fiji. After they'd flown 35 hours of endless concentration, Kingsford Smith had then to maneuver a heart-stopping landing on a short airstrip at a sports oval outside Suva.

The final leg to Australia was, by comparison, the easy one though they passed through appalling weather. The radio operator, Warner, and navigator Lyon could relax a little. Australia is a big land mass and hard to miss, unlike the first two legs of the flight where a few degrees of error would have led them to a watery grave. *Southern Cross* reached the Australian coast at the small fishing town of Ballina. There they turned north and flew for an hour to reach Brisbane, the capital of Queensland. The flight from Suva to Brisbane took 21 hours, and on landing, the crew was met by hysterical crowds who had gathered for a true Aussie welcome.

Charles Ulm, organizer and second pilot

Charles Kingsford Smith, pilot

Harry Lyon, navigator

Jim Warner, radio operator

Opposite page: This famous aircraft, pictured as it crosses the Australian coast at Ballina at the end of its great Pacific flight, was later to become the first airplane to complete a world circum-navigation. The completion of the world-girdling flight was one of the many record-making flights carried out by Charles Kingsford Smith to publicize the reliability and safety of passenger flying. The aircraft is preserved at Australia's Brisbane airport.

Left: In 1930, when Charles Kingsford Smith broke Bert Hinkler's record solo flight to Australia, he chose a similar machine to Hinkler's—an Avro Avian biplane, and christened it Southern Cross Junior. He had a depressing start. Not only was the weather atrocious but the previous week, the huge British Airship R101 crashed in France on a proving flight to India. His friend and colleague Sir Sefton Brancker, the British Director of Civil Aviation, was killed in the disaster. However, all went well with his flight and Smithy beat Hinkler's record by just over 5 days, flying the 10,000 miles (16,000 kilometers) in a little over 10 days.

Air Race was to be staged in 1934, he bought himself a new plane to participate. He chose a sleek blue and silver Lockheed Altair monoplane. He named it *Anzac*, but some considered this an affront to the memory of the World War I soldiers of the Australian and New Zealand Army Corps (the "Anzacs") so he renamed the plane *Lady Southern Cross*. However, as seafarers will tell you, it is bad luck to change the name of a ship; whatever the cause, *Lady Southern Cross* was not a lucky airplane.

The first bad omen occurred when the extra fuel tanks he had installed on the powerful Altair resulted in objections from both Lockheed and aviation safety authorities on the grounds that Smithy was overloading the aircraft. Smithy's appeal was overruled, and when, later, it was discovered that the engine cowling was split, he pulled out of the race. This, in turn, resulted in negative press reports and attempts to discredit him.

Fired up, he decided to overcome his bad press by making the first crossing of the Pacific in a single-engined aircraft. He would again fly from Australia to California via Fiji and Hawaii with the brilliant P. G. (Gordon) Taylor as his copilot and navigator. They flew to Oakland, California, arriving 14 days after taking off in Australia, and again, Kingsford Smith had achieved an historic flight.

He went on to London, where he made plans to fly back to Australia following the route taken by the Air Race fliers. He would make use of the extra fuel capacity denied him in the Air Race, and would break the 1934 Air Race record!

He chose Tommy Pethybridge to replace Gordon Taylor as copilot.

They and the *Lady Southern Cross* were tracking well to beat the record, when luck again turned bad. It is believed they crashed into the sea off Burma (now Myanmar). Nothing was ever found of the plane or crew, except the port undercarriage leg of the unlucky *Lady.* It was a gothic end to one of the world's greatest aviators, flying into the sea at the dead of night, leaving little trace of his passing.

The record-making Pacific crossing was not just to win acclaim. Charles Kingsford Smith and Charles Ulm were out to promote long-distance flying. They wanted to provide the general public with confidence in the reliability and safety of air travel between continents and over oceans. The pair had plans to set up their own airline and operate long-distance air routes, fully aware that for isolated continents like Australia, international flights would be revolutionary. Smithy and Ulm foresaw that in the future, airliners would break forever what one historian has called Australia's "tyranny of distance."

Kingsford Smith had not finished making and breaking records. After achieving the Pacific crossing he made a record flight from Australia to England during the next year (1929). He continued from England to fly the Atlantic—achieving the first truly successful flight "the wrong way"—that is, against the prevailing winds. Then he continued again to San Francisco, to complete a world circumnavigation. He

was the first flier ever to completely circumnavigate the globe in the same airplane. He still hadn't finished. In 1930 he broke the England to Australia solo record set by the famous Bert Hinkler. In 1933 he established another solo record, flying from England to Australia in just seven days. On this flight he flew a Percival Gull, designed by Australian, Edgar Percival (see pages 120–121).

In 1932, Kingsford Smith had been knighted by Britain's King George V for his contribution to aviation, and from then on was officially Sir Charles Kingsford Smith. It appears to have made little difference to his Australian admirers. With affection they still called him "Smithy." Charles Kingsford Smith was a compulsive competitor and though he had more than proved himself in the air, he just could not resist a challenge. When he heard that an England to Australia

Tommy Pethybridge

Left: Sir Charles Kingsford Smith and P. G. (Gordon) Taylor in front of the Lady Southern Cross, 1934. Note the lack of engine cowling.

Right: The only remains to come to light of the Lady Southern Cross is this solitary landing wheel—washed up on Aye Island in the Gulf of Mataban.

Right: It was common practice in the days of few aerodromes for visiting aircraft to land on a local racecourse. Takeoff from the same place was usually out of the question because the extra weight of a full load of fuel would necessitate a longer run than was available.

This was the reason why, in Fiji at the beginning of the second stage of their Pacific crossing, Kingsford Smith and P. G. Taylor took their lightly laden Lady Southern Cross to a long beach at Naselai. There, they filled the tanks.

Unfortunately, due to delays in trying to trace a fuel leak, their hard beach runway became much narrowed by the incoming tide. Also, the wind was gusting strongly across the beach, making for a tricky crosswind takeoff.

Just before she became airborne, the Lady Southern Cross slewed into the surf as a huge gust hit the large fin. Only Smithy's superb airmanship got her out of the surf and up onto dry sand, averting what could have been a major disaster and a premature end to their pioneering flight.

HERMANN KOEHL

THE WILL TO SUCCEED

In the 1930s, a few majestic square-rigged sailing ships still sailed the Atlantic. When crossing from America to Europe they took the direct route across the North Atlantic, although with some trepidation even with a following wind. Going the other way from Europe to America, they wisely followed the old trade route, south via the Canary Islands and the South Atlantic. This way they avoided battling the notorious head winds further north.

The pioneering aviators made sure they were helped by the winds as well. In 1919, first Commander Read, and then Alcock and Brown relied on prevailing westerlies to increase their ground speed across the Atlantic. When Charles Lindbergh made his historic single-engined flight from New York to Paris in 1927, he effectively increased the range of his Ryan monoplane by making clever use of westerly tail winds. The only attempt to fly east to west in one of the new, often unreliable flying machines was in early 1927 when *L'Oiseau Blanc*, piloted by Charles Nungesser and François Coli, tried to fly from Paris to New York. They were lost without trace somewhere in the Atlantic.

Then up stepped brave Capt. Hermann Koehl, ready to try his hand at the controls. Koehl prepared for his attempt in a new and revolutionary airplane—the Junkers W 33. Built for strength and extraordinary endurance, this was an all-metal machine, and featured Junkers' newly-invented skin of corrugated aluminum. Until then, most aircraft consisted of a complex wooden skeleton which was covered by fabric or plywood. The Junkers W 33, by contrast, had a metal skeleton which was much less complex than previous structures, and an aluminum cover, a combination designed to cope with both twist and stress. Moreover, the corduroy effect of the corrugations aligned with the airstream, though not esthetically pleasing, proved to be extremely resilient

and very effective. An added advantage of the corrugated skin was that it allowed the building of a large and very strong monoplane wing without the drag associated with a biplane wing.

Compared to existing aircraft, the Junkers W 33 model had a remarkable range—4,000 miles (6,435 kilometers). In 1928, Hermann Koehl was ready to fly his gleaming, all-metal Junkers from Ireland to America. Along for the ride was the financier of the attempt, Count von Hunefeld, who was also Koehl's navigator, and as the third crew member, Irishman Commander Fitzmaurice. They took off twice but had to turn back on each occasion. Then, on the third attempt, they set course and persevered. The flight became an epic of dogged courage. The infamous Atlantic threw every conceivable harsh element at them—ice, snow, cold front after cold front, and gusty westerly winds. Koehl had to fly low for most of the time. The west winds reduced their ground speed to about 46 miles (74 kilometers). Hour after tormented hour they battled on, until after 36 tortured hours, they crash-landed on a small island off the coast of Labrador, Canada.

From east to west across the Atlantic Ocean was not for the fainthearted. Koehl had already attempted the flight in 1927 but had had to turn back after 22 hours in the air because of prohibitively harsh weather. The final flight in 1928 was a fitting tribute to the courage and determination of Captain Koehl and his crew and to the Junkers' sturdy new plane.

Below: Hermann Koehl's successful east to west flight across the Atlantic was not his first attempt. In 1927, two Junkers W 33 planes took off from Dessau in Germany, heading west over the ocean. One soon turned back to land in Dessau. The second plane, with Koehl, navigator von Hunefeld, and a third crew member, Loose, flew into a succession of the frontal systems that string across the Atlantic, bringing strong headwinds and turbulent conditions. Realizing they'd never make it, Koehl turned back, landing exhausted after 22 hours in the air.

In the late 1920s and 1930s aircraft were not able to climb above bad weather. Unlike today's airliners which have radar to probe far-off weather and the ability to climb over 30,000 feet (9,140 meters) to avoid low-level storms and cloud, aircraft of the 1930s had either to stay on the ground, or fly against the prevailing weather systems. Any head winds could massively cut ground speed compared to later faster and higher-flying aircraft. For instance, a head wind of 56 miles (90 kilometers) per hour is nothing to a Concorde flying faster than the speed of sound. To an airplane of the late 1920s cruising at an airspeed of 103 miles (165 kilometers) per hour, a 56-mile (90-kilometer) head wind would more than halve its ground speed. The result was extra flying hours as well as a serious negative effect on the predicted fuel consumption to achieve the planned destination. The aircraft's range, normally calculated for still-air conditions, was seriously reduced.

Once you have flown, you will walk the earth with your face turned skyward.

LEONARDO DA VINCI

Below: The Bremen, Koehl's all-metal Junkers W33, made its historic east to west crossing of the North Atlantic on April 12, 1928. It was powered by a single Junkers water-cooled engine of around 300 horsepower. Unusual for the day, it featured a single unsupported monoplane wing of 58 feet (18 meters) and the unique Junkers corrugated aluminum skin, seen here. It cruised at about 93 miles (150 kilometers) per hour carrying 2.5 tons (2.54 tonnes) of fuel.

Left: A Junkers W 33 was selected for a nonstop flight across the Pacific in 1932. Commanded by Eiichiro Baba with Cmdr. Kiyoshi Homma as navigator and Sgt. Tomoyoshi Inoshita as radio operator, the aircraft set off on a great circle route similar to the one planned by the great navigator, Harold Gatty in his failed attempt with pilot Harold Bromley two years earlier. Like Bromley, Eiichiro and his crew took off from Sabishiro Beach, north of Tokyo, and were last reported near the Kurile Islands. Nothing was ever heard of them again.

CHARLES NUNGESSER AND FRANÇOIS COLI

HOW WHITE BIRD BECAME MIDNIGHT GHOST

Sailors in clipper ships always defined the trip from New York, across the Atlantic eastwards to Britain and Europe as "downhill"—the easier route, with prevailing winds assisting ships. To beat back, traveling east to west, was "uphill"— facing into winds and gales, and fighting against the weather that rolled in to thwart the mariners.

Fliers needed to be very tough or just foolhardy to try to fly "uphill" from Paris to New York in the year 1927. Nungesser and Coli were indeed tough and they flew "uphill" for the glory of France and to make their bid for the Orteig Prize of $25,000 as the first to fly Paris to New York. When Orteig asked why the two were attempting the flight the hard way, François Coli replied, "To fly from New York would make it seem as though we were going to visit ourselves!"

L'Oiseau Blanc ("The White Bird") was a Levasseur PL8, modified from the French Navy's Levasseur 4R4b airplane, with space for two crew members sitting side by side, and a third crew position replaced with tanks for an increased fuel load. The machine was a big, sturdy biplane, powered by a well-tested, 12-cylinder, 450-horsepower Lorraine Dietrich engine. The lower fuselage was crafted from plywood in the shape of a boat hull and the propeller could be fixed horizontally in case of being forced down in the sea, ensuring that the plane could not be flipped over by a moving prop. The landing wheels would be jettisoned after takeoff to reduce drag. But first, it would have to become airborne laden with 1,063 gallons (4,023 liters) of fuel.

Nungesser and Coli came to the project with a fine list of accomplishments. Charles Eugene Jules Marie Nungesser was France's third-ranking flying ace of World War I with a total of 45 "kills." François Coli was a Corsican born in Marseilles, with a record of maritime achievement first in the navy, then as navigator, and as one of the youngest men ever to command a merchant ship. He served in the army

when war broke out—rising from foot soldier to captain before transferring to the air service, learning to fly, and becoming Commandant of Escadrille Spa. 62, a French observation squadron. Coli was the man who, with a pilot from his squadron, Paul Tarascon, organized this Orteig challenge, but the first attempt was terminated when their Potez 25 plane was destroyed by lightning, and Tarascon badly burned.

While in hospital, Paul recommended that Nungesser take his place in the new Levasseur plane. With François's brilliant navigational skills and Charles's flying achievements these two were possibly the best airmen in France. They made a formidable pair to tackle the mighty Atlantic crossing.

Well aware that there were other planes and pilots in New York champing at the bit to make a bid for the Orteig Prize, they waited with their white bird for the right weather patterns before commencing their French bid. On May 8, 1927, at 5:17 A.M., *L'Oiseau Blanc* trundled along the runway at Le Bourget airfield, climbing and just missing the trees at the end of a heart-stopping 3,000-foot (914-meter) run.

A flight of military aircraft escorted them on their way. Nungesser dropped the landing gear as arranged at Sarcelles, the military escorts dipped their wings to bid adieu, and the gleaming white plane was on its own, soon flying out over the Channel.

Confirmation that they were on time was telegraphed from Ireland to Paris five hours later, when the white bird was observed heading out over the North Atlantic ocean. Officially that was the last time the Bird or its fliers were seen.

Charles Nungesser, wearing a kepi, and the Nieuport XXIII fighter in which he claimed many of his 45 World War I victories. The highly visible tricolor markings were the result of Nungesser's shock after shooting down and killing a British fighter pilot who had attacked him after mistaking the French ace's aircraft for a German fighter.

Left: François Coli was the brains behind the Atlantic attempt. He, like Nungesser, was a man of exceptional courage. He lost an eye as a result of a war wound and thereafter always wore a black monocle.

The next day, May 9, the French newspaper, *La Presse* reported that *L'Oiseau Blanc* had been sighted flying close to the city of Boston, and later the paper ran special editions reporting that the courageous pilots had landed in New York. The people of France took to the streets and celebrated in a rush of excitement and hysteria not seen since the Armistice in 1918.

La Presse had to recall the special editions when it became clear that the announced success was some sort of grim hoax. In the more than 70 years since, there have

Below: In the early light of dawn on May 8, 1927, Charles Nungesser and François Coli drop the landing gear of L'Oiseau Blanc a short distance north west of their takeoff point at Le Bourget airfield. Dropping the undercarriage reduced drag and increased the range of the aircraft. Also, without the wheels to catch the surface of the sea and trip the aircraft into a somersault, the crew stood a better chance of surviving a forced landing if she came down in the Atlantic. The hull-like underside of the fuselage was designed to withstand landing on water or land.

been attempts to discover what happened to Coli and Nungesser. Weeks after the disappearance, crews of the North Atlantic fishing trawlers reported that the white bird had flown over their fishing grounds. It was claimed that a radio call had been picked up in Newfoundland. Also from Newfoundland, witnesses claimed to have seen a white plane flying with no landing gear.

Another area where claims have been made of an aircraft crashing on May 9, 1927, is in the hills close to the Round Lake, Maine. Stories of this crash have circulated in Maine since the early 1930s. But meticulous searches as recently as 1990 have been unable to come up with any material evidence of any sort. The search of the Maine woods was called the "midnight ghost expedition" after the phrase used in Charles Lindbergh's book *The Spirit of St. Louis*. Certainly, over the past decades, the loss of *L' Oiseau Blanc* and its intrepid crew has become an aerial ghost story. What ever happened to the big white plane with the skull and crossbones painted on its fuselage when it flew into the night about the Atlantic Ocean—and vanished?

Right: The struts and wheels fell into a field near Paris. This sad pair of wheels is all that remains of L'Oiseau Blanc. *They can be seen today displayed in the Musée de l'Air et de l'Éspace, Paris.*

If we disappear, you'll tell them that our expedition was well prepared, won't you?

CHARLES NUNGESSER TO HIS CHIEF MECHANIC, MAY 8, 1927

DIEUDONNÉ COSTES AND MAURICE BELLONTE

ONE BIG QUESTION MARK!

When Dieudonné Costes and Maurice Bellonte climbed into the big, red Breguet *Super Bidon* long-range biplane, observers thought there were quite a few questions to be answered. The plane had been christened—it was called *Point d'Interrogation*. You don't need to be a French scholar to know this means "question mark" and there were a host of questions the two men—and the airplane—would need to answer. One of the first was: "Why would they want to try?" The airmen would be following a path that had already swallowed four aircraft and their crews without trace, the last being *L'Oiseau Blanc* which had wiped out the wartime heroes Charles Nungesser and François Coli, lost at night somewhere over the North Atlantic Ocean. Another question was: "Why would a man who had already gained such a formidable reputation once more risk his life against the harsh weather patterns of the North Atlantic?"

As a fighter pilot in World War I, Costes had been cited for gallantry on seven occasions and had been awarded the

Legion of Honor. In 1927 he had been the first to fly the South Atlantic nonstop with Joseph le Brix in another Breguet aircraft (he was employed as a test pilot by the Breguet company). In 1929 Costes and Bellonte—his trusted navigator and engineer—had already challenged the North Atlantic. They had taken off from Le Bourget airfield shortly after two Polish majors, Ldzikowski and Kubala. The Poles and the French were both aiming to beat the Atlantic and fly to New York. They flew into terrible weather. The Polish fliers tried to land in the Azores, but crashed. Leon Ldzikowski was killed. The Frenchmen tried to fly above the Azores, aiming to continue, but even their excellent red Breguet was practically uncontrollable in the shocking conditions. They were forced to turn back, landing again at Le Bourget after 28 hours nonstop flying, over 3,200 miles (5,400 kilometers).

The French Air Ministry then made it clear that the official view was that no further attempts to make such a flight across

Dieudonné Costes

Maurice Bellonte

the Atlantic would be tolerated.

Disgusted and frustrated, Dieudonné and Maurice later that year took off from Paris and flew nonstop to Manchuria, traveling 4,909 miles (7,900 kilometers) in 52 hours, 39 minutes. That was a new world record for a nonstop flight. On their return the two adventurers beat a record Costes himself had established in 1927 when he flew from Paris to Siberia. This time he cut seven hours off the 1927 nonstop record. Costes followed that with another remarkable flight. Together with copilot Paul Codos, he created a world endurance record by flying over and around France for a total of 58.5 hours.

With the acclaim and the eyes of an adoring nation on him, the Air Ministry kept quiet when Costes and Bellonte announced they would once more attempt to fly Paris to New York. The next question was: "What had they learned from their last attempt?" They had learned that the weather would be their toughest opponent. Costes wouldn't specify a date for the attempt. Instead, he studied the weather reports from the east coast of America, and the reports from Britain and the French coast. Costes said he would fly when the weather was right. He found out that it never was right. Flying conditions were always unfavorable on one side of the Atlantic or the other. They became impatient. Writing

Left: Costes and Bellonte were no strangers to long-distance flying. Before making their flight across the Atlantic the "wrong way" in the Breguet Point d'Interrogation, *shown in this photograph, they had already made a record long-distance flight of nearly 4,909 miles (7,898 kilometers) nonstop from Paris to Tsitsihar in Manchuria.*

Bellonte, seen here in the back seat storing his gear aboard the aircraft just before their Atlantic flight, was a fine navigator and took 17 astronomical sights throughout the trip. His last sunshot was so accurate that with the advanced navigational tables available to him, he was able to make landfall in America within two minutes of his predicted time of arrival.

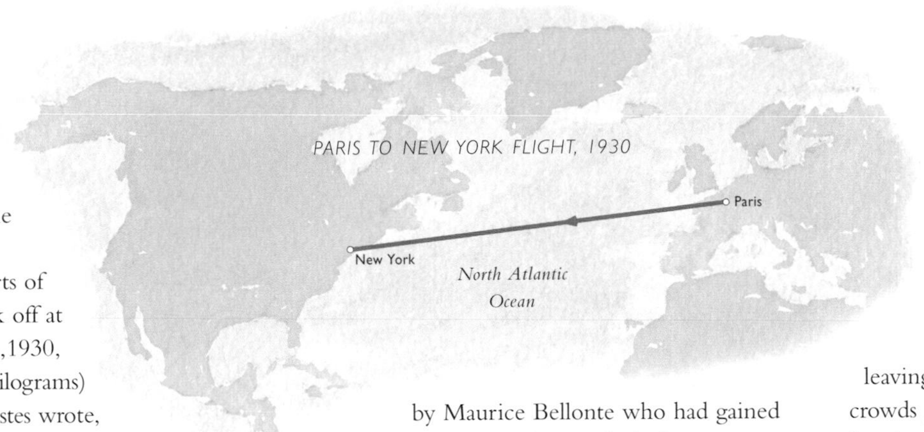

about his experiences later Costes said, "We did not hesitate to try to leave on September 5 because we knew we had done all that anyone could do for the trip."

Though he knew there was fog over parts of Britain and France, *Point d'Interrogation* took off at 10:30 A.M. on the morning of September 5, 1930, weighed down with 11,000 pounds (4,990 kilograms) of fuel. "We took off in the face of mists" Costes wrote, "…our battle with the elements had begun." And it was a never-ending battle. They had to fly low over the ground to reach the sea, breaking out of the fog when they reached the English Channel. The plane was able to gain some height before hitting clouds and rain storms. Five hours from Le Bourget, they were sighted passing over Ireland and, an hour farther on, were able to radio the liner *Berengaria* to report that they were pleased with their progress. After that, they were hit by successive Atlantic storms and had to take evasive action in case, with their huge fuel load, winds and turbulence could literally tear the wings off the sturdy craft. They flew on, into the night. Fortunately, the weary Costes could be relieved

Right: The historic Breguet Point d'Interrogation *flown by Costes and Bellonte can still be seen, beautifully preserved in the Museé de l'Air et de l'Éspace in Paris.*

by Maurice Bellonte who had gained his pilot's license only months before.

Both the front and rear cockpits had identical sets of instruments to assist flying in the pitch-black night. They were able to radio ships at sea with messages that were relayed to New York and Paris. By dawn, the Breguet was headed for Nova Scotia. Still buffeted by bad weather, they located the coast of Nova Scotia, only to run into the worst storm they had yet encountered. To be sure that they didn't lose their way they hugged the coast, at times forced to fly as low as 30 feet (10 meters) above the waves. Eventually, with a much lighter plane because of depleted fuel supplies, they proudly flew into New York.

Landing at Curtiss Field, they were greeted by Charles Lindbergh and a waiting crowd of over 20,000 Americans. The police couldn't hold back the crowd. The two Frenchmen were lifted from their cockpits in the scarlet *Point d'Interrogation* and carried as conquering heroes by the excited mob.

They had landed 37 hours, 17 minutes after leaving Paris. Later, Costes was able to speak to huge crowds gathered in Paris to share in the celebrations. Loudspeakers had been erected in Paris streets and Dieudonné was able to talk to his cheering countrymen via a special radio hookup.

Both men were honored by the French nation, Costes being elevated to Commandant of the Legion of Honor. These were aerial pioneers who had at last beaten the hoodoo of flying the North Atlantic from east to west. It is almost impossible to imagine more demanding challenges for fliers or a flying machine than the ones conquered by Costes, Bellonte, and *Point d'Interrogation* when they flew across the wild Atlantic. The question, "Could they make it?" had been answered.

PARIS TO NEW YORK FLIGHT, 1930

Paris

New York

North Atlantic Ocean

It is not pleasant to think how close we came to those cruel, jagged rocks.

COSTES, AFTER THE SUCCESSFUL PARIS TO NEW YORK FLIGHT, 1930

CHUBBIE MILLER

LET A WOMAN IN YOUR LIFE

Above: Chubbie Miller (right) with Bill Lancaster and his Avro Avian, *Red Rose*, in which the intrepid pair flew from England to Australia during 1928.

Jessie "Chubbie" Miller was not one of those women to marry, settle down, have children, and become a thorough homebody. She was, after all, an adult in the middle of the flapper era, when thanks to a combination of Hollywood films, gramophones, Tin Pan Alley, and radio, feminism was beginning to stir, and women were breaking out of the traditional mold. In spite of her rather staid Australian upbringing, her early interest in flying (and in another woman's husband) gained her a reputation of being a "fast" woman—a reputation she turned to advantage when she became one of the fastest women on earth.

Chubbie first attracted public interest in 1927, as the first female passenger to make a flight from England to Australia. On holiday in Britain, this petite young woman met Bill Lancaster, a young pilot trying to raise enough money to fly his Avro Avian to Australia. Chubbie, finding he and his mission attractive, decided to go all the way.

Showing either good business sense or good sales techniques, she raised finance for the flight and resolved to accompany Lancaster on what was to be a long and difficult journey. It was the beginning of Mrs. Miller's flying career. Perhaps in a tribute to flowering romance, Lancaster named his plane *Red Rose*.

Coincidentally, Australian Bert Hinkler had decided to fly from England to Australia at about the same time and in the same type of Avro Avian aircraft. Hinkler, though, wanted to achieve a record solo flight, and so was on his own. Both he and *Red Rose* were following the same daunting and inhospitable route. At one stage, while *Red Rose* was undergoing repairs after a crash, Lancaster and Miller acted as night guards on Hinkler's plane while he caught up on much-needed sleep.

Hinkler made his solo flight record. Chubbie became the first woman passenger to fly from England to Australia and *Red Rose* was given a warm welcome when it landed in

Australia. Not long after, Lancaster and Miller were in America. They traveled there courtesy of the two American members of the *Southern Cross* which, with Charles Kingsford Smith and Charles Ulm, had completed the first crossing of the Pacific.

Once in America, instead of being a passenger, Chubbie Miller learned to fly, and she vaulted into the sky and into the hearts and minds of the great American public. During the next three years, Chubbie air-raced, hounded by a breathless press. She earned accolades for her dashing, carefree pursuit of speed and competitors. Many male fliers were actively belligerent about any woman trying to become a pilot. They were particularly vicious about Mrs. Miller, but that didn't slow her down.

In 1930 Chubbie flew the fast and murderous Alexander Bullet aircraft, creating record-breaking times in a transcontinental air race from Los Angeles to New York and back. She roared her way to success in spite of the Bullet being considered unsafe to the point of being highly dangerous. Two previous prototypes had crashed, killing a hapless test pilot. When Chubbie tried to buy the plane from the Alexander company, it declined the offer and instead, gave the plane to her, to distance itself from any accident involving the Bullet while she was flying it. In Chubbie Miller's hands, the machine somehow became compliant and responsive. Its brand new Wright Whirlwind engine, combined with its new-fangled retractable landing gear created a highly competitive performer. And didn't Chubbie put it through its paces!

As well as winning the transcontinental air race, Mrs. Miller later flew her Bullet from Pittsburg to Cuba. On the return trip unforeseen strong winds took her miles off course, compromising her very survival. With poor visibility and fuel tanks nearly empty it was largely good luck that she found the Andros Islands, in the Bahamas. If she had missed

them, she would have flown on into the Atlantic with no hope of being seen again.

Had that happened, it would have been the complete opposite of the fate awaiting her *Red Rose* partner, Bill Lancaster. In 1932 he undertook to fly one of Charles Kingsford Smith's record-breaking Avro Avian planes from England to South Africa. He disappeared en route, not over water, but over the scorching, arid Sahara desert.

The complexities of Jessie "Chubbie" Miller's private life later eclipsed her reputation as a flier. The fame she achieved in the 1930s when she was the darling of the American press faded as rapidly as it grew.

Left: Jessie "Chubbie" Miller in the white flying gear she wore during her racing career in America.

Opposite page: Mrs. Miller's notorious Alexander Bullet flies over New York. Five refueling stops were made during her performance in the transcontinental race across the United States from New York to Los Angeles. She flew the same machine back to New York to make yet another record; the flight time to New York was three hours faster than her trip out; just 21 hours, 47 minutes. She now held the records for flights both ways.

DHMarshall 93

AMELIA EARHART

FAME FOR A DASHING DAME

Amelia Earhart was a feminist, and well before the word became fashionable in the 1970s. She wanted to do, and could do, what most men did when they took to the air. She became an expert mechanic, she studied navigation, and she crashed airplanes and walked away from them. She owned her own plane in the roaring 1920s, and was the first woman to fly the Atlantic.

Her disappearance in the Pacific on her last trail-blazing adventure is still one of the unexplained aviation mysteries of the twentieth century. It was quite a record for a girl born in the American town of Atchison, Kansas, in 1897. Amelia later said she had seen her first plane at the age of 10 at the Iowa State fair "a thing of rusty wire and wood— I was much more interested in an absurd hat I had just purchased for 15 cents."

Amelia took her first joyride at the age of 23. Within weeks she was taking flying lessons. She was not a "natural" but her teacher, John Montijo, a tough ex-army man, who had taken over from Amelias's first instructor, Nita Snook, taught her well and made her do stunt-flying before he would allow her to fly solo. Amelia decided to buy her own plane, an under-powered Kinner biplane which she painted yellow and called *The Canary*.

In 1928, now living in Boston, Amelia was chosen by a publisher of adventure books to fly a Fokker Trimotor across the Atlantic. By now used to being in command of her own plane, this time she would be, in fact, a passenger but with a pilot's understanding of the dangers. The plane was to be piloted by Bill Stultz, a superb 28-year-old flier and Lou Gordon, flight mechanic. The aircraft, named *Friendship*, was previously owned by Commander Byrd and was fitted with pontoons (floats), for alighting on water.

First they flew the *Friendship* from Boston to Trepassy, Newfoundland, and there, on Sunday June 17 they tried to take off. Having twice failed to lift from the water, they made a desperate decision. They dumped fuel, reducing

from 830 gallons (3,150 liters) to 700 gallons (2,650 liters) which, even with favorable forecast tail winds, left little margin for error. Eventually, after a three-mile (five-kilometer) takeoff run, they clawed their way into the air. One engine, saturated with spray, took nearly an hour to build to full power. The time was 2:15 P.M., British summer time.

They battled throughout the night, flying in fog by instruments. Then their radio gave up. At 8:00 A.M. they passed ships sailing below. Later, with clouds down to 500 feet (150 meters) they saw a small fleet of fishing vessels, and about an hour after that, uncertain of their position, they saw through the mists what they thought to be Ireland. Stultz brought the *Friendship* down and tied up to a buoy. They had about 50 gallons (227.5 liters) of fuel left—it would not feed the carburetors for long.

The trio was not in Ireland, but at Burry Port in South Wales. They had landed at 12:40 P.M after a flight of 20 hours, 49 minutes. Nobody came to meet them. Although people waved at them from the shore, it was not for nearly an hour after alighting that some men came out in a boat to investigate. The next day they fueled up and flew on to Southampton where they were greeted enthsiastically by surging crowds of people, reporters, and newsreel cameramen.

Overnight, Amelia Earhart was transformed into an international celebrity. She became one of the best-known and respected American women, an icon for every woman who wanted to take her place as an individual in a fast-changing world. After the success of the *Friendship* flight, Amelia took up competitive flying and set several records. Her main objective was to help promote flying as a safe means of transportation and, always a competitive person, she also wanted to keep her name in the news.

Left: Amelia Earhart, or "A. E." as she referred to herself, bore such a striking resemblance to Charles Lindbergh that she could have been his sister. As a small child, she did all the things girls are not supposed to do. She was a good shot with a rifle, climbed trees, and because of it was generally considered a tomboy. It seems even as a girl, she was out to do all the things that men are good at, and to do them better. After schooling, she became a nurse's aid and helped care for wounded soldiers during World War I. Then, one Christmas Day, her father took her to a flying display. Her dream to be a pilot never wavered from that moment.

George Palmer Putman, journalist, publisher, and publicist, was the man who managed Amelia and organized her initial publicity. They had met when he was helping choose the female pilot for the transatlantic flight in 1928. They later married. George, or "G. P." as Amelia called him, suffered from air sickness so never flew with Amelia, but he encouraged her and helped plan her major flights, arranged her publicity, and built her image.

On May 20, 1932, Amelia set out from Harbor Grace, in Newfoundland, to fly solo across the Atlantic to Paris. Her aircraft was a Lockheed Vega, bought in 1929 and modified with extra fuel tanks and a new 500-horsepower supercharged Pratt & Whitney Wasp engine. She had spent months gaining experience in instrument flying— necessary for night flying and to cope with cloud and heavy fog expected to be encountered during her flight. Though she suffered mechanical troubles—the altimeter failed so she couldn't be accurate about her true height and the exhaust manifold split causing engine vibration which worsened as the hours went by—Amelia flew on. At one point, with the wings iced up, the Vega went into a spin and when she switched to her reserve fuel tank, petrol

Right: The Fokker VII 3M in which Amelia Earhart flew as a passenger across the Atlantic was normally fitted with a wheeled undercarriage. The Friendship model used on the 1928 flight was fitted with pontoons to give it a chance of survival should it need to ditch in the Atlantic.

began to leak into the cockpit which, combined with the exhaust flames flaring from the split exhaust, caused her considerable tension.

As soon as she saw land, she searched for a suitable landing place, coming down gracefully in a long, sloping meadow. A lone, astonished farmer was the only observer. Amelia cut the engine, and climbed out of the Vega. "Where am I?" she asked. "In Gallagher's pasture!" he replied.

She had flown 2,026 miles (3,260 kilometers) in 14 hours, 54 minutes and had landed in Culmore, near Londonderry, Northern Ireland. In doing so, she carved a new record for having flown the Atlantic in the shortest time in either direction. And she had cemented her reputation as the world's most accomplished woman pilot.

Left: Soon after her passenger flight across the Atlantic, Amelia bought the Avro Avian flown from Africa to England by the famous English flier, Lady Heath. The aircraft is shown after Amelia had hit a ditch when she landed at Pittsburgh in 1928 while making a solo flight across America. Her sterling effort was recreated in 2002 by Dr. Carlene Mendietta flying a similar Avro Avian, superbly restored by Australian Lang Kidby.

On June 1, 1937, with her trusted navigator Fred Noonan, Amelia Earhart took off from Miami in her silver and red Lockheed Electra to fly around the world on an equatorial route. "I want to fly right around the middle of the world," she said. Noonan was in his forties with a reputation as one of the world's top aerial navigators. He had served with the British Navy in World War I, then studied aerial navigation at the Weems School of Navigation at Annapolis before working for Pan-Am as a navigation instructor.

With the Electra fitted with the latest in communication and navigational aids, plus a Sperry autopilot to help on the long hops, they moved effectively from Miami to Puerto Rico, then on to Brazil, across the Atlantic to Africa, to the Mediterranean, Pakistan, India, Burma (now Myanmar), Thailand, Singapore, Indonesia, to Darwin, Australia, and then to Lae in Papua New Guinea. The next leg was the longest. They would fly to Howland Island, a distance of 2,556 miles (4,115 kilometers).

With a heavy load of fuel, Amelia lined up on the runway and at precisely 00:00 G.M.T. (10:30 A.M. Lae time) started her takeoff. There was no wind and observers reported that the plane lumbered along, only becoming airborne at the very end of the runway which dropped 25 feet (7.6 meters) into the sea, and that the Electra was flying so low over the water that the propellers were throwing spray.

Amelia kept in touch with Lae by radio until she flew out of range. From then on, radio contact with the coast-guard vessel, *Itasca*, became increasingly confused. The ship's radio officers began to get faint messages from Amelia, but it appeared she was not receiving theirs. Eventually, after 18 hours of flying, they began to get strong signals from the Electra, but again, no indication whether their replies were getting through.

Then some ominous words from Amelia: "We must be on you but cannot see you but gas is running low. Been unable to reach you on my radio." At 18:50 G.M.T., briefly, Amelia and *Itasca* were in two-way communication. Responding to the message: "*Itasca* to K.H.A.Q.Q. Go ahead on 3,105 or 500 cycles," Amelia radioed: "K.H.A.Q.Q. calling *Itasca*. We received your signals but unable to get a minimum. Please take a bearing on us and answer 3,105 with voice."

The ship kept trying to contact the Electra again, to tell them the radio signals had been too poor for them to get a reading. Then, at 20:14 G.M.T., Amelia's voice was heard for the last time in a hurried, almost incoherent call. "K.H.A.Q.Q. to *Itasca*. We are on line position 175 dash 337. Will repeat this message on 6,210 kilocycles. We are running north and south."

That was the last anyone heard from Amelia Earhart and Fred Noonan.

PROPOSED ROUTE ACROSS THE PACIFIC, 1937

Above: This sketch map shows the intended route of Amelia Earhart's Electra from Lae, New Guinea, to the isolated Howland Island, a distance of 2,556 miles (4,115 kilometers).

Opposite page: Amelia Earhart's Lockheed Vega is shown here flying into the rising sun on her solo flight across the Atlantic in 1932. In his book Revolution of the Sky *Richard Sanders Allen notes that this distinctive aircraft was, in fact, a hybrid. Its fuselage was taken from a scrapped Vega and mated with a new engine and wings. The end result was said by some to be one of the best Vegas ever built.*

Earhart fitted new instruments and a new drift sight, two compasses and a directional gyro. A few months later Amelia flew this aircraft to a solo American transcontinental record. She then flew a similar Vega on a record-making flight from Newark to Mexico and, in 1935, became the first woman to fly 2,400 miles (3,860 kilometers) solo from mainland America to Hawaii.

Earhart's Lockheed Electra 10E, 1937

SIR FRANCIS CHICHESTER

MAD ABOUT MOTHS AND MATH

Francis Chichester, 1931

"Mad Dogs and Englishmen Go Out in the Midday Sun"—this hit-song chorus, written by British playwright-songwriter Noel Coward in the 1930s, fitted perfectly with the antics of a thin, wiry Englishman in New Zealand in 1929. He could be seen in Auckland at the wheel of an open car trying to take sun shots with a sextant while driving down the street. Even without his car he would try to line up the sun on his sextant while running on the footpaths or across fields. Mad? No. Methodical and dedicated? Yes. Like a first-class athlete, he was in training for a navigational marathon.

Francis Chichester was to become one of Britain's most revered twentieth-century heroes. He was a born adventurer—courageous, physically tough, and a brilliant mathematician.

At the age of 18 in 1919, he walked out of Marlborough College in England, farewelled his family and with £10 in his pocket, left, vowing to return when he had made £20,000. He worked his passage to New Zealand as a stoker on a steam ship. There he earned a living as a lumberjack, coal miner, gold prospector, and salesman before making a small fortune as a property developer. With a wad of money in the bank, he paid for flying lessons, then in 1929 he headed back to Britain where he bought a little De Havilland Gypsy Moth biplane built of timber and linen. He resolved to fly it to Australia.

He flew a shake-down cruise around Europe, reveling in this new-found outlet for his love of math—pilot navigation. Thrilled with his small plane, and self-assured, he immediately set off for Australia. For a pilot of so little experience it was a devil-may-care thing to do. Only two solo flights had ever been made on the route before, both with seasoned fliers in the cockpits. Yet, with iron will, icy concentration, and an almost superhuman ability to overcome desperate situations, he made good progress all the way to Australia.

The harsh, unforgiving land at the top end of Australia was the most difficult terrain he had encountered and nearly cost Francis his life. Leaving Brunette Downs—a cattle station the size of Belgium—he flew into thick haze. Unable to locate his position from a sketchy map, he was forced to land near a desolate and muddy water bore as night fell. Next morning he took off as a strong wind again whipped up hazy conditions.

He had just over 30 minutes of fuel left. Chichester flew out about 15 miles (24 kilometers) in an attempt to fix his position. Now desperate, he turned, intending to land back again at the bore when he saw a flash of sun reflected through the haze. It was a tin shed roof at Rocklands station, where he landed safely. Had he stayed at the remote water bore he would surely have starved to death.

The forced landing made him realize, as he had now decided to continue flying on around the world, that he would need to improve his navigation methods. To be able to plot his course over featureless deserts and oceans, he would need to work out latitude and longitude from the sun or stars by using a sextant. He would have to become a mariner in the sky.

Chichester flew on from Australia to New Zealand where he embarked on intensive training. He started taking sights while driving a car, or while running on footpaths. Finally, he achieved the impossible—making accurate sightings while on the run.

He aimed for the same results while flying his plane. He found he could be a hundred miles (160 kilometers) out following his early aerial sun shots. But soon he became the master. He juggled the delicate sextant and the flying controls, checked his watch to the split second, then, working with complex formulae from a nautical almanac and using his sight tables, he'd pinpoint his position. He could do all this in a cramped open cockpit, blasted by noise, wind, and weather. In his book *The Lonely Sea and the Sky,* Sir Francis told of the blood-curdling antics the plane went through while he was taking his sights. His book recounts the first navigational experience with the sextant as he continued his world-girdling attempt; flying from New Zealand, Chichester had to be sure to locate his first stop, Norfolk Island, which was but a speck in the mighty Pacific Ocean. If he made an error of half a degree over nearly 500 miles (805 kilometers) he would be a dead man. Until now, Hawaii had been the smallest and most difficult target attempted by any solo pilot. It was 7 degrees wide for fliers coming from San Francisco. Many pilots disappeared trying to hit Hawaii. To reach Norfolk Island was 14 times smaller and far more difficult to hit.

During the flight, an unforeseen wind change caused the Gypsy Moth to drift off track. Changing course in mid-ocean with nothing other than faith in his own sextant reading and drift sights to go on was a huge effort of will for Chichester. However he was able to make those decisions and found landfall as predicted. Landing safely at Norfolk Island confirmed his abilities as a top-rank aerial navigator.

Francis's world circumnavigation attempt was brought to an abrupt halt in Japan when his plane met with a horrific accident by hitting power lines. After recovering, Chichester returned to England where he was honored by being the first pilot to receive the now coveted British Empire's Johnson Memorial Trophy for the year's best feat of airmanship.

He set up a successful map printing business, then started applying his navigational skills to sailing small boats. His wife named his yachts Gypsy Moth after his beloved biplane. During World War II he created vital new navigational systems for military pilots. After the war, he sailed a history-making solo voyage across the Atlantic and around the world. For this achievement he received his knighthood.

Sir Francis Chichester's little De Havilland Gypsy Moth no longer exists, but his Gypsy Moth IV, the famous well-traveled yacht, stands proudly on longitude zero in Greenwich, England—the hallowed birthplace of astronomical navigation—as a fitting memorial to the remarkable man and his unique navigational skills.

Francis Chichester flies his De Havilland Gypsy Moth, Elijah, over the spectacular Lord Howe Island. The little biplane was severely damaged here in a gale, so Chichester, with help from the islanders, spent nine weeks virtually rebuilding the wings before continuing his attempted circumnavigation of the globe. Lord Howe Island, along with Norfolk Island, was one of the two tiny specks of land that Chichester had to locate on his flight from New Zealand to Australia. Finding these pinpoints in the Tasman Sea called for masterly navigation. He was piloting an aircraft flying so slowly that contrary winds could create up to 25 degrees of drift. Chichester faced the real danger of missing the tiny islands and flying into oblivion. However his unique navigational skills pulled him through.

JEAN GARDNER BATTEN C.B.E.

BEAUTIFUL, DUTIFUL DAUGHTER SPREADS HER WINGS

"The weather was too good to last. One hundred and fifty miles out from Africa the sky became flecked with clouds and gradually completely overcast. Heavy rain clouds seemed to open and pour their contents down …the rain resembled a great black curtain. I remember the weather forecast, and I thought, either go back now while there is time, or go through it."

This was the account of a woman of 24, alone, without radio or autopilot, flying above the Atlantic Ocean, headed for Brazil. The year was 1935 and the woman was a New Zealander, Jean Batten. Many say she was the greatest woman flier of all time.

When she landed safely at Port Natal, Brazil, Jean Batten had registered a new record— England to Brazil, via Casablanca and Senegal, in an elapsed time of 16 hours, 15 minutes. She had chopped a day off the previous best time to claim a world record for any type of plane flown by man or woman.

This daughter of Ellen Batten was born in 1909 in the tiny tourist town of Rotorua in New Zealand's North Island. She was christened Jane Gardner, but came to be called Jean. Her father, dentist Fred Batten, and the family moved to Auckland some years later. As the result of a domestic split, Jean stayed with her mother Ellen, while Fred took his three sons to live with him. But when she was 17, Jean accompanied Fred to listen to Charles Kingsford Smith talk at a dinner in honor of Smithy's record-breaking flight across the Pacific. That evening Jean announced to the famous aviator that she was going to learn to fly.

Fred tried to discourage Jean's flying ambitions, but during a trip to Sydney with Ellen in 1929, Jean talked her way into a joy flight with Kingsford Smith in his famous *Southern Cross*. Her flame was lit.

Jean Batten, 1936

A year later, mother and daughter were in England where Jean joined the Airplane Club and started flying lessons at the Stag Lane aerodrome. With a private flying *A* license in her handbag, Jean and her mother went back to New Zealand in 1932. Within months, Jean gained her commercial license. Now she was ready for action: she would fly, solo, from England to New Zealand.

With dark hair, sparkling eyes, and a winning smile, Batten found she could attract and manipulate men, inducing them to provide the money to feed her flying ambitions. In 1932, Victor Doree—scion of a wealthy linen-merchant family—gave Jean a secondhand De Havilland Gypsy Moth aircraft previously owned by Edward, the Prince of Wales.

Jean intended to use it to beat the 1930 record of Amy Johnson who had flown from England to Australia in 20 days. Her first two attempts in 1933 failed—once through engine failure and once when she damaged the Gypsy Moth in Italy after running out of fuel.

She obtained more funds—one bewitched admirer gave her his entire life savings. On May 8, 1934, in her second Gypsy Moth, Jean took off aiming for a new world record. She flew London to Darwin in 14 days, 20 hours, and 30 minutes, with 16 stops along the way. She cut five days off Amy Johnson's 1930 record. Overnight, this attractive New Zealander, in her immaculate white flying suit, helmet, and goggles, became an international star. In the depths of the Great Depression, Jean Batten's solo victory lifted the spirits of all New Zealanders. She sailed into Auckland from Sydney to a rapturous welcome and weeks of speeches and celebrations. Returning to Sydney, she then flew her Gypsy Moth back to England—taking 17 days, 15 hours, and becoming the first woman to make that return flight.

Above: Jean Batten's 1934 record-breaking De H Gypsy Moth with a spare propeller strapped to the fuselage.

With celebrity status, cinema appearances, and an endorsement deal with Wakefield Castrol Oil Jean had enough funds to invest in a racy Percival Gull 6 monoplane (G-ADPR) with a 200-horsepower Gypsy 6 engine. In 1935 in her Gull, she broke the England to Brazil record. In 1936, she flew England to New Zealand solo, in a record 11 days, 45 minutes elapsed time (which included two and a half days in Sydney).

In the last dangerous Tasman Sea leg Batten flew through heavy rainstorms nearly all the way. After nine and a half tension-filled hours, she was afraid she'd lost her way, then— relief: "A dark blur loomed ahead through the rain … within a few seconds I swept over New Plymouth, absolutely on course!" She had clocked another record, the fastest ever flight across the Tasman of 10 hours, 10 minutes.

Never had New Zealanders given their hearts to anyone as they did to this lovely, courageous woman. When she returned to Britain in 1937, she established another remarkable solo record—Australia to England in 5 days, 18 hours, and 15 minutes. She decided that she'd achieved her goals. She had made her last long-distance flight.

After World War II, Jean lived with her mother in Jamaica, then Spain. When her mother died in 1966, she lived alone in Spain. Once she traveled to New Zealand in 1977 as guest of honor for the opening of the Aviation Pioneers' Pavilion in Auckland. She returned to Spain, then moved to Majorca. Until documentary film makers tracked her down, no one knew that she had died from an infected dog bite and had been buried in a pauper's grave at Palma. In New Zealand, The Jean Batten Terminal at Auckland's International Airport keeps her name alive.

Above: Landfall! An amazing moment of truth on a rough 9 hour, 29 minute-flight across the Tasman from Australia to New Zealand. Flying low in murky weather Jean Batten holds her charted course but with an increasing belief that she had overshot New Zealand and was heading for oblivion into the vast waters of the Pacific. Suddenly, a rocky outcrop appeared and moments later she sped over New Pymouth, her planned landfall. Jean used no radio aids, no autopilot, and no satellite navigation or global positioning, yet her accurate landfalls using dead-reckoning (a chart, arithmetic, a compass, and a watch) proved her navigation to be of the highest order.

Flying over oceans today is commonplace yet there were many risks involved in such flights in the 1930s. Jean Batten would have been aware that so much could go wrong; simple things such as a blocked fuel line or a broken valve spring could have sent her to a watery grave; meteorological forecasts were sketchy so a contrary wind or an unexpectedly vicious cold front could have meant running short of fuel—or death. Contemplating the odds stacked against her makes an observer realize that Jean Batten was an exceptionally courageous woman who deserved every accolade awarded her. Her aircraft was the trusty Percival Vega Gull Jean.

NANCY BIRD-WALTON AO, OBE

Nancy Bird-Walton

EARLY BIRD OF THE AUSTRALIAN OUTBACK

Nancy had the surname for it—"Bird"—so she aimed to fly. At 17, in 1933, she obtained her aviator's license—one of the first women in Australia to make it. The following year, she won her commercial license and Charles Kingsford Smith—already a flying legend—became her first instructor. It was still a man's world and Kingsford Smith told her so: "Nancy, you know I don't approve of women in aviation—it's not the right place for them."

But Nancy proved him wrong. A few years later, she was running a regular aerial run of tours for the Far West Children's Health Scheme in some of Australia's most isolated country areas. Nancy's task was to bring medical assistance to what one author classified as the "Never-Never." Early in Australia's development phase—after the arrival of the British First Fleet to colonize the country—intrepid men and women aiming to carve a future out of this often inhospitable land, established vast sheep and cattle properties far away from the early cities. As a result, many people in these remote areas were far from medical help when it was needed.

So the Flying Doctor Service was started in 1928, and expanded to cover mainly inland areas in central Australia.

But there was still a need for regular clinics to service smaller settlements, outback towns, and remote properties in other parts of the country so the Far West Children's Health Scheme was set up in the sprawling state of New South Wales. As part of the scheme, the young Nancy Bird flew nurses in her plane on a regular basis to run health clinics in isolated towns around the state.

The weather in the outback made flying extremely hazardous. Climatic conditions were influenced by vast distances, extremes of temperature mostly at the top end of the scale, sudden and unexpected changes in weather, bushfires, lightning, and thunderstorms—all very inhospitable when flying a small light plane. Bird's first aircraft was a De Havilland Cirrus Moth biplane, which she later swapped for a handsome silver De Havilland Leopard Moth—still small, but better for getting nurses to the clinics on time. Before she had taken on the Far West job, Nancy had barnstormed in her Cirrus Moth. She had entered and won the Ladies' Trophy in the 1936 Brisbane to Adelaide Air Race.

In 1938, she was invited by the Dutch Airline, K.L.M., to tour in Europe, during which time she covered 43,000 miles (68,800 kilometers). While in Britain Nancy met and later married English photographer, Charles Walton. Shortly after returning to Australia, she was appointed commandant of the Women's Air Training Corp, a post she held for the duration of World War II. In the 1950s she flew in the American Powder Puff Derby—the all-women's transcontinental air race. She founded the Australian Women Pilots Association, and is an honorary life member of the Royal Aero Club, NSW. Her honors include the Order of Australia and the Order of the British Empire. Nancy Bird, now in her eighties, still flies at every opportunity—but these days as a passenger.

Left: A patient is lifted from Nancy's Leopard Moth on one of her missions in the outback of Australia.

A living legend, Nancy remains most proud of the way she used her plane to bring medical assistance to families in outback Australia. In a book of her memoirs, she tells of a man on a dusty outback property waiting for desperately needed medical help. When he telephoned for help, he was shocked to hear the pilot's voice on the other end of the line. All he could say was, "My God, it's a woman!"

Opposite page: Nancy told of one of her experiences: "There was a violent storm over the far west of New South Wales. Towering cumulo-nimbus clouds with all kinds of dangerous down drafts if you were unlucky enough to be caught in one of them. Micro-bursts of wind flattened trees and any tin sheds that happened to be in the way. The visibility was so poor with rain and hail that I decided to fly only a few feet above the telegraph line. This was the only way which gave me a clue of where we were going. I simply couldn't see ahead, but I knew if I stuck to the telegraph posts and the wires, I'd eventually reach clear air and our destination. My passenger was a nurse. I told her to keep her eyes peeled out the other side of the cabin and let me know if she could see any landmarks she knew. She wasn't much help, really. I think she was petrified! I can understand why she was frightened. I wasn't all that confident myself that we would make it. I was about 20 at the time."

JACQUELINE COCHRAN

FROM FOSTER TO FASTER

It could only happen in America. A young orphaned girl—Jacqueline—was handed over to foster parents, so poor they had to live in a shack with tar paper instead of glass in the windows and a packed dirt floor in hard scrabble woods in Northern Florida. Her foster father was a saw miller and at eight years of age, when the family moved to Georgia looking for work, the barefoot girl worked in a cotton mill for six cents an hour. She became a beauty shop operator, had a stint at nursing, sold dress patterns, graduated to the cosmetics counter, gave herself a name she liked, founded her own cosmetic company then—in part to promote her own brand of cosmetics—learned to fly. She married a millionaire, became America's fastest woman pilot, then in wartime as a ferry pilot took a Lend Lease bomber across the Atlantic to Britain. She organized American women pilots to deliver war planes in Britain. She wound up beating most male pilots by flying faster than the speed of sound. Among her decorations were the French Legion of Honor and the U.S. Distinguished Flying Cross with two Oak Clusters. Some story. Some woman.

"Jackie" among the flying fraternity in the lively air-mad days of the mid-thirties meant only one person, Jacqueline Cochran. She gave herself that name because she never did find out who her parents were. She chose Cochran from a telephone book when she was 18 years old. She thought she was born near Muscogee in Florida. Her foster mother guessed she was born in May 1910.

Jackie tackled everything with a driving urge to win, a desire to learn, and a staggering tenacity. When she was planning her cosmetics business she met Floyd Odlum, a millionaire business man. He was the first to suggest she learn to fly, and eventually bet her she wouldn't learn to fly in the six weeks of an advertised pilot's course. Jackie did it in three weeks! On her first solo flight, the engine stopped and she brought the plane in for a perfect dead-stick landing. She thought that the instructor had organized the engine shutdown but he hadn't. He later said she was just a natural flier. That was in 1922. By 1934 she was such an experienced pilot that she entered the MacRobertson

Above: Jackie Cochran 1945

Left: In 1938 Maj. Alexander Seversky and Jackie Cochran were presented with the Gar Wood Trophy by Wood who was an aviation and motoring enthusiast. The aircraft shown is the Seversky 1XP, a prototype of the P-35, which Cochran flew. Seversky asked Jackie to fly a P-35 in the Bendix race to prove that if a woman could fly a "souped-up" version safely, then Army Air Corps pilots could. Later the highly effective Republic Thunderbolt fighter of World War II was developed from this aircraft. Alexander Kartveli, engineer, was the design genius who worked with Seversky throughout their professional lives.

Right: This Northrop T-38 Talon jet was similar to the one in which Jackie Cochran flew before converting to the Lockheed Starfighter. Because this jet had similar flying characteristics, the T-38 was used to train pilots before they flew Kelly Johnson's SR-71 Blackbird reconnaissance aircraft.

London to Australia Air Race, but her plane was so unstable she had to withdraw after flying to London from America. The next year she started her cosmetics business and also entered her first Bendix air race. In 1936 she married Floyd Bostwyck Odlum, but insisted that she continued to be addressed as Jackie Cochran. During her flying career Jackie held more distance, speed, and altitude records than any other U.S. pilot. She started off by being the first woman to be a competitor in the Bendix Transcontinental Air Race in 1935 and in 1938 was the first woman to win the race outright. In 1953 in a Sabre jet she broke the world speed record for both men and women. Aided by Colonel (later General) Charles "Chuck" Yeager and other test pilots, Jackie learned to fly first the F-86 Sabre jet, then a Northrop twin jet T-38. Once she mastered them, she became the first woman to fly faster than Mach 1—the speed of sound. The first time was in the Sabre. In 1961, in the T-38, she set eight major speed records. Finally, during 1964 in a Lockheed F-100 Starfighter, Jackie flew at a speed of 1,429 $\frac{1}{3}$ miles (2,286.9 kilometers) per hour over a 9 $\frac{1}{3}$-mile (15-kilometer) course, establishing a women's international speed record, traveling at Mach 2—twice the speed of sound.

Jackie Cochran built a network of powerful friends, among them General "Hap" Arnold who, with the agreement of

Lord Beaverbrook, the British Minister of Supply, encouraged Jackie to ferry a Lockheed Hudson bomber across the Atlantic when England desperately needed war supplies. Against angry protests from male pilots who didn't want her involved, she piloted the Hudson from Newfoundland to Britain, but was not allowed to take off or land the plane. She had to let her male copilot do that.

Cochran stayed on in Britain and was made a captain in the British Air Force Auxiliary, where she organized a group of 25 American women pilots to join her, ferrying military aircraft from factories to the airfields where they were needed for combat. In 1942, General Arnold pressured her to return to America to help organize a training scheme for women pilots to provide a similar service for the U.S. Army Air Force. The following year she was made director of the specially formed Women's Air Force Service Pilots. Jackie called them W.A.S.P.s. Twenty-five thousand women applied to be trained, 1,830 were accepted, and 1,074 graduated to fly every type of plane from trainers to Superfortress bombers.

It was the lobbying Jackie Cochran did after the end of World War II that prompted the decision to set up a separate U.S. Air Force instead of the Army, Navy, and Marines each having their own. Jackie retired from the Air Force Reserve with the rank of colonel in 1970. She continued as special consultant to N.A.S.A. until her death in 1980.

The fact that women are now U.S. Air Force fighter pilots and N.A.S.A. has women astronauts is undoubtedly due in part to her efforts. After her death, General Chuck Yeager said: "Sometimes even Jackie Cochran couldn't believe what she had accomplished."

Above: Jackie Cochran raced across America in this Seversky P-35—lucky Number 13—at around 16,000 feet (4,877 meters) in the cold, early-morning light, maneuvering to fill the left-wing fuel tank. On this day in August 1938 she won the Bendix Trophy for flying the fastest time between Los Angeles and Cleveland. She touched down in Cleveland at the end of the race, then immediately flew on to New York to create the fastest transcontinental record of 10 hours, 27 minutes, and 55 seconds. Jackie had experienced fuel problems that caused her P-35 to become right-wing heavy. So, as she says in her autobiography, she "kept repeating these strange aerobatic maneuvers" so the fuel would flow simultaneously from both wings to keep the aircraft balanced.

A beauty operator ceased to exist and an aviator was born.

JACKIE COCHRAN, AFTER OBTAINING HER PILOT'S LICENSE

Dr. Clyde Fenton

A PAIN IN THE NECK FOR SOME

Dr. Clyde Fenton, 1935

Seven years before Australia's Royal Flying Doctor Service set up a headquarters in the center of Australia at Alice Springs in 1938, Clyde Fenton, a medical doctor of adventurous spirit and with a huge sense of humor, set up his own flying doctor service and flew his own aircraft to outlandish places in the "Never Never" of Northern Australia. He based his operations in the small town of Katherine, near Darwin.

Single-handedly, Fenton looked after the whole of the vast Northern Territory, one sixth of the area of Australia. He flew 3,000 hours and 250,000 miles (402,250 kilometers) during his six years of devoted work at a time when, in his own words, "every flight was an adventure." Yet he was refused permission to join the Flying Doctor Service.

Dr. John Flynn, who formed the Flying Doctor Service in 1928, worked to the philosophy that doctors were doctors and pilots were pilots. It had been suggested that this dictum may have arisen only when he received an application from Clyde Fenton to join the Service.

Flynn was aware that Fenton was a dedicated doctor of medicine, and that he was also typically Australian in his high-spirited behavior and his contempt for bureaucratic

convention. Such a man who regularly flouted authority and was the bane of all officials could cause problems in Flynn's organization. So, as an excuse for not employing Fenton, John Flynn is said to have thought up his "one man, one job" working philosophy to keep Fenton out.

Fenton went on to disprove the philosophy. As he said in his autobiography, *Flying Doctor*, he passionately wanted to fly and from 1933 until the beginning of World War II, hundreds of sick and injured were to benefit from his love of flying and dedication to his medical practice.

His adventures and misadventures were legion. He often flew at night, landing by moonlight or fire light, or guided by motor-vehicle headlamps. His privately owned aircraft, a De H Gypsy Moth, had two open cockpits which made transportation of sick or badly injured patients very difficult. The government eventually recognized his excellent work and supplied an airplane with a small cabin for his patients.

Fenton's most outrageous run-in with authority came in 1936. His sister died suddenly. Clyde decided to fly and join his mother who had been with her at the time but there was a problem—they were both in China, a dilemma for normal people but not for the intrepid doctor. He was granted leave by his base hospital, fitted an extra fuel tank in his plane without the authority of the Civil Aviation Department, borrowed a life jacket and flew there in his Gypsy Moth.

The trip was an epic of ignoring bureaucracy and red tape. It was aggravated by tropical storms and the fact that Fenton hadn't obtained permission to land at any of the countries through which he planned to pass. His extraordinary, illegal flight took him to the destinations of Koepang, Singapore, Penang, Bangkok, Hanoi, Hong Kong, and finally Satow, in China. Typically he would be asked, "Where is the Certificate of Airworthiness for your machine? Where is your pilot's license? Where is your logbook?" Of course, Clyde had none of these items with him. Not surprisingly, events finally caught up with him and he was arrested on arrival in China.

The journey back was a repeat of the outward trip. He left (escaped would be more accurate) without permission, flouting every regulation, but still managed to attend a medical convention in Singapore (on the subject of malaria), as he passed through.

During World War II he gave up his medical practice and joined the R.A.A.F. but that's another story.

Left: The De H Fox Moth, seen at a remote property near Katherine in Australia's far north, was supplied to Dr. Fenton by the Australian Government as a replacement for his own private Gypsy Moth that had been used for his flying doctor missions. The tiny, enclosed cabin of the new aircraft could accommodate a stretcher, patient, and an attendant. Fenton still had to sit in an open cockpit, exposed to heat, cold, wind, rain, and dust.

Opposite page: Clyde Fenton in his De H Gipsy Moth in the early morning over Bathurst Island in the far north of Australia. Typical monsoonal cumulo-nimbus clouds which built up behind him made flying conditions dangerous later in the day.

SIDNEY COTTON

SPY IN THE SKY

Sidney Cotton was infuriating. He was one of those men who was masterful, insightful, very clever, completely sure of being right, and endowed with unbelievable courage. He was the first to use camouflage on his World War II airplanes and invented a remarkable flying suit that kept out the cold. Named the Sidcot flying suit, it was worn by aircrews in two world wars. Cotton also became a trailblazer in aerial photography in peace and wartime.

Cotton's impatience with second-rate thinking showed up in 1915 in World War I. At the age of 21, he was in command of a special unit in the Royal Naval Air Service and was ordered to send one of his aircraft to bomb a Zeppelin base in Germany. He refused. "The aircraft simply hasn't the range to do the job and get back," he said. Cotton was overruled. The bomber was sent, and as Cotton had predicted, the plane ran out of fuel over the North Sea. By luck, after three days the crew was found but not without loss of life—one rescuing aircraft was lost.

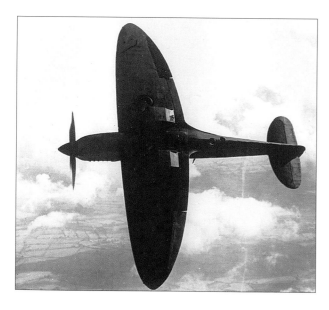

Left: The Supermarine Spitfire was Sidney Cotton's choice of aircraft for high speed, high altitude photographic reconnaissance. All armament was removed and special care was taken to preserve a smooth-skin surface. Many other aircraft types, such as the Lockheed Lightning and the De Havilland Mosquito, were later used for both high- and low-level photographic reconnaissance work throughout World War II. This Spitfire Mk. XI has two vertical camera apertures on the underside of the fuselage.

In disgust, Cotton resigned from the Navy and volunteered for the Royal Australian Flying Corp. He was rejected because of his "difficult temperament." Shortly after the end of World War II, Sidney planned to be the first pilot to fly from England to Cape Town—a dream that was shattered when he crashed on a beach in Italy.

Cotton pioneered aerial spotting for a Newfoundland sealing operation before he moved to aerial photography and survey work for map making. That led, in turn, to a management job—he became head of the Dufay Color Film company in Europe. His business contacts often took him across Europe in his Lockheed 12a twin-engined airliner—the 1930s equivalent of today's executive jet.

With the rise of Adolf Hitler and the obvious build-up of war planning by Germany, Cotton was approached by Col. Fred Winterbotham—an attaché in the British Embassy in Berlin. The colonel wanted Cotton to take photographs of military installations for the British Military Information Service, MI-6. Always ready for an adventure, Cotton equipped his Lockheed aircraft with three specially adapted Leica cameras, hidden behind sliding panels and operated from the pilot's seat. Often accompanied by a companion posing as another businessman but who was really Flt. Lt. "Shorty" Longbottom of the R.A.F., Sidney Cotton went

Sidney Cotton, 1916

... had he (Cotton) lived a few centuries earlier, he would have made a splendid buccaneer. He loved adventure for adventure's sake, continually defied the orthodox, and had a notable record of getting things done by hook or by crook. He also had a flair for inventing things ...

EVIDENCE IN CAMERA BY CONSTANCE BABINGTON-SMITH

photographing. He was able to supply photos of secret installations in Europe and the Middle East in the six months before the outbreak of war in 1939. It is said that his was the last plane to leave Berlin before war broke out. On the way to Britain he claimed to have photographed the German fleet as a passing shot.

Jeff Watson, a respected film and documentary maker has been researching Sidney Cotton's life as the subject of a television documentary. His probing suggests that although Sidney claimed and used the Lockheed 12a as his own, the aircraft was secretly provided and financed by the British intelligence services.

There was no doubting Cotton's razor-sharp mind—an ability to cut right to the core of a problem and then find a quick solution—often caused embarrassment to slower thinkers. For example, as soon as war was declared, the R.A.F. asked his advice on photo-reconnaissance techniques. They were using slow, medium bombers for photographic work. Discussing the pressing need for a specific set of photographs of Dutch seaports, Cotton told the R.A.F. their bombers would be shot out of the skies. "You must have fast, high-flying aircraft to get the shots you need," he told them. The senior officers, ignoring his advice, asked him to talk to their bomber crews anyway, at a briefing set up for the following day.

Sidney drove to Heston airport, fueled his pale green Lockheed—it was still a civilian aircraft—and made a dash to Holland, took the necessary shots, and next day turned up at the briefing with a pile of enlargements. Casually, he asked the senior officers if this was the sort of result they wanted. "Yes, indeed," was the reply, "but we couldn't expect this quality in wartime. When were these taken?" Cotton's reply was, "At 3:15 P.M. yesterday afternoon." There was an explosion of noisy protest. Before it subsided, Cotton had left.

Eventually the R.A.F. set up a special Photographic Reconnaissance Unit headed up by Sidney Cotton. Through the intervention of Winston Churchill, Cotton got the planes he wanted: Spitfire fighters. He modified them to carry his special cameras. As these units grew in number and in recognition of how vital photo reconnaissance was to military operations, their command was soon taken out of Cotton's prickly hands.

When the war was over, and after the partition of India, Cotton popped up once more, this time masterminding an airlift operation with a fleet of Lancaster bombers flying arms, food, and medical supplies to a group blockaded in Hyderabad. As always, he ran foul of people, particularly the Pakistani Government. He narrowly missed a bomb attempt on his life. Sidney Cotton died of natural causes in 1949 before he could carry out his lifelong intention—to return to his place of birth in Queensland, Australia.

Above: Sidney Cotton's civilian-registered Lockheed 12a—painted pale green in one of the several camouflage schemes he devised for high-flying photo-reconnaissance aircraft—was considered by Luftwaffe officers to be a "hot ship" and they often coaxed Cotton to allow them to fly with him. This he did while taking clandestine photographs of German military airfields. If the often very high-ranking officer sitting next to him in the copilot's seat showed any concern about flying over these forbidden zones, Cotton would say he had temporarily lost his bearings. Several hidden cameras were fitted behind sliding panels under the wings and fuselage and these were operated by a hidden button in the cockpit. He would calmly press the release button under his seat as he chatted away to his enthusiastic and unsuspecting passengers. The Lockheed is said to have been the last aircraft to leave Berlin in 1939 before the beginning of World War II and Cotton was close to being arrested by the Gestapo.

JOHN CUNNINGHAM

WAS IT A MOTTO THAT HELPED HIM TO SEE IN THE DARK?

Between World War I and World War II, groups of part-time fliers and ground staff in Britain formed auxiliary squadrons. They became a reserve force, which could be called upon in a national emergency. One of these R.A.F. auxiliary squadrons had as its motto the Latin phrase *si pacem para bellum* meaning "If you want peace, prepare for war." It was a motto well suited to John Cunningham who started his flying career at the age of 18 when he joined 604 County of Middlesex Squadron, Royal Air Force, in 1935. No one could predict that in dedicating himself to the motto's ideal, he would become Britain's greatest night-fighter in wartime and, in peacetime, an outstanding test pilot who would introduce the world and its travelers to the jet age as the first pilot to fly the Comet jetliner.

Born in South London in 1917, Cunningham left school in his teens to join the highly respected technical school run by the De Havilland Aircraft Company. It was while he was at the school that he signed up with the Middlesex auxiliary squadron and learned to fly, making his first solo in an Avro 504K before converting to the squadron's operational aircraft, the Hawker Demon. The Demon was a powerful two-seat biplane and though classed as a fighter, it was not a great advance on the Avro 504K, which had been designed for use in World War I. The Avros were still being used to train England's air force pilots and generally, Britain's operational aircraft showed little real progress over those used in the World War I conflict. It must have been very clear to Cunningham and his fellow pilots, playing out their mock-combat maneuvers, that their obsolete biplanes would scarcely provide effective resistance to an enemy attack. It was also clear in the dying days of the 1930s that an attack was almost inevitable.

When the inevitable happened and war was declared, Cunningham's squadron was equipped with Bristol Blenheims—cumbersome fighters hastily converted from a recently introduced twin-engined medium bomber. None-too-soon these were replaced with the heavily armed Bristol Beaufighter—one of the most successful twin-engined flying machines of the war. It was flying in Beaufighters that John Cunningham first came to the notice of the British public.

In the dark days when they desperately needed heroes, Cunningham was the first night fighter to shoot down an enemy bomber over Britain— a Junkers Ju88. It was not his last. Cunningham's "kills" brought headlines and praise. His successes in bringing down enemy raiders at night in the grim days of the German blitz on British cities became legendary. He was credited with an amazing ability to see in the dark, an almost superhuman night vision. Before long, the press dubbed him "Cat's Eyes" Cunningham—a nickname that stayed with him throughout the war.

The secret of Cunningham's cat's eyes was revealed years later. His Beaufighter was one of the first in the world to be fitted with a newly developed radar. John Cunningham's navigator, Jimmy Rawnsley, was also his radar operator. With teamwork they were able to use their radar to lock on to an enemy bomber. Rawnsley would track the marauding aircraft as a blip on his radar screen and guide Cunningham toward his victim. But this was nowhere as easy as it sounds; the pair, through hard work, trial and error, and some terrifying near misses, were able to hone their skills as they improved their kill rate. Technical improvements in the radar equipment helped as well. Together they were writing the rule book on the techniques of aerial night fighting.

Toward the end of the war, Cunningham was flying one of the most brilliant aircraft of the era—the famous molded plywood Mosquito. Designed by R. E. Bishop for De Havilland, powered by two 1,300-horsepower Rolls-Royce Merlin engines, and equipped with advanced radar in its night fighting role, it was a fitting plane for Group Captain Cunningham to finish his wartime career. He had become Britain's most famous night fighter, with a score of 19 victims. Among his decorations were the D.S.O. and two Bars, and the D.F.C. and Bar. Later he would be honored as a Commander of the British Empire (C.B.E.).

Left: John Cunningham 1968

Above right: The Bristol Beaufighter was one of those flown by John Cunningham in 604 Sqdn. R.A.F. The Beaufighter was one of the most deadly and heavily armed fighters of World War II. Its combination of four (20-millimeter) cannons and six .303 machine guns literally tore targets apart. However, it also took a toll on many inexperienced pilots and those who were not watchful of its idiosyncrasies. As with many operational airplanes, the "Beau" was not a forgiving machine. In Cunningham's hands, however, she was a pussycat. But then he was a perfectionist with the skills to go with it. His navigator, Jimmy Rawnsley, says in his autobiography Night Fighter *that even after a long operational flight, if Cunningham was not satisfied with the way he had landed the aircraft he would go round again and then "grease" it on to the runway. And he was talking about night landings, in weather conditions when most pilots would have been happy to arrive on the ground in any manner that would allow them to walk away from the airplane.*

As a pilot, his voice becomes crisp, impersonal, and firm, revealing how much he is the master of his situation.

A PILOT WHO SERVED IN THE 85TH SQUADRON COMMANDED BY
WING COMDR. JOHN CUNNINGHAM R.A.F., SPEAKING OF HIM

The De Havilland Mosquito Mk. 12 night fighter was one of the first of John Cunningham's 85 Sqdn. to be fitted with a modified nose that housed early model English night-fighting radar. Designed as a multi-role machine, the fighter version of this remarkable wooden aircraft had a flat, bulletproof windscreen and four 20-millimeter cannons. Its top speed, driven by two Rolls-Royce Merlin engines, was 370 miles (592 kilometers) per hour— though Cunningham, in pursuit of enemy aircraft, flew it beyond this speed. The bomber variation, with a perspex nose and split windscreen, could carry a larger bomb load than the four-engined Boeing B-17 Flying Fortress.

The Bristol Beaufighter, 1941

Left: L to R Jimmy Rawnsley and John Cunningham

The De H Mosquito Mk. 12, 1943

At the end of hostilities, John Cunningham rejoined De Havilland, this time not as a student but as test pilot. On the death of Geoffrey de Havilland in a high-speed flying accident in 1946, he took over the position of chief test pilot. In March 1948, in a De Hx 100 Vampire, he created a new world altitude record of 59,492 feet (18,145 meters), and in the following year on July 27, 1949, John took G-ALVG, the first De H 106 Comet passenger jet on its initial flight. He was the pilot to put all the marques of this first civil jet aircraft through their paces as well as being responsible for a team of test pilots who, with him, flight-tested the 17 successful aircraft types produced by De Havilland up to the time of his retirement in 1980.

The late 1940s were to be historic times for De Havilland and for jet propulsion. The company was set to introduce an aircraft that would change forever the business of transporting people by air. When it rolled out for its maiden flight on July 27, 1949, it looked truly magnificent with air intakes for its four Ghost jet engines sculpted into the wings of a handsome, silver bird. With test pilot John Cunningham at the controls, the De Havilland Comet was ready for take-off. It was the world's first jet-powered airliner.

The idea of a jet-propelled airliner was being discussed in Britain as early as 1941. By 1943 in the middle of the titanic war, a planning group (the Brabazon Committee) was drawing up specifications for a civilian aircraft of transatlantic capability, which could carry passengers and mail. They labeled it Brabazon Type 4. By the end of 1946, the new jetliner was taking shape on the drawing board, being designed to fly above 34,000 feet (10,500 metres), a height where jet engines could work most efficiently. When the Comet took off in July 1949 it flew as brilliantly as it looked.

As the first jet-powered airliner ever made, it faced an intensive testing program by the British Air Ministry. The plane had to undergo three years of close scrutiny and demanding checking by the Ministry, De Havilland, and British Overseas Airways Corporation.

B.O.A.C. was to take the Comet into commercial flying. No previous passenger carrier had ever been so thoroughly reviewed. Once all the hurdles had been jumped, the Comet flew its first passenger-carrying flight for B.O.A.C. from London to Johannesburg, South Africa, on May 2, 1952.

Comet was an overnight, world sensation. It flew twice as fast as its rivals, the Lockheed Constellation and the Douglas DC-7. It flew higher and so avoided bad weather. It had none of the vibration caused by piston engines and was considerably quieter in flight. If everything had gone to plan, De Havilland might today rule the world of air transport instead of Boeing and Airbus. But the Comet had a nasty sting in its tail.

Aircraft watchers swear that representatives of the Boeing company who saw the Comet jet airliner on display at the

The De H Vampire jet fighter

Above: In 1948, John Cunningham set a world altitude record in the De Havilland Vampire jet fighter of 59,492 feet (18,145 meters). The previous record had been set by an Italian, Lt. Col. Mario Pezzi, in a Caproni 161bis biplane. The Vampire was powered by a De Havilland Ghost jet engine of 4,400-pound (1,997.6-kilogram) static thrust. The flight was part of the high-altitude testing of this power plant. Eight feet (2.4 meters) was added to each wingtip of the airplane and 25 pounds (11.4 kilograms) weight of external paint rubbed off. Other unnecessary internal weighty objects were removed. A metal canopy with a porthole replaced the normal perspex hood.

Farnborough Air Show in 1950, blanched and returned to Seattle shaken by what they had seen. That is when Boeing put U.S.$15,000,000—one quarter of Boeing's net worth at the time—into designing and planning the 707 Airliner project.

Boeing had already built their radical B-47 bomber; it was first flown at Boeing field by test pilots Robert Robbins and Scott Osler in 1947. Boeing was the only American manufacturer with any experience in designing large jet aircraft and in their B-47 bomber they knew they had the fundamentals from which to build a better jetliner than the Comet. So while the Comet was up and flying the first jet air routes, Boeing were beavering away at their new design.

In its first year, Comet carried 28,000 passengers, and filled De Havilland's books with orders for more than 50 of the aircraft. Work commenced

The De H Comet prototype, 1949

The De H 108 Swallow, 1949

Left: Originally the Comet was conceived as a tail-less design so de Havilland instituted a research program, which culminated in the beautiful De H 108 Swallow research aircraft.

The VW 120 aircraft was the third built and the first British machine to fly faster than the speed of sound. The pilot on that occasion was one of Cunningham's most brilliant and talented test pilots, John Derry. Geoffrey de Havilland, son of the founder of the company and chief test pilot before Cunningham, was killed flying the first prototype.

The idea of the tail-less Comet was abandoned in 1946 but these planes formed valuable test vehicles for many of the innovative ideas used in the final Comet design.

on Comet 2—with larger Rolls-Royce Avon engines—followed by Comet 3, to hold 76 passengers instead of 44.

Then, a year after B.O.A.C. started flying the Comet, one crashed after leaving Calcutta, and bad weather was the culprit. The next year on January 10, 1954, from a Comet G-ALYP flying out of Rome, the captain, Alan Gibson, was chatting on the radio to another B.O.A.C. aircraft. His plane was nearing its cruising altitude of 34,000 feet (10,500 meters) and Gibson was heard to say, "Did you get my …" when the radio went dead.

Off the island of Elba, fishermen saw pieces of the Comet crash into the sea. After that, all Comets were grounded. Comprehensive testing of all aircraft revealed no failures, but 50 modifications were made on all Comets to be doubly sure. They were then cleared once more for flying. Just two weeks later, in April 1954, again after leaving Rome, Comet G-ALYY crashed after nearing its cruising altitude. All Comets were grounded, indefinitely.

The Royal Navy had been dredging the sea around Elba for wreckage from the first crash and was able to come up with close to two-thirds of the plane. Once more, this was a world first. The parts of the recovered plane were all taken back to Britain and laid out in their order for a thorough examination. Marks on the tail began to tell a story. Analysis showed they had come from the seats, indicating the seats had been flung violently from the cabin. Paint from the fuselage was found on one of the Comet's wings. The final conclusion was that there had been an explosive decompression of the plane's cabin.

The Air Ministry then conducted a complex test on one of the grounded Comets, fitting the pressurized cabin in a water-tight tank and arranging hydraulic jacks to flex the wings constantly, 24 hours a day, to replicate the stresses that the plane would expect when flying, particularly the stresses caused by changes in pressure as the plane climbed rapidly to its operating height. The torture test—equal to 9,000 flying hours—worked. The cabin pressure dropped suddenly and when examined it was found that the fuselage had split. If the plane had been flying high, the pressurized cabin would have exploded like a bomb.

Studying the break showed that design weakness was responsible. The Comet had windows of a square design. The fatigue cracks had started at the corners of one of the squared-off windows. Once the problems had been discovered they could be corrected.

Work was started on a redesigned Comet 4 but there was much to be done. It took four more years before the Comet was ready to fly again but it was too late. Boeing had introduced their new, innovative 707. It carried twice as many passengers, it had more powerful engines and greater range, and the fuselage walls were four and a half times thicker than the original Comet. They were also strengthened with titanium strips at intervals along the walls.

The Boeing 707 had another advantage. The engines were hung on pods beneath the wings—not as pretty as the hidden engines of the Comet but, in case of engine trouble, a great deal safer. Boeing 707 is what the world's airlines ordered and paid for. The Comet 4, now a thoroughly tested and safe airliner, simply could not compete. Although B.O.A.C. ordered 19 of the new 81-passenger Comets and was first to fly passenger jets from London to New York and return taking as little as 6 hours, 11 minutes to cross the Atlantic from west to east, they were not able to stem the irresistible march of the 707.

Intimately involved with all the testing, triumphs, and tribulations of the Comet was De Havilland's chief test pilot John Cunningham. In 1955, the year following the rigorous testing which led to destruction of a grounded Comet, he flew an improved Comet 3 in a demonstration flight around the world, flying a distance of 30,000 miles (48,270 kilometers) in 56 hours. After a further three years of comprehensive re-engineering, Cunningham flew the first Comet 4 (G-APDA) from Hong Kong to London in a remarkable and newsworthy "dawn to sunset" flight of 7,925 miles (12,754 kilometers) with stops at Bombay (now Mombai) and Cairo in an elapsed time of just 16 hours, 16 minutes. But the sadness for Cunningham was that he was flying the Comet into the twilight. Its days of glory were over.

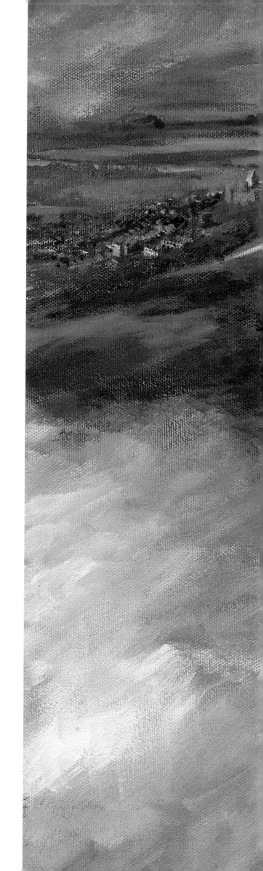

Right: A Comet IV of B.O.A.C is on its way to London's Heathrow Airport. Windsor Castle is in the background. On October 4, 1958, this particular aircraft, captained by T. B. Stoney, left New York and flew nonstop to London while a similar Comet took off from London and flew the other way, (it stopped to refuel at Gander, Newfoundland). Thus, the De Havilland Comets inaugurated the first-ever jet service on the lucrative transatlantic route. They also won an unofficial race with Pan American's Boeing 707s for the honor. However, it was the Boeing airliners that soon dominated world airways.

JOHN HERSCHEL GLENN JR.

LEAPING INTO SPACE

Just over 17 years after the Wright brothers took to the air at Kitty Hawk, John Glenn was born on July 18, 1921, in Cambridge, Ohio, U.S.A. Educated at Muskingham College, Ohio, he gained a Bachelor of Science degree in Engineering. In March 1942, aged 21, at a New Philadelphia airfield, John earned his wings as a cadet in the U.S.A. Naval Aviation Cadet Program. From there, he was posted to 155 Fighter Squadron of the U.S. Marines stationed in the Marshall Islands in the South Pacific. In World War II and the Korean War, he racked up 149 missions, winning the Distinguished Flying Cross five times and the Air Medal with 18 clusters, first flying F4U Corsairs, and later, Grumman F9F Panthers and North American F-86 Sabre jets.

After the Korean War, Glenn was selected for the Test Pilot School at the Naval Air Test Center in Maryland, later becoming project officer on a number of aircraft before being assigned to the Fighter Design branch of the Navy Bureau of Aeronautics as a test pilot on Navy and Marine Corp jet fighters.

In 1957, while project officer on the new F8U fighter, John flew from Los Angeles to New York in 3 hours, 23 minutes. He set a transcontinental air-speed record, which was the first to average supersonic speed all the way across America.

Left: John Herschel Glenn Jr., aviator and astronaut—the American hero, who helped take the enormous leap from Earth and its supporting cushion of air, into the dangerous but beckoning vacuum of space.

Left: John Glenn sits in the cockpit of his F-86 Sabre jet after shooting down his first North Korean Mig fighter.

Left: When John Glenn became an astronaut at the age of 38 he had flown 5,000 hours in high performance aircraft with the U.S Marine Corps. Marine Major Glenn of the 1st Marine Aircraft Wing stands with the Grumman Panther jet, which received a large hole in its tail section after Glenn completed a low-flying mission over North Korea. In the month before this photograph was taken, he had received more than 375 hits on his machine.

Left: The North American F-86 prototype Sabre, 1947, became a classic post-World War II fighter. It began life as a straight-winged aircraft but the more radical swept wing and tail unit was later adopted. In 1949, a standard airplane broke the world speed record at 671 miles (1073.6 kilometers) per hour. The Sabre incorporated new structural and aerodynamic features—full-span leading edge slats, and hydraulically boosted ailerons and elevators, the latter within the structure of an all-moving tail plane. The cockpit was pressurized and the machine such as the F-86E version, was powered by a single General Electric jet of about 5,200-pound (2358-kilogram) thrust. Its armament originally consisted of six 0.5 Colt-Browning machine guns set in the fuselage but there were many variations and combinations of rockets, bombs, and 20-millimeter cannons and external drop tanks.

The F-86 Sabre came to public prominence through its successes with the U.S. Forces in the Korean War. The F-86 distinguished itself as the first allied aircraft to dominate the skies against the Russian-designed Mig 15 and was first flown on October 1, 1947, by North American test pilot, George Welch. John Glenn's aircraft was decorated on its side with his nickname, "The Mig Mad Marine."

The F-86 Sabre

Right: The Vought F4U Corsair, 1943, was designed by Rex Beisel and Igor Sikorsky and it became one of the great combat fighters of World War II. This powerful machine was flown operationally from 1943 by the U.S. Navy and Marines as well as the armed forces of many other Allied nations. It incorporated the biggest engine and the largest propeller ever used in a single-engined fighter— hence the gull-wing shape to keep the large propeller clear of the ground or the flight deck. The Pratt and Whitney engine, of about 2000 horsepower (later versions could be boosted to about 2,800 horsepower) enabled it to become the first U.S. fighter to exceed 400 miles (640 kilometers) per hour.

The F4U first saw action with the U.S. Marines and gained air supremacy against the Japanese in the Solomon Islands. John Glenn flew them in the Marshall Islands. First flown in 1940, the aircraft's production with many variations continued until 1952. As a carrier-based fighter it owed much of its success to its great versatility. Its long "hose nose" made it tricky to land on an aircraft carrier but its superb stability at low speeds allowed a very slick routine to develop where smart Corsair operators, astonishingly, could land-on at less than a 20-second interval.

The Vought F4U Corsair

Two years later, John Glenn was selected as one of the seven astronauts in Project Mercury—America's first space program. To make the team, he had to meet the demanding criteria: under 40 years of age; less than 5 feet, 11 inches (180 centimeters) tall; top physical condition; Bachelor's degree in Engineering; Test Pilot School graduate; minimum of 1,500 hours flying time; and a qualified jet pilot.

After selection, Glenn and the other six astronauts faced nearly three years of intensive training. They did a graduate-level course in space science, constant stints in flight simulators, scuba diving to prepare them for weightlessness, and training in communications and technology. On the morning of February 20, 1962, atop an enormous Atlas Rocket, in his Mercury capsule smaller than a Volkswagen Beetle, John Glenn was hurled into orbit more than a hundred miles (160 kilometers) above the Earth to become the first American to circle the Earth from space.

Soviet astronaut Yuri Gagarin had beaten him to that record, but Glenn was the first to achieve part of the promise made by President John F. Kennedy that the U.S. would land a man on the moon before 1970. John Glenn, in the capsule he named *Friendship 7*, made three orbits of the Earth at a speed of 17,500 miles (28,000 kilometers) per hour before splashing down safely in the Atlantic, 19 miles (30.4 kilometers) north of the planned impact point. He wanted to remain as an active astronaut, but President Kennedy believed it was not fitting to endanger a national hero, and insisted that Glenn be removed from further space flight lists.

In January 1964, John Glenn resigned from the Manned Spacecraft Center. He was promoted to the rank of colonel in the Marine Corps, and was later elected to the United States Senate, where he again made history by being the first popularly elected Senator from Ohio to be elected for four consecutive terms. But the fighter-pilot-turned-astronaut still yearned to fly.

And fly he did, in October 1998 at the age of 77, after N.A.S.A. invited him to once more climb into a spacesuit and accompany the Space Shuttle *Discovery* on a planned mission. He participated both as a payload specialist, and in a study on the effects of space flight on the aging process. The launch took place on October 29, and as a member of the crew, Glenn spent the next 8 days, 22 hours, and 4 minutes orbiting the Earth—compared with his first five-hour flight 36 years before. During that flight in the space shuttle, Glenn traveled 3½ million miles (5.6 million kilometers)—more than all of his previous extensive flights combined.

I read ... that John F. Kennedy had passed the word that he didn't want me to go back up.

JOHN GLENN, EXPLAINING HIS 1964 RESIGNATION AS A N.A.S.A. ASTRONAUT

Left: The tiny black Mercury capsule sitting on top of its huge Atlas rocket is blasted into space from Cape Canaveral.

Right: Thirty-six years later, Space Shuttle Discovery, *with payload specialist John Glenn among the crew of seven, on track for the 92nd shuttle mission.*

ALWAYS ROOM FOR ONE MORE

Reinhold Platz, 1919

With international corporations employing expensive design teams, scientists, and supercomputers to produce today's mighty airliners, it would be feasible to believe that the day of the talented individual had passed. Yet, on a December morning in 1986, when a strange-looking plane landed at Edwards Air Force base in California, it brought flying proof of the exceptional value of the creative entrepreneur. Burt Rutan's *Voyager* had just completed a 25,000-mile (40,225-kilometer) nonstop flight around the world. Burt's brother Dick Rutan, the pilot, accompanied by his copilot Jeana Yeager, had flown for nine days without landing or refueling at an average speed of 115⅓ miles (185.3 kilometers) per hour.

Burt had designed the plane himself. Although he was sponsored by a company which specialized in sophisticated composite materials that resulted in whisper-light but extremely strong construction, the *Voyager* was an individual designer's creation. On takeoff, with its load of fuel and its provisions, the plane weighed more than 10 times its structural weight. Its drag was lower than almost any other powered aircraft. Rutan had produced an airplane that challenged existing perceptions. The pilots demonstrated bravado and tenacity of a remarkably high degree.

Rutan's achievement bore a much closer parallel to aviation's early pioneers than the way most aircraft were developed at the end of the twentieth century. Many of those dedicated originators started by designing an aircraft (the Wright brothers sketched theirs on a brown paper bag). Then they built a prototype, fired up the engines, and took off on their own test flights. As manufacture and design became more complex, sophisticated, and much more expensive, the three basic functions of design, construction, and flight became separated. Hence, recognition of the creative individual began to erode.

Anthony Fokker (pages 76–83) provides a human blueprint of the almost inevitable pattern of events. He started as a designer, manufacturer, and pilot of his own early inventions. He then discovered the German Reinhold Platz—and appreciated that Platz was a better designer than himself. So Anthony employed him to create the most successful of the Fokker airplanes. Yet it was Anthony Fokker who flighttested and demonstrated the new machines. With his name emblazoned on the aircraft, Fokker made very public appearances in them. The brilliant Reinhold Platz was paid but not publicized. Fokker, the intuitive self-publicist, sensed that any publicity for Platz would blur the public focus on the Fokker brand and weaken the company's reputation.

He probably also sensed the danger in crediting Platz as the designer of the splendid Fokker machines because a competitive manufacturer could spirit away Anthony's

creative genius. He could wake one morning to find his company's reputation at zero. So Fokker ensured that Platz remained anonymous while the planes he designed were making aviation history.

John Northrop's story (pages 44–49) demonstrates how the alternative scenario could happen. When Northrop was forced to leave the Lockheed brothers he first worked for the Douglas Company before striking out on his own and rapidly building his designing reputation and aircraft company.

Certainly with today's complications of electronic and navigational developments, the requirements of international travel, airport and safety regulations, together with the breathtaking complexity of large-scale aircraft manufacturing, individual designers have had to submit to the team approach to design. No one individual could hope to cover all aspects of modern aircraft design, even with the leap forward in computing power available today. Nor does the diminishing influence of the individual appear to have affected the progress of mainstream aviation. The large manufacturers provide positive proof with the staggering performance of modern jetliners, freighters, and military jets.

Yet the historical facts recorded in this book reveal that without public awareness of the inspiration, creative flair, talent, and pure courage of individual designers, builders, and fliers, aviation as we know it would not have happened.

The first inspiration for the pioneers was to fly like a bird. As flying machines developed, there came the spur of improved performance of different designs, better engines, and the publicity given to the individuals who created and flew them. The danger of allowing designers and pilots to disappear from public consciousness is that, without them, there may be no creators for a new generation to admire and emulate.

Burt Rutan's Voyager, 1986

Above: In the U.S.A., the Experimental Aircraft Association fosters the development of unusual light aircraft. The Discovery is produced in kit form for assembly by do-it-yourself enthusiasts and is designed by Progress Aero.

There are still a few adventurous aviators willing to risk their lives, reputations, and bank balances to reenact some of the well-known historic flights of the early pioneers—fliers of the caliber of Lang Kidby, who tracked early trail breakers in beautiful reproductions of the original aircraft that made flying history. There are today's dreamers with fresh, innovative ideas such as Burt Rutan and his *Voyager*—or daredevils such as lone flier Dick Smith in his world-circling helicopter, prepared to create new records in the air. In Europe, small groups of individuals in small companies, design, build, and fly highly sophisticated soaring machines— lovely, long-winged sailplanes of wondrous grace and exceptional performance.

These aircraft, especially some produced in Germany, are able to be flown by glider pilots to distances of more than 621 miles (1,000 kilometers) on a wisp of a thermal updraft and without an engine.

In America, the Experimental Aircraft Association encourages an army of talented people who create new, often unorthodox-looking aircraft for private fliers. Like European sailplanes and the record-breaking *Voyager*, these new creations are built of exotic materials using revolutionary manufacturing techniques. The enthusiasts chalk up new records, assist in educating the young,

and create their own publicity. Every year, their work culminates in the world's largest air show at Oshkosh, Wisconsin, U.S.A. It is not uncommon for there to be 10,000 visiting aircraft parked for the show. The audience is vast, flocking in their thousands to see the week-long flying displays of historic "war birds" and experimental aircraft.

Oshkosh is the modern equivalent of the Great Week of Aviation at Reims in 1909, when so many individuals came together and invented a new industry. The Oshkosh Air Show is a reminder, at the start of the third millennium, that there will always be an important role for the individual—always room for one more—to achieve and enhance the future of flying.

To the dreamers, doers, and daredevils of today—keep the love of flying alive.

Left: Lang Kidby piloted two historic 12,000-mile (19,200-kilometer) reenactment flights—one in 1994 with financier Peter McMillan, flying a replica Vickers Vimy of the 1919 Great Australian Air Race and the other, a solo flight marking the 70th anniversary of Hinkler's flight across the world in 1928, in Kidby's beautiful reconstruction of a 1930s Avro Avian similar to Bert Hinkler's version.

German ASH 25 high-performance sailplane

Dick Smith, 1983

Left: Explorer and loner Dick Smith is a great admirer of early aviation pioneers and, in 1982–83, was the first man to fly solo around the world in a helicopter. Much of his route covered ground first tracked by fliers of the 1930s. Smith made a flight of 35,285 miles (56,742 kilometers), piloting his Bell Jet Ranger III.

The Dreamers, Doers, and Daredevils

1810 to 2000

Sir George Cayley
1773–1857

Clement Ader
1841–1925

Lawrence Hargrave
1850–1915

Otto Lilienthal
1848–1896

Octave Chanute
1832–1910

Percy Pilcher
1867–1899

Samuel Langley
1834–1906

1910 continued

Anthony Fokker
1890–1939

Claude Dornier
1884–1969

Lawrence Sperry
1892–1923

Harry Hawker
1889–1921

Kenneth McKenzie-Grieve
1880–1942

Lt. Cmdr. Albert Read
1887–1967

John Alcock
1892–1919

Arthur Brown
1886–1948

Ross Smith
1892–1922

Keith Smith
1880–1953

Henry Wrigley
1892–1987

Arthur Murphy
1892–1963

1920 continued

Stanley Goble
1891–1948

Ivor McIntyre
1899–1928

Francesco de Pinedo
1890–1933

Francis Chichester
1901–1972

Sir Alan Cobham
1894–1973

Arthur Elliott
1900–1926

Charles Kingsford Smith
1897–1835

Harry Lyon
1885–1963

Jim Warner
1892–1970

Charles Ulm
1897–1934

Sir Hubert Wilkins
1888–1958

1930 continued   1940

Howard Hughes
1905–1976

Nancy Bird-Walton
1915–present

Dr. Clyde Fenton
1901–1982

Thomas Pethybridge
1906–1935

Reginald J. Mitchell
1895–1937

Jacqueline Cochran
1908–1970

Edgar Percival
1897–1984

Jean Batten
1909–1982

Sidney Cotton
1894–1969

Roy Chadwick
1893–1947

210

1910

Wilbur Wright
1867–1912

Orville Wright
1871–1948

Richard Pearse
1877–1953

Alberto Santos-Dumont
1873–1932

Glenn Curtiss
1878–1930

Gabriel Voisin 1880–1973 Charles Voisin 1882–1912 Henri Farman 1874–1958 Léon Levavasseur 1863–1922

Louis Blériot
1872–1936

Alphonse Pégoud
1850–1880

1920

Reinhold Platz
1886–1966

Ray Parer
1894–1967

John McIntosh
1896–1921

Cago Coutinho
1869–1959

Sacadura Cabral
1881–1922

Hudson Fysh
1895–1974

Hermann Koehl
1888–1938

Jack Northrop
1895–1981

Bert Hinkler
1892–1933

Charles Nungesser
1892–1927

François Coli
1881–1927

1930

Roald Amundsen
1872–1928

Harold Gatty
1903–1957

Harold Bromley
1888–1987

Amelia Earhart
1897–1937

Dieudonné Costes
1892–1973

Maurice Bellonte
1896–1984

Jessie Miller
1910–1972

Clairmont Egtvedt
1892–1975

Charles Lindbergh
1902–1974

Arthur Raymond
1900–1999

Charles Ulm
1897–1834

1950 **1960** **1970** **1980** **1990** **2000**

John Cunningham
1916–2002

Willi Messerschmitt
1898–1978

Patrick G. Taylor
1896–1966

Igor Sikorsky
1889–1972

Marcel Dassault
1892–1986

Kelly Johnson
1910–1990

André Turcat
1921–present

Dick Smith
1944–present

John Glenn
1921–present

Lang Kidby
1947–present

WINGS THAT BLAZED TRAILS IN THE SKY

1896 to 2003

1896

Otto Lilienthal makes over 2,000 flights in his gliders before his death during that year.

1896

Lawrence Hargrave rides his box kites to demonstrate their stability and lifting ability.

1901

Octave Chanute creates a biplane wing with a constant chord.

1903

Wright brothers make the first sustained powered flight.

1914

Lawrence Sperry demonstrates the first autopilot in a Curtiss C5 flying boat.

1915

Claudius Dornier designs the RS III, an all-metal flying boat, at a time when wood and fabric were the preferred materials.

1915

Igor Sikorsky designs the first four-engined aircraft.

1915

Anthony Fokker designs an interrupter gear to enable guns to fire through the propeller arc.

1917

The Sopwith Camel shoots down the greatest number of enemy aircraft in World War I.

1918

German air ace Baron von Richtofen is killed in his Fokker Dreidekker by ground fire.

1922

Sabadura Cabral and Cago Coutinho fly the South Atlantic in stages from Lisbon to Rio de Janeiro.

1923

John Macready and Oakley G. Kelly fly a Fokker T2 on the first nonstop flight across America.

1924

Stanley Goble and Ivor McIntyre circumnavigate Australia in a Fairey-IIID.

1924

Two U.S. Army Douglas World Cruisers circumnavigate the globe, led by Lt. Lowell Smith.

1924

K.L.M. makes the first regular airline schedule flight from Holland to Batavia (Indonesia).

1925

Francesco De Pinedo flies his Savoia Marchetti S 16ter flying boat from Italy to Japan and back.

1927

Charles Nungesser and François Coli are lost on their Paris to New York flight.

1927

Alan Cobham makes his pioneering flight around Africa.

1928

Jack Northrop pioneers economical production of a wooden, monocoque, drag-reducing fuselage in the Lockheed Vega.

1928

Igor Sikorsky produces his S-38, the first of many successful flying-boat designs that would revolutionize ocean travel.

1928

Charles Kingsford Smith and crew fly a Fokker VII 2m to make the first crossing of the Pacific—America to Australia.

1928

Hubert Wilkins and Ben Eielson, in a Lockheed Vega, make the first crossing of the arctic ice cap and their first flight in the Antarctic.

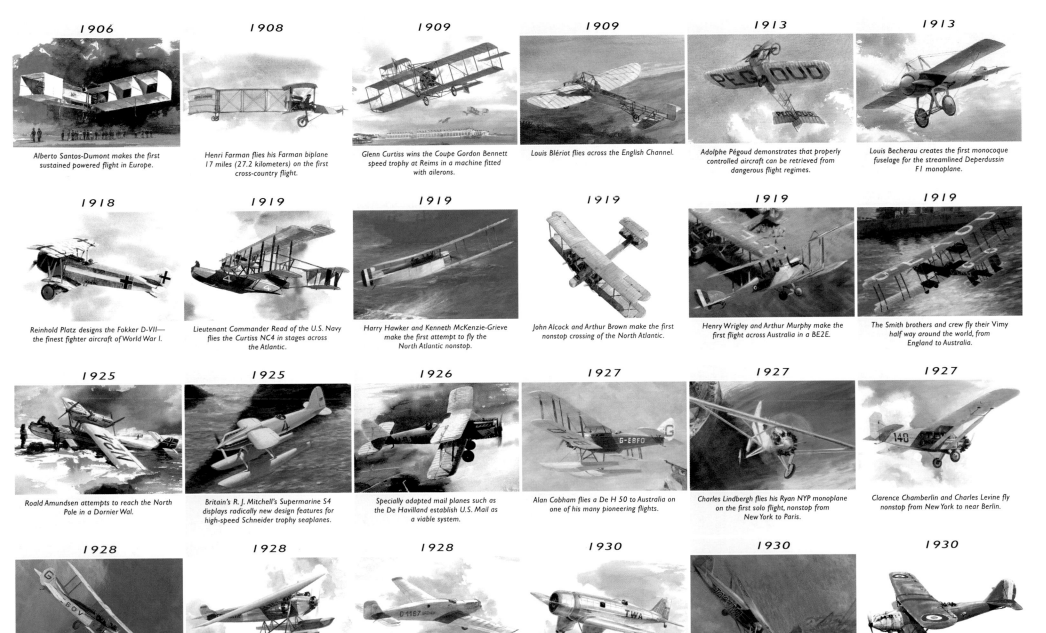

1906
Alberto Santos-Dumont makes the first sustained powered flight in Europe.

1908
Henri Farman flies his Farman biplane 17 miles (27.2 kilometers) on the first cross-country flight.

1909
Glenn Curtiss wins the Coupe Gordon Bennett speed trophy at Reims in a machine fitted with ailerons.

1909
Louis Blériot flies across the English Channel.

1913
Adolphe Pégoud demonstrates that properly controlled aircraft can be retrieved from dangerous flight regimes.

1913
Louis Becherau creates the first monocoque fuselage for the streamlined Deperdussin F1 monoplane.

1918
Reinhold Platz designs the Fokker D-VII— the finest fighter aircraft of World War I.

1919
Lieutenant Commander Read of the U.S. Navy flies the Curtiss NC4 in stages across the Atlantic.

1919
Harry Hawker and Kenneth McKenzie-Grieve make the first attempt to fly the North Atlantic nonstop.

1919
John Alcock and Arthur Brown make the first nonstop crossing of the North Atlantic.

1919
Henry Wrigley and Arthur Murphy make the first flight across Australia in a BE2E.

1919
The Smith brothers and crew fly their Vimy half way around the world, from England to Australia.

1925
Roald Amundsen attempts to reach the North Pole in a Dornier Wal.

1925
Britain's R. J. Mitchell's Supermarine S4 displays radically new design features for high-speed Schneider trophy seaplanes.

1926
Specially adapted mail planes such as the De Havilland establish U.S. Mail as a viable system.

1927
Alan Cobham flies a De H 50 to Australia on one of his many pioneering flights.

1927
Charles Lindbergh flies his Ryan NYP monoplane on the first solo flight, nonstop from New York to Paris.

1927
Clarence Chamberlin and Charles Levine fly nonstop from New York to near Berlin.

1928
Bert Hinkler's Avro Avian makes the longest solo flight—England to Australia.

1928
William Stultz flies a Fokker F-VII with passenger, Amelia Earhart. She becomes the first woman to fly the North Atlantic.

1928
Hermann Koehl flies a Junkers W 33 across the North Atlantic, east to west, nonstop.

1930
Jack Northrop creates the stressed-skin concept and metal monocoque fuselage in the Alpha—the progenitor of modern aircraft design.

1930
Harold Bromley and Harold Gatty attempt to fly across the Pacific to Japan from America, nonstop.

1930
Dieudonné Costes and Maurice Bellonte fly nonstop from Paris to New York in their Breguet Point D'interrogation.

1931

Wiley Post and Harold Gatty fly around the world in record time in a Lockheed Vega.

1931

Boeing introduces the all-metal, monocoque B9 bomber.

1931

The gigantic 12-engined Dornier X makes a trial passenger flight from Germany to South America.

1931

Boeing designs the first all-metal, stressed skin Model 247d airliner.

1932

Amelia Earhart, in a Lockheed Vega, becomes the first woman to fly the North Atlantic nonstop, solo.

1933

The Douglas company introduces its famous DC-1 and DC-2 airliners.

1937

Amelia Earhart and Fred Noonan, in a Lockheed Electra, disappear in the Pacific attempting an equatorial circumnavigation of the globe.

1937

The Focke Achgelis Fa 61 becomes the first successful helicopter.

1937

Pan-Am's Sikorsky S 42 inaugurates the trans Pacific route from America to New Zealand.

1938

Jaqueline Cochran wins the Bendix Trophy flying a Seversky P 35.

1938

The Boeing Stratoliner, the first fully pressurized airliner, makes its first flight.

1939

Sidney Cotton creates high altitude photo reconnaissance techniques, making secret flights over Germany in a Lockheed 12a.

1945

The Messerschmitt 262 becomes the first operational jet fighter.

1945

The first operational, fully pressurized high-altitude bomber, the Boeing B 29 Superfortress, is used in Pacific theatre in World War II.

1946

The XB 35, John Northrop's advanced flying wing long-range bomber, makes its first flight.

1947

The Boeing B 47 radical swept-wing jet bomber makes its first flight.

1947

Howard Hughes flies the Hughes H-4 flying boat—the largest aircraft ever constructed and dubbed the Spruce Goose.

1949

The first jet airliner, the De H Comet, takes to the air.

1958

The De H Comet, much modified after early disasters, is finally accepted by airlines and the public as a safe and efficient jet airliner.

1964

André Turcat flies a world speed record of 1,441 miles (2,305.6 kilometers) per hour in a Nord 1500 Griffon jet.

1964

Jaqueline Cochran in a F 100 Lockheed Starfighter becomes the first woman to fly at more than 1,000 miles (1,600 kilometers) per hour.

1964

The Lockheed SR 71 makes its first flight and becomes the highest-flying, fastest operational aircraft of all time.

1969

The Boeing747 makes its first flight.

1969

André Turcat pilots the Anglo French Concorde supersonic airliner on its first flight.

1934

The first Douglas DC-3 flies.

1934

Charles Kingsford Smith and P. G. Taylor, in a Lockheed Altair, make the first crossing of the Pacific in a single-engined aircraft.

1934

Charles Ulm and Leon Skilling, in an Airspeed Envoy, disappear in the Pacific trying to prove land planes can fly ocean routes.

1935

Willi Messerschmitt creates the Me. 109 fighter, highly successful in the Spanish Civil War and World War II.

1936

R. J. Mitchell's prototype Spitfire fighter makes its first flight.

1936

Jean Batten is claimed by many to be the finest long-distance woman aviator of her era after flying solo from Britain to New Zealand.

1941

Airborne radar is first used to intercept and destroy night-flying bombers.

1942

Igor Sikorsky conceives and test-flies the first truly successful helicopter, with a single main rotor and one tail rotor.

1944

Roy Chadwick's Lancaster bomber carries more bombs farther, faster, and safer than any World War II bomber in Europe.

1944

The Boeing Flying Fortress becomes a household word for its spectacular daylight bombing raids over Europe.

1944

The Sikorsky helicopter is put into production for the U.S. Army as the R4.

1944

The Horten brothers in Germany create the progenitor of the modern stealth aircraft in their Horten Ho. IX tail-less jet bomber.

1951

P. G. Taylor in Frigate Bird pioneers a long-haul air route across the Pacific from Australia to South America.

1954

The prototype Boeing 707 jet liner, the Dash 80, makes its first flight.

1955

The Lockheed U 2 high-altitude spy plane makes its first flight.

1956

Test pilot Peter Twiss becomes the first pilot to fly more than 1,000 miles (1,600 kilometers) per hour in a Fairey Delta-II.

1958

The success of Dassault's Mirage III consolidates France's claim of leadership in jet combat aircraft.

1958

Qantas Airways inaugurates the first round-the-world air route with two Lockheed Super Constellations.

1983

Dick Smith, flying a Bell Jet Ranger, makes his first solo circumnavigation of the globe in a helicopter.

1986

Burt Rutan's Voyager makes the first nonstop flight around the globe, flying 25,000 miles (40,250 kilometers).

1998

Astronaut John Glenn at age 77 crews Space Shuttle Discovery on its 8 days, 22 hours, and 4 minutes orbit of Earth.

1998

ASW20 Glider, flown by Terry Delore of New Zealand, creates a new long-distance record of 1270 ⅔ miles (2,049.4 kilometers).

1999

The Grumman Northrop B 1 stealth bomber flies its first operational sortie, 30 hours from Missouri to Servia with air-to-air refueling.

2002

The first Unmanned Air Vehicles Global Hawk and Predator are used for surveillance and strike operations.

AIRCRAFT SPECIFICATIONS

In alphabetical order of manufacturer

ADER L'EOLE
French single-seat batlike flying machine of 1890. Powered by a four-cylinder, 20-hp steam engine. Wingspan 46 ft (14 m), length 21 ft (6.4 m), weight approx 498 lb (226 kg), with Ader aboard 650 lb (294.8 kg). This machine is said to have left the ground for 165 ft (50 m).

AEROSPATIALE/BAE CONCORDE
British and French 128-passenger supersonic jet airliner. First flown in 1969. Powered by four 38,000-lb thrust Rolls-Royce S.N.E.C.M.A. Olympus 583–610 afterburning turbo jets. Wingspan 83 ft 10 in (26.6 m), length 202 ft (61.66 m), operating speed at 60,000 ft—Mach 2.04 1,355 mph (2,179 kph), max fuel load 26,400 gal/95,680 kg, range max fuel 3,843 m (6,580 km), max takeoff weight 408,000 lb (185,070 kg), pay load 29,000 lb (13,150 kg). Three crew—two pilots, one flight engineer. British Airways flew seven, Air France five; 18 aircraft produced in total.

AIRSPEED ENVOY
British eight-passenger transport of 1933. Powered by two Armstrong Siddeley Cheetah IX seven-cylinder, air-cooled radial engines. Wingspan 52 ft 4 in (15.9 m), length 34 ft (10.3 m), max speed 203 mph (326.6 kph), ceiling 22,000 ft (6,705 m), range 620 ml (997 km), total weight 6,600 lb (2,993 kg).

AIRSPEED FERRY
British joy flight transport of 1932. Powered by two inverted 120-hp De Havilland Gypsy II and one upright 120-hp De Havilland Gypsy III six-cylinder, in-line, air-cooled engines. Wingspan 55 ft (16.7 m), max speed 108 mph (173.8 kph), max weight 5,400 lb (2,449 kg). Aircraft shown here was so seriously eaten by ants on a tour of India that it was written off in 1934.

ALEXANDER 700 H BULLET
American four-seat monoplane of 1930. Powered by one five-cylinder, Wright J-6-5 engine. Wingspan 34 ft 4 in (10.5 m), length 26 ft 10 in (8.2m), max speed 125 mph (201 kph).

AVRO AVIAN
British two-seater biplane designed in 1926. Powered by one Cirrus II 85-hp four-cylinder, in-line, air-cooled engine. Wingspan 28 ft (8.53 m), length 24 ft 3 in (7.39 m), gross weight 1,435 lb (650 kg), speed 102 mph (164 kph), range 400 ml (644 km). Later Avians built with steel frame rather than wood and powered by a variety of more powerful Cirrus engines. Over 370 constructed.

AVRO BABY
British single-seater biplane designed in 1919. Powered by a 35-hp Green engine. Wingspan 25 ft 9 in (7.6m), gross weight 870 lb (398 kg). Progenitor of today's light aircraft.

AVRO LANCASTER
British heavy bomber first flown in 1942. Powered by four 1,460-hp Rolls-Royce Merlin 20, or Packard Merlin 22, V-12 liquid-cooled engines. Wingspan 102 ft (31.1 m), length 69 ft 4 in (21 m), load weight 68,000 lb (30,800 kg), cruising speed at 20,000 ft (6,095 m) 210 mph (338 kph), range with 14,000 lb (6,350 kg) of bombs 1,660 ml (2,875km), armament eight 0.303 machine guns. Seven crew.

AVRO MANCHESTER
British heavy bomber first flown in 1940. Powered by two 1,845-hp Rolls-Royce Vulture X-type 24-cylinder, liquid-cooled engines. Wingspan 90 ft (27.4m), length 68 ft 10 ins (20.98 m), cruising speed at 15,000 ft (4,750 m) with max weight 50,000 lb (22,680 kg), 205 mph (330 kph), armament eight 0.303 machine guns. Seven crew.

AVRO TRIPLANE (AVROPLANE)
British triplane of 1909. Powered by a 9-hp, three-cylinder, air-cooled JAP engine. Wingspan 20 ft (6.09 m), weight 450 lb (203 kg), distance flown 900 ft (274m), speed unknown. Built by designer Alliott Verdon Roe. First British-built airplane to fly.

AVRO 504K
British two-seat training aircraft. Designed as bomber in 1913 by Roy Chadwick, and later produced in many variants. Powered by a 100-hp Gnome Monosoupape seven-cylinder rotary engine. Wingspan 36 ft (10.9 m), length 29 ft 5 ins (8.9 m), max speed 82 mph (131.9 kph), ceiling 13,000 ft (3960 m).

BAC 221
British single-seat experimental aircraft of 1964 for research into ogee-curved delta wing. Powered by a Rolls-Royce Avon RA 228-R turbo jet engine with reheat. Wingspan 25 ft (7.62 m), length 57 ft 7 in (17.56 m), max speed up to Mach 1.6. Cockpit area hinged downward for takeoff and landing. A modified Fairey Delta II.

BELL 206 JET RANGER
American five-seat light helicopter. First flown in 1962. Powered by 400-hp Allison 250-C20 turbo shaft driving two-blade main rotor and two-blade tail rotor. Main rotor diameter 33 ft 4 in (10,16 m), length 31 ft 2 in (9.5 m), max cruising speed 136 mph (219 kph), range 436 ml (702 km), max weight 3,000 lb (1,360 kg).

BELLANCA WB-2
American long-distance monoplane of 1927. Powered by one 220-hp Wright Whirlwind J-5C seven-cylinder, air-cooled radial engine. Wingspan 45 ft 9 in (14. 1 m), length 27 ft 10 in (8.5 m), max speed 112 mph (180 kph), range 5,000 ml (8,050 km). Flew nonstop New York–Berlin.

BE 2E
British two-seat reconnaissance spotter of 1916. Powered by a 90-hp Royal Aircraft Factory 1A, six-cylinder engine. Wingspan 40 ft 9 in (12.42 m), length 29 ft 6 in (8.1 m), max speed 82 mph (131 kph), range with extra fuel tanks 400 ml (643 km), ceiling 10,000 ft (3,048 m), endurance 3-4 hours, armament one 0.303 Lewis gun and bomb load to100 lb (945 kg). Developed from BE 2A of 1912. Used wing warping for lateral control instead of ailerons.

BLÉRIOT XI
French single-seat monoplane of 1909. Powered by one 25-hp three-cylinder, Anzani air-cooled radial engine. Wingspan 25 ft 6in (7.8 m), length 26 ft 3 in (8 m), max speed 36 mph (58 kph), weight 661 lb (300 kg). First aircraft to cross English Channel.

BLÉRIOT XII
French single-seat racing monoplane of 1909, constructed of wood and fabric. Powered by a 30- to 50-hp water-cooled ENV engine. Wingspan 31 ft 2 in (9.5 m), length 32 ft 7 in (10 m), max speed 44 mph (70 kph), weight 1212 lb (550 kg).

BLOCH 152
French single-seat fighter. Powered by one 1,080-hp Gnome-Rhone 14N-25, 14-cylinder, two-row, radial air-cooled engine. First flown in 1935. Wingspan 34 ft 6 in (10.5 m), length 29 ft 10 in (9.1 m), max speed 323 mph (520 kph), rate of climb approx. 2,700 ft (823 m) per min, ceiling 32,800 ft (10,000 m), range 370 ml (595 km), max weight 5,842 lb (2,650 kg), armament two 20-mm Hispano 0 404 cannon and two 7.5 mm machine guns.

BLOCH 200 BN4
French bomber of 1934. Powered by two 870-hp Gnome-Rhone 14 Kirs 14-cylinder, air-cooled radial engines. Wingspan 73 ft 8 in (22.4 m), length 52 ft 6 in), max speed 143 mph (230 kph) at 14,000 ft (4,300m), ceiling 22,640 ft (6,000 m), range 621 ml (1,000 m),

max weight 16,060 lb (9,280 kg), armament three machine guns and 3,300 lb (1,500kg) bomb load. Five crew.

BOEING DASH EIGHTY

Prototype Boeing 707/717. American experimental jet transport first flown in 1954. Powered by four 11,000-lb thrust Pratt & Whitney JT3P turbo jet engines. Wingspan 130 ft (39.6 m), length 128 ft (39 m), cruising speed 600 mph (965.4 kph), ceiling 42,000 ft (12,801 m), range 2,000 ml (3,218 km), gross weight 160,000 lb (72,480 kg)

BOEING MODEL C

American two-seat float plane of 1917. Data for Model C/EA land plane. Powered by one 100-hp Hall Scott L-4, four-cylinder, water-cooled, in-line engine. Wingspan 43 ft 10 in (13,4 m), length 27 ft (8.2 m), max speed 73 mph (117 kph), range 200 ml (321 km), ceiling 6,500 ft (1,981 m), total weight 2,395 lb (1,086 kg), range 200 ml (321.8 km).

BOEING B9

American medium bomber of 1931. Powered by two 600-hp Pratt & Whitney R-1860-11 Hornet, nine-cylinder, air-cooled radial engines. Wingspan 76 ft (23.2 m), length 51 ft 5 in (15.6 m), cruising speed 158 mph (254.2 kph), range 1,150 ml (1,850 km), ceiling 20,150 ft (6,141 m), gross weight 13,919 lb (5,975 kg), bomb capacity 2,400 lb (1,087 kg), armament two 0.303 Browning machine guns. Ground-breaking military aircraft.

BOEING B-17G FLYING FORTRESS

American heavy bomber. YIB-17 prototype flew in 1936, B-17 G in 1943. Powered by four 1,200-hp Wright R-1820-97, 18-cylinder, twin-row, air-cooled radial engines. Wingspan 103 ft 9 in (31.6 m), length 74 ft 9 in (922.78 m), cruising speed 160 mph (257 kph), range 3,750 ml (6033 km), ceiling 35, 600 ft (10,850 m), gross weight 65,000 lb (29,445 kg), bomb capacity 17,600 lb (7,972 kg),

armament thirteen 0.5-in machine guns.

BOEING B-29 SUPERFORTRESS

American high-altitude, long-range heavy bomber. Prototype flew in 1942. Powered by four 2,200-hp Wright R-3350-23/59 Twin Cyclone 18-cylinder, twin-row, air-cooled radial engines. Wingspan 140 ft 3 in (42.7 m), length 99 ft (30.17 m), cruising speed 220 mph (353.9 kph), range 5,830 ml (9,380 km), ceiling 31,850 ft (9,707 m), bomb capacity 20,000 lb (9,060 kg), gross weight 140,000 lb (963,420 kg), armament twelve 0.5 in remotely operated machine guns and usually one 20-mm cannon (in tail turret).

BOEING B-47 STRATOJET

American radical swept-wing, long-range strategic bomber. First flown in 1951. Powered by six 7,200-lb (3,268.8-kg) thrust General Electric J-47 turbojet engines plus rocket-assisted takeoff gear. The B-47H model carried 33 Aerojet 14 AS1000 rocket bottles in a cradle that could be jettisoned. Wingspan 116 ft (35.3 m), length 107 ft (32.6 m), cruising speed more than 525 mph (844.7 kph), ceiling 40,500 ft (12,344 m), range 4,100 ml (6,596 km), gross weight 206,700 lb (93,635 kg), bomb capacity 20,000 lb (9,060 kg), armament two 20-mm cannon in tail turret.

BOEING B-52 STRATOFORTRESS

American long-range strategic bomber first rolled out in 1951. Variants still operational in 2003. B-52 H model powered by eight 13,750-lb (6,242.5-kg) thrust Pratt & Whitney TF-33 turbofans. Wingspan 185 ft 9 in (56.3 m), length 160 ft 11 in (49.05 m), max speed 650 mph (1,040 kph), ceiling 55,000 ft (16,764 m), range more than 11,000 ml (17,699 km), gross weight 488,000 lb (9,221,064 kg), bomb capacity 13,500 lb (5,889 kg) conventional, or eight nuclear bombs, or 20 RAMs, armament one six-barrelled 20-mm Vulcan cannon in rear turret.

BOEING F4B4

American single-seat carrier-borne fighter

of 1931. Powered by a single 550-hp Pratt & Whitney R-1340-16 Wasp nine-cylinder, air-cooled radial engine. Wingspan 30 ft (9.1 m), length 20 ft 5 in (6.2 m), max speed 187 mph (300.8 kph), cruising speed 160 mph (257.4 kph), range 585 ml (941 km), ceiling 27,500 ft (8,382 m), gross weight 2,898 lb (1,312 kg), armament two 0.303 Browning machine guns.

BOEING PW-9

American single-seat fighter of 1926. Powered by one 435-hp Curtiss D 12 C V-12 water-cooled engine. Wingspan 32 ft (9.75 m), length 32 ft 1 in (7.04 m), max speed 163 mph (268 kph), ceiling 21,000 ft (6,468 m), endurance 2 hrs, 35 min, max weight 3,170 lb (1,438 kg), armament two 0.303 Browning machine guns or one 0.303 and one 0.5 Browning.

BOEING P-26A

American single seat all-metal fighter of 1932. Powered by a single Pratt & Whiney R-1340-27 Wasp nine-cylinder, air-cooled radial engine. Wingspan 28 ft (8.5 m), length 23 ft 7 in (7.19 m), max speed 234 mph (376.5 kph), range at 200 mph (320 kph) 635 ml (1,021 km), ceiling 27,400 ft (8,351 m), armament two 0.303 Browning machine guns, or one 0.5 and one 0.303.

BOEING XB-15

American experimental heavy bomber. First flew in 1937. Powered by four 850-hp Pratt & Whitney R-1830-11 Twin Wasp two-row, 18 cylinder, air-cooled radial engines. Wingspan 149 ft (45.4 m), length 87 ft 7 in (26.7 m), max speed 200 mph (321 kph), cruising speed 152 mph (246 kph), range 5,130 ml (8,254 km), ceiling 18,900 ft (5,760 m), 8,000 lb (3,624 kg) bomb load.

BOEING 221A MONOMAIL

Ground-breaking American all-metal mono-plane. Light transport of 1930. Powered by a single 575-hp Pratt & Whitney Hornet B nine-cylinder, air-cooled radial engine. Wingspan 59 ft 1 in (17.98 m), length 43 ft

5 in (13.22 m), cruising speed 135 mph (217.2 kph), ceiling 14,700 ft (1,432 m), range 575 ml (925 km), gross weight 8,000 lb (3,624 kg). Capacity eight passengers and 750 lb (339 kg) of mail.

BOEING 247-D

American ten-seat passenger transport of 1933. Powered by two 550-hp Pratt & Whitney R-1340-S1H1G Wasps two-row, 18-cylinder, air-cooled, radial engines. Wingspan 74 ft (22.5 m), length 51 ft 7 in (15 720 m), cruising speed 189 mph (304 kph), ceiling 25,400 ft (7,741 m), range 745 ml (1,198 km), gross weight 13,650 lb (6,183 kg). First "modern" airliner.

BOEING 307 STRATOLINER

American first fully pressurized passenger transport. First flew in 1938. Powered by four 1,100-hp Wright GR-1820-G102, 18 cylinder, two-row, radial air-cooled engines. Wingspan 107 ft 3 in (32.68 m), length 74 ft 4 in (22.7 m), cruising speed 215 mph (345.9 kph), ceiling 23,300 ft (7,101 m), gross weight 42,000 lb (19,026 kg). Capacity 33 passengers.

BOEING 314A

American long-range passenger flying boat. Powered by four 1,600-hp Wright GR-2600 Cyclone 18-cylinder, twin-row, radial air-cooled engines. Wingspan 152 ft (46.3 m), length 106 ft (32.3 m), cruising speed 199 mph (320 kph), ceiling 19,600 ft (5,974 m), range 5,200 ml (8,320 km). Capacity up to 74 passengers.

BOEING 707/320C

American long-range jet transport of 1959. Powered by four 18,000-lb (8,172-kg) thrust Pratt & Whitney JT3D turbofans. Wingspan 145 ft 9 in (44.4 m), cruising speed 600 mph (965.4 kph), ceiling 41,000 ft (12,496 m), range 4,000 ml (6,436 km), gross weight 336,000 lb (152,208 kg), capacity 219 passengers or 96,800 lb (43,850 kg) cargo.

BOEING 747/400

American. One of many versions of original

Boeing 747 long-range transport first flown in 1959. The 400 model of 1988 powered by four Pratt & Whitney 54,750-lb (24,856-kg) thrust turbofans (or Rolls-Royce, or General Electric equivalents). Wingspan 211 ft 5 in (64.44 m), length 231 ft 10 in (70.66 m), cruising speed 600 mph (965 kph), ceiling 45,000 ft (13,725 m), range more than 8,000 ml (12,800 km), gross weight 870,000 lb (394,980 kg), capacity more than 400 passengers.

BREGUET 19 GR ?

Final development of 1929 French two-seat bomber fitted with variety of motors. Long-range model dubbed *Super Bidon* (super petrol can). Powered by one 650-hp Hispano-Suiza 12 Nb V-12 liquid-cooled engine. Wingspan 60 ft (18.3 m), length 35 ft 11 in (10.7 m), max speed 155 mph (250 kph), ceiling 22,000 ft (6,700 m), range 5,592 ml (9,000 km). Two earlier GR models *Joseph le Brix* and *Nungesser Coli* also long-distance record makers.

BRISTOL BEAUFIGHTER 1F

British two-seat night fighter of 1941. Powered by two 1,770-hp Bristol Hercules XVII 14-cylinder, sleeve-valve, air-cooled radial engines. Wingspan 57 ft 10 in (17.63 m), length 41 ft 8 in (12.6 m), max speed 312 mph (502 kph) ceiling 26,500 ft (8077 m), range 1,540 ml (2478 km), max weight 26,400 lb (11,530 kg), armament four 20 mm cannon and six 0.303 machine guns. Several versions. Mk. X was highly successful torpedo/strike fighter.

BUTOSOV GLIDER

American monoplane glider of circa 1896. No data available.

CAUDRON G3

French two-seat reconnaissance aircraft. First flown 1914. Powered by one 100-hp Anzani rotary engine. Wingspan 43 ft 10 in (13.4 m), length 20 ft 11 in (6.4 m), max speed 81 mph (130 kph), ceiling 14,750 ft (4,500 m), range 250 ml (402 km), max weight 1,543 lb

(700 kg), armament one Lewis or Vickers 0.303 machine gun.

CAUDRON G4

French two-seat reconnaissance bomber. First flight 1914 developed from the G-3 model. Powered by two 80-hp Gnome-Rhone 9C air-cooled rotary engines or two 100-hp Anzani engines. Wingspan 56 ft 5 in (17,2 m), length 23 ft 7 in (7.2 m), max speed 82 mph (132 kph) ceiling 14,750 ft (4,500 m), range 250 ml (402 km), rate of climb 800 ft (243 m) per min, max weight 2,932 lb (1,330 kg), armament one 0.303 Lewis or Vickers machine gun, bomb load 220 lb (100 kg).

CHANUTE GLIDER

American biplane glider of 1896-7. Wingspan 15 ft 9 in (4.8 m), chord of wings 4 ft 11 in (1.5 m), total wing area 154 ⅕ sq ft (47.17 sq m), length details not available. Best glide about 360 ft (109 m), gliding angle of 6:1.

CIERVA C30 AUTOGIRO

British two-seat autogiro. Powered by one 150-hp Armstrong Siddeley Genet seven-cylinder, air-cooled radial engine. Rotor diameter 37 ft (11.2 m), max speed 100 mph (160 kph), length 19 ft 8 in (5.9 m).

CONSOLIDATED MOD 28 CATALINA

Maritime patrol flying boat. First flown 1935. Powered by two 1,200-hp, 14-cylinder, two-row air-cooled radial Pratt & Whitney R-1830-92 Twin Wasp engines. Wingspan 104 ft (31.7 m) length 63 ft 11 in (19.5 m), max speed 196 mph (314 kph), rate of climb approx 1,100 ft (335 m) per min, ceiling 18,200 ft (5550 m), range at 100 mph (161 kph) 3,100 ml (4,960 km), max weight 34,000 lb (15,436 kg), armament four 0.5-in machine guns, 2000 lb (907 kg) of bombs or mines.

CURTISS GOLDEN FLYER

American single seat biplane of 1909. Powered by one Curtiss 40-hp, 4-cylinder, water-cooled, 6-cylinder, in-line engine.

Wingspan 33 ft 4 in (10.2 m), length 25 ft 9 in (7.9 m), max speed 45 mph (72 kph). Data based on the Curtiss Model D of 1909.

CURTISS C2

American two-seat flying boat of 1913. Powered by one 100-hp, V-8 liquid-cooled Curtiss OXX engine. Wingspan 47 ft 6 in (14.5 m), length 33 ft 1 in (10 .1 m), max speed 69 mph (111 kph), ceiling 4,500 ft (1,372 m). Data based on the Curtiss F boat.

CURTISS JENNY JN 4D

American two-seat trainer of 1916. Powered by one 50-hp Curtiss OX-5 engine. Wingspan 43 ft 7 in (13.30 m), length 27 ft 4 in (8.33 m), max speed 75 mph (121 kph), endurance 2 1/4 hours, max weight 2130 lb (966 kg).

CURTISS NC4

American maritime patrol flying boat of 1919. Powered by four 400-hp Liberty 12 A, V-12 water-cooled engines. Wingspan 126 ft (38.4 m), length 68 ft 3 in (20.8 m), max speed 91 mph (146 kph), max weight 28,500 lb (12,925 kg), armament eight machine guns (none carried on transatlantic flight). Five to six crew.

CURTISS PW 8

American single-seat fighter of 1922. Powered by one 435-hp V-12 Curtiss D-12, 12-cylinder, water-cooled engine. Wingspan 31 ft 10 in (9.74 m), length 23 ft 1 in (7.04 m), max speed 171 mph (275 kph), cruising speed 152 mph (244 kph), ceiling 20,350 ft (6,200 m), range 440 ml (708 km), armament two 0.303 Marlin machine guns.

DASSAULT BREGUET MIRAGE III

French single-seat fighter of 1956. Powered by one 13,225-lb (6,004-kg) thrust SNECMA Atar 9B single-shaft turbojet. Wingspan 27 ft (8.22 m), length 50 ft 10 in (15.5 m), max speed 863 mph (1,390 kph) Mach1.14 at sea-level, initial climb 16,400 ft (5,000 m) per min, ceiling 55,775 ft (17,000 m), combat radius 745 ml (1,200 km), ferry range with external tanks 2,485 ml (4,000 km), max

weight 19,700 lb (8,936 kg), armament two 30-mm DEFA 5–52 cannon, 3,000 lb (1,360 kg) bomb load. Tactical strike, reconnaissance and trainer versions also produced.

DASSAULT MIRAGE IVA

French two-seat strategic bomber of 1959. Powered by two 15,432-lb (7,000-kg) thrust SNECMA Atar 9K single-shaft augmented turbojets. Wingspan 38 ft 10 in (11.85 m), length 77 ft 1 in (23.5 m), max speed 1,454 mph (2,340 kph) Mach 2.2 at 40,000 ft (13,125 m), ceiling 65,620 ft (20,000 m), time to 36,090 ft (11,000 m) 4 min, 15 secs, ferry range 2,485 ml (44,000 km), tactical radius 770 ml (1,240 km), max weight 73,800 lb (33,475 kg), armament none, one 60-ton (62-tonne) free-fall bomb, or up to 16,000 lb (7,257 kg) other weapons.

DASSAULT MIRAGE 2000

French single or two-seat fighter of 1983. Powered by one 21,385-lb (9,715-kg) thrust SNECMA M 53–P2 turbofan. Wingspan 29 ft 11 in (9.1 m), length 47 ft 1 in (14.3 m), max speed 1,452 mph (2,336 kph), armament two 30-mm DEFA cannon, four Matra A/A missiles, 13,900 lb (6,300 kg) attack weapons.

DASSAULT MYSTÉRE

French single-seat fighter of 1951. Powered by one 6,600-lb (3,000-kg) thrust SNECMA Atar 101 D3 single-shaft turbojet. Wingspan 49 ft 9 in (13.1 m), length 38 ft 6 in (11.7 m), max speed 658 mph (1,060 kph), initial climb 8,460 ft (2,546 m) per min, ceiling 42,650 ft (13,000 m), range 745 ml (1,200 m), armament two 30 mm Hispano 603 cannon.

DASSAULT MYSTÉRE IVA

French single-seat fighter-bomber of 1952. Powered by one 7,716 lb (3,500 kg) thrust Hispano Suiza Verdon 350 single-shaft turbojet. Wingspan 36 ft 5 in (11.1 m), length 42 ft 2 in (12.9 m), max speed at sea level 696 mph (1,120 kph), initial climb 8,860 ft (2,700 m), ceiling 45,000 ft (13,750 m), range 820 ml (1,320 km), armament two 30-mm DEFA 551 cannon and 2,000 lb (907 kg) bombs or rockets.

DASSAULT SUPER MYSTÉRE
French single-seat fighter bomber of 1953. Powered by one 9,920-lb (4,500-kg) thrust SNECMA Atar 101G single-shaft augmented turbojet. Wingspan 34 ft 6 in (10.5 m), length 46 ft 1 in (14 m), max speed 686 mph (1,104 kph) at sea level, initial climb 17,500 ft (5,333 m) per min, ceiling 55,750 ft (17,000 m), range 540 ml (870 km), max weight 22,046 lb (10,009 kg), armament two 30-mm DEFA cannon, 325 SNEB 69-mm rockets and 2, 000 lb (907 kg) bomb load.

DASSAULT OURAGON
French single-seat fighter of 1949. Powered by one 5,070-lb (2,300-kg) thrust Hispano-Suiza Nene 104B single shaft turbojet. Wingspan 43 ft 2 in (13.2 m), length 36 ft 3 in (10.74 m), max speed 584 mph (940 kph), initial climb 7,847 ft (2,400m) per min, ceiling 49,210 ft (15,000 m), range 620 m (1,000 km), max weight 14,991 lb (6,800 kg), armament four 20-mm Hispano 404 cannon, two 1,100 lb (500 kg) bombs or 16 rockets.

DASSAULT RAFALE
French single-seat multi-role fighter of 1986. Powered by two 21,065-lb (9,555-kg) thrust SNECMA M-88-3 turbofans. Wingspan 36 ft 9 in (11.2 m), length 51 ft 10 in (11.80 m), max speed 1,320 mph (2,135 kph) at 55,000 ft (16,764 m), combat radius at sea-level 4,101 ml (6,600 km), max weight 44,090 lb (20,000 kg), armament one 30 GIT DFA 79.16 cannon and variety of A/A and A/S missiles including Excocet and nuclear to 7,715 lb (3,500 kg).

DE HAVILLAND DE H 4
British two-seat day bomber of 1916. Powered by a single 375-hp Rolls-Royce Eagle VII V-12 in-line water-cooled engine, (U.S. Mail versions of the 1920s powered by 400-hp Packard-designed Liberty engine). Wingspan 42 ft 4 in (12.9 m), length 30 ft

8 in (9.4 m), max speed 143 mph (230 kph), max weight 3,472 lb (1,575 kg), initial rate of climb 1,042 ft (306 m) per min, ceiling 20,000 ft (6096 m), one fixed 0.303 Vickers and two manual 0.303 Lewis machine guns, 460 lb (209 kg) bomb load.

DE HAVILLAND DE H 9
British two-seat bomber of 1918. Powered by one 240-hp Beardmore-Halford-Pullinger six-cylinder, in-line water-cooled engine. Wingspan 42 ft 4 in (12.9 m), length 30 ft 10 in (9.41 m), max speed 110 mph (177 kph), ceiling 18,000 ft (5,486 m), endurance 5hrs, 15 min, max weight 3,890 lb (1185.6 kg), armament two or three 0.303 machine guns and 660 lb (200 kg) bomb load.

DE HAVILLAND DE H 50
British four-seat biplane of 1923. Powered by 230-hp Armstrong Siddeley Puma six-cylinder, inline water-cooled engine and later (as in Alan Cobham's machine) by a 380-hp Armstrong Siddeley Jaguar 14-cylinder, air-cooled radial engine. Wingspan 42 ft 9 in (13.3 m), length 29 ft 9 in (9.2 m), max speed 112 mph (180 kph), cruising speed 102 mph (164 kph), total weight 3,900 lb (1,769kg).

DE HAVILLAND DE H 60 MOTH
British two-seat light biplane of 1925. Powered by a 140-hp four-cylinder, in-line air-cooled Cirrus I engine. Wingspan 30 ft (9.1 m), length 23 ft 8 in (7.2m), max speed 97 mph (156 kph), cruising speed 85 mph (136.7 kph), ceiling 15,000 ft (4,572m), range 410 ml (659.8 km), total weight 1,550 lb (703 kg).

DE HAVILLAND DE H 82A TIGER MOTH
British two-seat basic trainer. First flown in 1931. Powered by a single 130-hp De Havilland Gypsy Major I inverted in-line four cylinder, air-cooled engine. Wingspan 29 ft 4 in (8.94 m), length 23 ft 11 in (7.29 m), max cruising speed 99 mph (160 kph), ceiling 13,600 ft (4,145 m), range 285 ml

(459km), max weight 1,825 lb (828 kg).

DE HAVILLAND DE H 83 FOX MOTH
British 5-seat light cabin biplane of 1932. Powered by one 120-hp De Havilland Gypsy III four-cylinder, in-line air-cooled engine. Wingspan 30 ft 10 in (9.4 m), length 25 ft 9 in (7.84 m), max speed 107 mph (172 kph), ceiling 10,000 ft (3,048 m), range 438 ml (704 km), max weight 2,070 lb (938.9 kg).

DE HAVILLAND DE H 85 LEOPARD MOTH
Three-seat British light aircraft of 1932. Powered by a 130-hp De Havilland Gypsy Major four-cylinder, inverted in-line air-cooled engine. Wingspan 37 ft 6 in (11.5 m), length 24 ft 6 in (7.5 m), max speed 140 mph (225 kph), cruising speed 110 mph (177kph), ceiling 14,500 ft (4,419 m), range 700 ml (1,126 km), rate of climb 625 ft (190.5 m) per min, max weight 2,225 lb (1,009 kg).

DE H 98 MOSQUITO NF XII
British two-seat night fighter. First flown in 1941. Fitted with Mk VII Airborne Interception centimetric Radar. Powered by two Rolls-Royce Merlin 21 or 23 1,280-hp V-12 liquid-cooled engines. Wingspan 54 ft 2 in (16,5 m), length 41 ft 9 in (12.7 m), max speed 410 mph (660 kph), ceiling about 40,000 ft (12,190 m), range typically 1,800 ml (2,990 km), max weight 25,000 lb (11,340kg). Armament four 20-mm cannon. Original Mosquito designed as high speed, unarmed day bomber. Many variations, including fighter and reconnaissance versions followed.

DE H 100 VAMPIRE
British single-seat jet fighter. First flown 1943. Powered by a single De Havilland Goblin turbojet of 3,100 lb static thrust. Wingspan 40 ft (12.2 m), length 30 ft 8 in (9.4 m), max weight 8,000 lb (3,632 kg), max speed 540 mph (800 kph), ceiling 40–50,000 ft (13,725–15,250 m), range 730 ml (1,175 km), with drop tanks 1,400 ml (2,253 km), armament four 20-mm

cannon. Altitude record 59,491 ft (18,133 m) set in 1948 by modified version with De H Ghost engine of 4,400-lb (1997.6-kg) thrust.

DE HAVILLAND 108 SWALLOW
British experimental single-seat tail-less jet of 1949. Powered by one 3,100-lb (1,406-kg) thrust De Havilland Goblin turbojet. Wingspan 39 ft (11.8m), max speed Mach 1, max weight 8,960 lb (4,064 kg). Fuselage of De Havilland Vampire fighter.

DE HAVILLAND DE H 106 COMET
British 36-passenger transport of 1949. Powered by four 4,450-lb (2,019-kg) thrust DeHavilland Ghost 50 Mk I turbojets and two 5,000-lb (2,268-kg) thrust Sprite rocket motors. Wingspan 115 ft (35 m), length 93 ft (28,35 m), max speed 490 mph (789 kph), cruising altitude 35,000 ft (10,668 m), range 3,540 ml (5,710 km), max weight 105,000 lb (47,628 kg). Four crew. First jet passenger transport; only modified Comet 4, 4b and 4c models produced in numbers after disasters with Comet Mk I series. See Comet 4 details below.

DE HAVILLAND COMET 4
British passenger transport of 1958. Powered by four 10,000-lb (4763-kg) thrust Rolls-Royce Avon 525b turbo jets. Wingspan 107 ft 10 in (32.87 m), length 118 ft (35.69 m), cruising speed 532 mph (856 kph), max weight 156,000 lb (70,762 kg), range 3,350 ml (5,391 km). Carried up to 101 passengers with three or four crew.

DEPERDUSSIN 1913 RACER
French single-seat monoplane of 1913 with first monocoque fuselage. Powered by one 160-hp Gnome-Rhone 14-cylinder, two-row air-cooled rotary engine. Wingspan 21 ft 10 in (6.7 m), length 20 ft 6 in (6.1 m) max speed 127 mph (204 kph)★, weight 1,350 lb (612 kg). ★World speed record created by seaplane version.

DORNIER RS I
All-metal construction flying boat. First aircraft designed by Claudius Dornier.

Produced at Zeppelin-Werke, Lindau, Germany in 1914. Powered by three 240-hp, inline six-cylinder, water-cooled Maybach engines. Span 145 ft 9 in (43.5 m).

DORNIER RS III

All-metal flying boat designed and produced by Claudius Dornier at Zeppelin-Werke Lindau, Germany, 1917. Powered by four 245-hp six-cylinder, inline Maybach water-cooled engines. Wingspan 121 ft 4 in (37 m), length 74 ft 8 in (22.7 m), max speed 84 mph (135 kph), endurance 12 hours, ceiling 6,560 ft (2,000 m).

DORNIER DO. X

All-metal construction, transocean flying boat. Designed and produced by Claudius Dornier at Alterheim, Germany in 1927. Only three constructed. Do. X which flew to South America powered by twelve Curtiss GV-1570 640-hp liquid-cooled engines mounted in tandem pairs. Wingspan 157 ft 5 in (48 m), length 131 ft 4 in (40 m), cruising speed 118 mph (190 kph), ceiling 4,1000 ft (1,250 m), range 1,055 ml (1,697 km), max takeoff weight 123,460 lb (56,000 kg). Capacity up to 160 passengers.

DORNIER DO. 17

1936 airliner later developed in Germany as the Do. 17Z medium bomber. Produced in large numbers during World War II. Powered by two 1,000-hp Bramo 323 radial engines. Wingspan 59 ft (18 m), length 52 ft (15 .8 m), max speed 263 mph (423 kph), range 1,860 ml (2,993 km).

DORNIER DO. 18 WAL (WHALE)

Highly successful all-metal German flying boat designed in 1922. Powered originally by two 360-hp Rolls-Royce Eagle engines then various engines of similar power such as Hispano, B.M.W., Junkers, Napier, Bristol, Piaggio, Hispano. Wingspan 73 ft 9 in (29.5 m) length 80 ft 5 in (24.6m), max speed 130 mph (209 kph), ceiling 6,500 ft (2,000 m), range 620 ml (1,000 km).

DORNIER DO. 24

German maritime patrol flying boat of 1937. Powered by three 750-hp Wright Cyclone air-cooled radial engines or three 1,000-hp Bramir Fafnir 323 R, nine-cylinder air-cooled radial engines. Wingspan 88 ft 7 in (27 m), length 72 ft 2 in (22.m), max speed 150 mph (241 kph), range 2,240 ml (3,600 km), max weight 40,560 lb (18,400 kg), armament two machine guns and one 20-mm cannon with 1,320-lb (600-kg) bomb load.

DORNIER DO. 31E

German. The only VSTOL (Very Short Take-Off and Landing) passenger aircraft to make full transition from vertical takeoff to normal flight. First flew in 1967. Powered by two banks of Rolls-Royce lift jets at wing tips and two Bristol-Sideley Pegasus vectored thrust units under wing. Wingspan 64 ft 7 in (19 .7 m), length 67 ft 5 in (20.54 m), cruising speed 460 mph (740 kph), weight 51,808 lb (23,599 kg), loaded weight 52,500 lb (24,000 kg), range 1,120 ml (1,902 km).

DORNIER DO. 335 PFEIL (ARROW)

German. First production aircraft to be installed with an ejection seat. First flown in 1943. Powered by two 1,900-hp Daimler-Benz DB 603G 12-cylinder, inverted-vee, liquid-cooled engines mounted in tandem. Wingspan 45 ft 4 in (13.8 m), length 45 ft 6 in (13.8 m), height 16 ft 4 in (4 m), max speed 413 mph (665 kph), ceiling 37,400 ft (11,410 m), range 1,280 ml (2,050 km). Less than 100 were completed before production stopped at the end of World War II.

DOUGLAS DWC WORLD CRUISER

American two-seat land/floatplane of 1924. Powered by a single 420-hp V-1650 Liberty12A, V-12 water-cooled engine. Wingspan 50 ft (15.24 m), length 35.5 ft (20.66 m), height 13.6 ft (4.15 m), max speed 100 mph (161 kph), ceiling 7,000 ft (2,134 m), range 2,200 ml (3,540 km), weight

(float plane) 8,180 lb (3,710 kg). Fuel capacity (floatplane) 375 gal (1,700 ltr). Average speed on total world trip of 371 hrs, 70 mph (112 kph). Four only modified for world circum-navigation. Fitted with dual controls.

DOUGLAS DC-2

American 14 seat passenger transport of 1934. Powered by two nine-cylinder 720-hp Wright SGR 1820 air-cooled radial engines. Wingspan 85 ft (25.9 m), length 61 ft 11 in (18.9 m), max speed 196 mph (315 kph). Two crew.

DOUGLAS DC-3

American 28-30 passenger transport. First flight in 1935. Powered by two 1,200-hp Pratt & Whitney R-1830SIC 3G Twin Wasp 14-cylinder, radial air-cooled engines (or two Wright SGR-1820 Cyclones). Wingspan 95 ft (28 96 m), length 64 ft 6 in (19.66 m), cruising speed 165 mph (266 kph), range 333 ml (563 km), max weight 28,000 lb (12,700 kg).

DOUGLAS DC-7C

American passenger transport of 1955. Powered by four 3,400-hp Wright R 3350 18EA-1 turbo compound 18-cylinder, air-cooled radial engines. Wingspan 127 ft 6 in (938.8 m), length 112 ft 3 in (34.2 m), cruising speed 360mph (580 kph), range 4,606 ml (7,412 km), max weight 143,000 lb (64,864 kg). Seating for up to 105 passengers and eight crew.

DOUGLAS DC-8

American jet passenger transport of 1958. Powered by four 13,500-lb (6,124 -kg) thrust Pratt & Whitney JTC3C-6, 2-shaft turbojets. Wingspan 142 ft 5 in (43.41 m), length 150 ft 6 in (45.87 m), cruising speed 580 mph (933 kph), range 4,300 ml (6,920 km), max weight 273,000 lb (123,830 kg). Seating for up to 179 passengers and five crew.

DOUGLAS C 47

American military version of Douglas DC-3 passenger transport. First flown in 1936. Powered by two 14-cylinder, 1,200-hp Pratt

& Whitney R-1830 90D Twin Wasp two-row, air-cooled radial engines, featuring large cargo doors. Wingspan 95 ft (29 m), length 64 ft 6 in (19.7 m), max speed 230 mph (370 kph), cruising speed 185 mph (298 kph), weight 33,000 lb (14,969 kg), armament variable but often three 7.62-mm Miniguns. Three crew plus 27 troops. Many versions such as ambulance, glider tug etc.

DOUGLAS A4 SKYHAWK

American single-seat naval jet attack bomber of 1954. Powered by one 8,500-lb (3,860-kg) thrust Pratt & Whitney J52-6 turbo jet. Wingspan 27 ft 6 in (8.4 m), length 40 ft 1 in (12.2 m), max speed 685 mph (1,102 kph), initial climb 5,620 ft (1,713 m) per min, ceiling about 49,000 ft (14,935 m), max weight 17,000 lb (7,711 kg) range approx 920 ml (1,480 km), armament two 20-mm cannon and 8,200 lb (3,270 kg) bomb load.

DUNNE D8

British single-seat experimental tail-less biplane of 1912. Powered by one 80-hp Gnome air-cooled rotary engine. Wingspan 46 ft (14 m), length approx 26 ft 6 in (8.07 m), max speed approx 45 mph (72.4 kph), max takeoff weight approx 1,900 lb (8,618 kg). U.S. Navy floatplane version developed in secret in 1916—the Burgess-Dunne, AH-7, powered by 100-hp Curtiss OXX-2 engine which gave max speed of 69 mph (110 kph).

EMSCO MODEL B-3

American transport monoplane of 1931. Powered by one 420-hp Pratt & Whitney Wasp nine-cylinder, air-cooled radial engine. Wingspan 60 ft (18 .2 m), length 40 ft 9 in (12 4 m), max speed 150 mph (241.4 kph), cruising speed 120 mph (193 kph), rate of climb 900 ft (274 m) per min, ceiling 20,000 ft (6,096 m). Fuel capacity 997 U.S. gal (3,774 ltr) in seven fuselage tanks, range 4,000 ml (6,437 km), max weight 10,000 lb (4,535 kg).

FAIREY DELTA II

British single-seat experimental delta-wing aircraft of 1954. Powered by one Rolls-Royce Avon 200 series turbojet with reheat and variable area nozzle. Wingspan 26 ft (8.18 m), length 51 ft 7 in (15.71 m), max speed 1,132 mph (1,821 kph)—a world speed record in 1956. Nose area hinged downward for takeoff and landing (see also BAC 221).

FAIREY IIID

British two-seat maritime reconnaissance aircraft of 1917. Powered by one 375-hp Rolls-Royce Eagle V-12 water-cooled engine. Wingspan 46 ft 1 in (14. m), length 31 ft 9 in (9.6 m), max speed 120 mph (193 kph), ceiling 17,000 ft (5,182 m), range 400 ml 643 km), endurance 5 hrs, armament one fixed Lewis and one manually-aimed Vickers 0.303 machine gun plus two 100-lb (45-kg) bombs.

FARMAN HF 1

French single-seat biplane of 1908 based on a Voisin design. Powered by one 50-hp Antoinette V-8 engine. Wingspan 35 ft 6 in (10.8 m), length 44 ft (13.5 m), max speed 38 mph (60 kph), flew first 3/5 ml (1 km) circuit in Europe.

FERBER GLIDER

Single place French glider of 1904 based on the Wright brothers' *Flyer*.

FOKKER SPIDER

Dutch single-seat monoplane of 1911. Powered by a 50-hp four-cylinder in line water-cooled Argus engine. Wingspan 36 ft (11 m), length 26 ft (8 m). Wing warping used for lateral control. Fokker flew it to an altitude of about 490 ft (150 m). The machine he demonstrated at Haarlem was his third version of the Spider, named because it had so many wire bracings.

FOKKER E I

German single-seat fighter. First designed as the M5 and flown in 1913. Powered by one 110-hp le Rhone seven-cylinder, air-cooled rotary engine. Wingspan 26 ft 2 in (8 m), length 23 ft 2 in (7.1 m), max speed 103 mph (165 kph), ceiling 20,013 ft (6,100 km), rate of climb 720 ft (220 m) per min, ceiling 12,000 ft (3,659 m), endurance 2 plus hours, range about 130 ml (209 km), max weight 1,239 lb (562 kg), armament one and later two 7.92 mm Spandau machine guns. When fitted with the world's first interrupter gear for its machine gun it was produced as the EI in 1915; operational in 1915 and the E II and E III followed.

FOKKER DR. I TRIPLANE

German single-seat triplane fighter of 1917. Powered by one 110-hp Le Rhone nine-cylinder, air-cooled rotary engine built under licence by the Thulin Company in Germany. Wingspan 23 ft 7 in (7.1 m), length 18 ft 11 in (5.7 m), max speed 103 mph (165 kph), ceiling 20, 013 ft (6,100 m), max weight 1,289 lb (585 kg), armament two 7.92 mm Spandau machine guns. Inspired by success of British Sopwith Triplane of 1916.

FOKKER D VII

German single-seat fighter first flown operationally in1918. Powered by a single 160-hp Mercedes D III six-cylinder, in-line water-cooled engine. Wingspan 29 ft 3 in (8.91 m), length 22 ft 11 in (6.9 m), max speed at 9,843 ft (3,000 m) 109 mph (175 kph), initial rate of climb around 800 ft (243 m) per min, ceiling 19,685 ft (6,000 m), endurance 1½ hours, max weight 1,936 lb (878 kg), armament two 7.9 mm Spandau machine guns.

FOKKER T-2 (FIV)

Dutch transport monoplane of 1922. Powered by one 400-hp Liberty V-12 water-cooled engine. Wingspan 79ft 6 in (24 .26 m), length 49 ft 3 in (15 m), max speed 96 mph (154 kph), cruising speed 75 mph (120 kph), range more than 2,500 ml (94,023 km), total weight 10,850 lb (4,922 kg), average speed for trans-America flight 92 mph (148 kph). Only four constructed.

FOKKER F VII

Dutch single-engined six-seat passenger transport of 1924. Powered by one 360-hp Rolls-Royce Eagle V-12 engine or similar up to 450 hp. Wingspan 63 ft 4 in (19,3 m), length 47 ft (14.3 m).

FOKKER F-VIIB 3M

Dutch eight-to ten-seat passenger transport. First flown in 1927 and was an adaptation of the Fokker FVII. Powered by three 200-hp Wright J 5 Cyclone 9-cylinder, air-cooled radial engines or three Armstrong Siddely Lynx engines of similar power. Wingspan 71 ft 2 in (21.7 m), length 47 ft 7 in (14.5 m), max speed 115 mph (185 kph), cruising speed 93 mph (149kph), range 477 ml (768 km), ceiling 10,170 ft (3,100 m). Two crew. There were several versions.

FOCKE-ACHGELIS FA 61

German single-seat two intermeshing three-blade rotors helicopter of 1936. Powered by one 160-hp Bramo Sh 14a seven-cylinder, air-cooled radial engine. Main rotor blade length 23 ft (7 m), length 24 ft (7.3 m), max speed 76 mph (122 kph), rate of climb 750 ft (228 m) per sec, ceiling 8,600 ft (2,621 m), endurance 1 hr, 30 min, max weight 2,100 lb (952 kg). First helicopter to fly successfully.

GENERAL ATOMICS RQ-1 PREDATOR

American Unmanned Combat Air Vehicle. First operations in 1995. Powered by a Rotax four-cylinder engine. Wingspan 48 ft 7 in (14.84 m), length 27 ft (8.23 m), payload 450 lb (204 kg), ceiling 25,000 ft (7,620 m). Can remain on station for 24 hours at a range of 460 ml (740 km).

GLOSTER GLADIATOR

British single-seat biplane fighter. First delivery in 1937. Powered by one 830-hp Bristol Mercury nine-cylinder, air-cooled radial engine. Wingspan 32 ft 3 in (9.83 m), length 27 ft 5 in (8.36 m), max speed 257 mph (414 kph), ceiling 33,500 ft (10,211 m), range 440 ml (708 km), max weight 4,864 lb (2,206 kg), armament four 0.303 machine guns.

GRUMMAN F9F PANTHER

American single-seat naval fighter of 1947. Powered by a 5,000-lb (2,270-kg) thrust Pratt & Whitney turbojet. Wingspan 38 ft (11.58 m), length 37 ft 3 in (11.35 m), max speed at 22,000 ft (6,700 m), 526 mph (846 kph), ceiling 44,600 ft (13,600 m), range 1,353 ml (2,180 km), max weight 19,452 lb (8,842 kg), armament four 20-mm cannon, 2,000-lb (907-kg) bomb load.

HANDLEY PAGE HARROW II

British military transport of 1936. Powered by two 925-hp Bristol Pegasus XX nine-cylinder, air-cooled radial engines. Wingspan 88 ft 5 in (26.9 m), length 83 ft 6 in (25.4 m), max speed 210 mph (337.9 kph), max weight 23,000 lb (4,732 kg), capacity 20 troops.

HANDLEY PAGE 115

British single-seat experimental delta-wing jet of 1960. Powered by one 1,900-lb (861-kg) thrust Bristol Siddely Viper ASV-9 turbojet. Wingspan 20 ft (6,096 m), length 49 ft 11 in (15.2 m) including probe, length to nose 45 ft (13.7 m), max speed 300 mph (482 kph). Because of its extreme sweepback (about 75 degrees) this aircraft was always flown stalled and achieved lift from wing vortices.

HORTON HO. IX (GO 229)

Single-seat German tail-less bomber of 1944. Powered by two 1,800-lb (816.4-kg) thrust Junkers Jumo 004B turbojets. Wingspan 52 ft 6 in (16,0 m), max speed 590 mph (949.5 kph), ceiling 52,500 ft (15,849.4 m), rate of climb 4,300 ft (1,310 m) per min, range 1,200 ml (1,931 km), weight loaded 18,700 lb (8,482 kg), 4,400 lb (1,995 kg) bomb load, armament four MK 108 cannon.

HUGHES H-1 RACER

American single-seat experimental racer of 1935 designed and flown by Howard Hughes. Powered by one 700-hp Pratt & Whitney Twin Wasp 14-cylinder, air-cooled radial engine. Wingspan of transcontinental record machine 31 ft 9 in (9.67 m), length 27 ft (8.23 m), max speed 352.322 mph (567 kph)—a world speed record. Average speed for transcontinental record 322 mph (518.2 kph), max weight 5,500 lb (2,495 kg).

HUGHES H-4 *SPRUCE GOOSE*

American heavy transport flying boat of 1947. Powered by eight 3,500-hp Pratt & Whitney Wasp major R-4360 four row "Corncob" 28-cylinder, air-cooled radial engines. Wingspan 320 ft 6 in (97.69 m), length 218 ft 6 in (66.6 m), max speed 218 mph (350 kph), range 5,900 ml (9,495 km), payload 152,000 lb (60,947 kg). Flown only once by Howard Hughes for about one ml (1.6 km) at 70 ft (21 m).

HUGHES XF11

Single-seat American experimental reconnaissance aircraft of 1946. Powered by two 3,000-hp Pratt & Whitney R-4360 28-cylinder, four-row, radial air-cooled engines driving contra-rotating air screws. Wingspan 101 ft 4 in (30.8 m) length 65 ft 5 in (19.9 m), max speed 420 mph (675 kph), ceiling 48,000 ft (14,630 m), range 5,000 ml (8,046 km),max weight 58,000 lb (26,308 kg). Performance figures calculated only, as prototype crashed before testing completed.

JUNKERS W 33

German all-metal transport monoplane of 1926. Powered by one 310-hp Junkers L-5 water-cooled in-line engine. Wingspan 58 ft 3 in (17.75 m), length 34 ft (10.3 m), cruising speed 92 mph (148 kph), endurance—world record in 1927 of 52 hr, 23 min. W34 version fitted with a 660-hp BMW 132A nine-cylinder, air-cooled radial engine to increase performance.

LANGLEY AERODROME

American single-seat flying machine. Powered by one 52-hp five-cylinder, air-cooled radial engine designed by Charles Manly. Wingspan 48 ft 5 in (14.7 m), length 52 ft 5 in (16 m). This machine did not fly.

LEVASSEUR PL8 *OISEAU BLANC*

A French two-seat long-distance biplane modified from the French Navy's Levasseur 4R 4b for transatlantic crossing by Nungesser and Coli. Powered by one Lorraine type 450 CV-12 engine. Wingspan 47 ft 10 in (14.6 m), length 32 ft 9 in (10 m), cruising speed 102 .5 mph (165 kph), max weight 11,089 lb (5,030 kg), range 4,350 ml (7,000 km). Jettisoning undercarriage probably increased speed by up to 10 mph (15 kph). Fuselage designed as a boat-shape hull in case of ditching.

LEVAVASSEUR ANTOINETTE

French single-seat monoplane of 1909. Powered by 50-hp fuel-injected water-cooled Antoinette V-8 evaporative (steam) engine. Wingspan 40 ft (12.2 m), length 37 ft (11.3 m), max speed 45 mph (72 kph).

LILIENTHAL GLIDER

German monoplane glider of 1896. Wingspan 26 ft (7.93 m), length 13 ft (3.9 m), glided 1,150 ft (350m) from a 165-ft (50-m) high hill, also soared to 50 ft (15.2 m), max speed, at the "speed of a galloping horse". Controlled only by body movement of Lilienthal as pilot.

LOCKHEED ALTAIR

American two-seat light personal transport of 1931. Powered by one 450-hp Pratt & Whitney Wasp S1D1 nine-cylinder, air-cooled radial engine or 625-hp Wright Cyclone. Wingspan 42 ft 10 in (13 m), length 27 ft 6 in (8.3 m), cruising speed 205 mph (329 kph), ceiling 18,000 ft (5,486 m), range approx 1,400 ml (1,596 km), max weight 5,170 lb (2,345 kg).

LOCKHEED VEGA

American six-seat passenger transport of 1927. Powered by a single uncowled 200-hp Wright J 5 C Whirlwind nine-cylinder, air-cooled radial engine (later models with N.A.S.A.-cowled 450-hp Pratt & Whitney Wasp). Wingspan 41 ft 912.5 m), length 27 ft 6 in (8.38 m), max speed 185 mph (298 kph), max weight 4,500 lb (2,041 kg), ceiling 19,000 ft (5,791 m), range 725 ml (1,167 km).

LOCKHEED SIRIUS

American two-seat personal transport designed for Charles Lindbergh in 1930. Powered by a 710-hp Wright Cyclone SR-1820-F2 nine-cylinder, air-cooled radial engine. Wingspan 42 ft 10 in (13 m), length 27 ft 10 in (8.5 m), max speed 175 mph (282 kph), ceiling 18,000 ft (5,486 m), range 975 ml (1,596 km), max weight 5,170 lb (2,345 kg).

LOCKHEED 10A ELECTRA

American 10-passenger airliner of 1934. Powered by two Pratt & Whitney Wasp Jr SB/450-hp engines. Wingspan 55 ft (16.75m), length (38 ft 7in (11.7m), max speed 205 mph (329.9 kph), cruising speed 182 mph (192.9 kph), ceiling 22,000 ft (6,705 m), rate of climb 1,000 ft (3,048 m) per min, range 675 ml (1,086 km), total weight 10,500 lb (4,762 kg). Two crew.

LOCKHEED 12A

American six-passenger airliner of 1936. Powered by two Pratt & Whitney Jr/SB 450-hp engines. Wingspan 49 ft 6 in (15 m), length 36 ft 4 in (11.1 m), max speed 226 mph (363.7 kph), cruising speed 203 mph (326.7 kph), ceiling 22,900 ft (6,979.9 m), rate of climb 1,470 ft (448 m) per min, range 800 ml (1,287 km), total weight 8,400 lb (3,810 kg). Two crew.

LOCKHEED 14 ELECTRA

Medium range 14-passenger transport. First flown in 1934. Powered by two Wright ASGR Cyclone radial air-cooled, 18-cylinder two-row radial engines of 900-hp each. Wingspan 65 ft 6 in (19.96 m), length 44 ft 4 in (13.51 m), cruising speed 228 mph (367 kph), ceiling 24,500 ft (7468 m), range 1,590 ml (2558 km). Two crew. Howard Hughes virtually tripled the fuel capacity in his record-breaking Electra and his 14,672-ml (23,611-km) circumnavigation in 1938 was flown at an average speed of 206 mph (331.5 km).

LOCKHEED P 38 LIGHTNING

American single-seat long-range fighter first flown in 1939. Powered by two 1,450-hp Allison V-171089/91 liquid-cooled V-twelve engines. Wingspan 52 ft (15.85 m), length 37 ft 10 in (11.53 m), max speed 414 mph (666 kph), ceiling 44,000 ft (13,410 m), range 475 ml (764 km), max weight 21,600 lb (9798 kg), armament one 20-mm cannon and four 0.5 machine guns plus 3,200-lb (1,451-kg) bomb load.

LOCKHEED SUPER CONSTELLATION

Long-range passenger transport. Powered by four 3,520-hp Wright R3350-DA3 turbo-compound 18-cylinder, turbine-boosted air-cooled radial engines. Wingspan 126 ft 2 in (38.47 m), max weight 145,000 lb (66,772 kg), cruising speed 354 mph (570 kph) at 22,600ft (6890 m), range 5,100 ml (8,200 km). 95 passengers, five flight crew plus cabin crew.

LOCKHEED F80 SHOOTING STAR

Single-seat fighter. First flown in 1944. Powered by one Allison J-33 A-35 turbo-jet of 5,400-lb (2449-kg) static thrust. Wingspan 38 ft 10 in (11.85 m), length 34 ft 6 in (10 51 m), max speed 594 mph (955.9 kph), ceiling 46,800 ft (14,265 m), rate of climb 5,000 ft (1,524 m) per min, range 825 ml (1328 km), max weight 16,856 lb (7,645.9 kg), armament six 0.5 machine guns plus 2,000-lb (908-kg) bomb load or eight rockets.

LOCKHEED F 104 STARFIGHTER

American single-seat fighter. First flown in 1954. Many versions—104c powered by a single 15,800-lb (7,167-kg) afterburning thrust General Electric J79-GE-7 turbojet engine. Wingspan 121 ft 9 in (6.63 m), length 54 ft 6 in (16.6 m), max speed 1,150 mph (1850.7 kph), or Mach 1.74 at 50,000 ft (15,240 m), rate of climb 54,000 ft (16,459 m) per min, ceiling 58,000 ft (17,678 m), max takeoff weight 27,853 lb (12,634 kg), armament one 20-mm M61A1 cannon plus up to four AIM Sidewinder A/A missiles or 2,000-lb (907.2-kg) bomb load.

LOCKHEED U-2

American single seat, high altitude reconnaissance aircraft. First flown in 1955. U-2 A model powered by one 11,200-lb (5080-kg) static thrust Pratt & Whitney J 57 13 A two-shaft turbojet. Wingspan 80 ft (24.38 m), length 49 ft 7 in (15.1 m), max speed 494 mph (795 kph), ceiling 70,000 ft (21,340 m), range 2,600 ml (4,185 km), max weight 17,270 lb (7833 kg). No armament.

LOCKHEED SR 71A BLACKBIRD

American two-seat high altitude supersonic surveillance aircraft of 1964. Powered by two 32,500-lb (14,740-kg) thrust Pratt & Whitney JT11T-20B turbojets. Wingspan 55 ft 7 in (16.95 m), length 107 ft 5in (32.74 m), max speed 2,310 mph (3,717 kph), range 2,980 ml (4,800 km), ceiling 85,069 ft (25,920 m), range at 78,740 ft (24,000 m) at 1,938 mph (3,191 kph) is 2,982 ml (4,800 km), endurance normally 1 hr, 30 min but can loiter for 7 hours, max weight 170,000 lb (77,110 kg). Absolute world speed record over 15-ml (25-km) course 2,193 mph (3,5300 kph) Mach 3 31. Two crew.

MARTYNSIDE TYPE A *RAYMOOR*/F4A

British two-seat long distance aircraft of 1919. Powered by a single 285-hp engine. Total weight 4,600 lb (2,086 kg), endurance with 2, 000 lb (907 kg) fuel load, 7 hours. Believed to be similar to the Martynside F4A which itself was a two-seat version of

single-seat F4 fighter. Powered by one 300-hp Hispano-Suiza engine. Wingspan 32ft 9 in (9.98 m), length 25 ft 6 in (7.77 m), max speed 145 mph (233 kph), total weight 2,300 lb (1,043 kg), endurance 3 hours.

MESSERSCHMITT M20 A

German 10-passenger transport of 1920. Powered by one 500-hp BMW VIa water-cooled V12 engine. Wingspan 83 ft 8 in (25.5 m), length 52 ft 2in (15.9 m), max speed 109 mph (175 kph), range about 621 ml (1,000 km), max weight 10,141 lb (5,600 kg), payload 3,307 lb (1,500 kg).

MESSERSCHMITT BF 108 TAIFUN

German four-seat touring monoplane of 1934-5. Powered by one 270-hp Argus As 10C inverted V-8 cylinder air-cooled engine. Wingspan 34 ft 10 in (10.62 m), length 27 ft 2 in (8.29 m), max speed 188 mph (303 kph), absolute ceiling 29,766 ft (9,073 m), range 621 ml (1,000 km), max weight 2,981 lb (1,352 kg). Produced in France post-1945 as the Nord 1002 with a 240-hp Renault built Argus engine.

MESSERSCHMITT BF 109E

German single-seat fighter prototype. First flown in 1935. Powered by one 1,100-hp Daimler Benz DB601A 12-cylinder, liquid-cooled inverted V-twelve cylinder engine. Wingspan 32 ft 4 in (9.87 m), length 28 ft 4 in (8.64 m), max speed 354 mph (570 kph), ceiling 34,450 ft (10,500 m), initial rate of climb 3,100 ft (944 m) per min, range 460 ml (740 km), armament four Rheinmetal-Borsig 7.92-mm MG17 and one 20-mm cannon firing through propeller hub.

MESSERSCHMITT 323 GIGANT

German heavy transport. First flown in 1942. Powered by six 1,140-hp Gnome-Rhone 14N 48/49 14-cylinder, air-cooled two-row radial engines. Wingspan 180 ft 5 in (55m), length 92 ft 4 in (28.15m), max speed 177 mph (285 kph), initial climb 710 mph (216 kph), ceiling 13,100 ft

(4,000 m), range 684 ml (1,100 km), max weight 94,815 lb (43,00 kg)—could take payload of 48,500 lb (922,000 kg), armament five MG 15 machine guns in nose plus six MG 34 Infantry machine guns in side windows. Development of Me. 321 glider first flown in 1941.

MESSERSCHMITT 209 V-1

German single-seat experimental high speed racing machine of 1939. Powered by one Daimler Benz DB 601A RJ 1,550-hp evaporative water-cooled engine capable of producing 2,300 hp for two min. Wingspan 32 ft 11 in (10.04 m), length 23 ft 9 in (7.2 m), max speed created 1939 world record of 469.22 mph, ceiling 36,080 ft (10,997 m), endurance of racer 35 min, cooling water capacity 100 Imp gal (378.4 ltr), max weight 5.54 lb (2,515 kg).

MESSERSCHMITT ME. 262

German single-seat fighter. First flight of prototype in 1941. Powered by two 1,980-lb (900-kg) thrust Junkers Jumo 004B single-shaft axial turbojets. Wingspan 40 ft 11 in (12.5 m), length 34 ft 9 in (10.6 m), max speed 540 mph (870 kph), ceiling 37,565 ft (11,500 m), initial rate of climb 3,940 ft (1,200 m) per min, range 650 ml (1,050 km), max weight 9,700 lb (4,400 kg), armament four 30-mm MK 108 cannon with variations, including rockets. Also single-seat bomber and two seat night-fighter versions.

MCDONNELL F4 PHANTOM

American two-seat multi-role land-based and carrier-borne jet fighter. First flown in 1958 and operated for 20 years in many variations and in 13 air forces, also creating many international record performances. The world's most outstanding jet fighter design. Wingspan data based on the F4E model. Powered by two General Electric J29GE-17A axial flow turbojets of 11,870-lb (5,389-kg) thrust. Wingspan 38 ft 7 in (11.77m), length 63 ft (19.20 m), max speed 1,432 mph (2,306 kph) or Mach 2

at 36,000 ft (10,972 m), ceiling 58,750 ft (17,907 m), initial rate of climb 49,800 ft (15,180 m) per min, ferry range 1,612 ml (2,594 km), max takeoff weight 61,795 lb (28,030 kg), armament one General Electric M61A-1 20-mm multi-barrel cannon and large variety of underwing stores including rockets and nuclear bombs.

NIEUPORT GOSHAWK

British single-seat racing biplane of 1920. Powered by one 295-hp ABC/RAF Dragonly nine-cylinder, air-cooled radial engine. Wingspan approx 28 ft 9 in (8.53 m), length 19 ft (5.79 m), max speed 166 mph (267 kph). One only built.

NIEUPORT XVII

French single-seat fighter first flown in 1916. Powered by a single 80-hp Gnome-Rhone 9C nine-cylinder, air-cooled rotary engine. Wingspan 26 ft 11 in (8.22 m), length 18 ft 10 in (5.74 m), max speed 109 mph (176 kph), ceiling 17,388 ft (5,300 m), initial climb about 800 ft (243 m) per min, range 186 ml (300 km), endurance 2 hrs, 30 min, max weight 1,179 lb (534 kg), armament one 0.303 Lewis or one or sometimes two Vickers machine guns. Some models carried rockets on interplane struts.

NORD 1500 GRIFFON II

French single-seat experimental ram-jet/turbojet of 1959. Powered by 7,716-lb (3,503-kg) thrust SNECMA Atar 101E (mounted inside a ramjet which provides 80 percent of thrust at Mach 2.0). Wingspan 26 ft 7 in (8.1 m), length 51 ft 7 in (15.72 m), max speed Mach 2.19, ceiling 60,000 ft (18,288 m), weight 14,839 lb (6,730.8 kg).

NORTHROP ALPHA

American. First stressed-skin monocoque, all-metal monoplane of 1930. Powered by one 450-hp Pratt & Whitney Wasp nine-cylinder, air-cooled radial engine. Wingspan 41 ft 10 in (12.7 m), length 28 ft 5 in (8 7m), max speed 170 mph (273,5 kph), total weight 4,500 lb (2,041 kg). One pilot, four to six passengers.

NORTHROP AVION

American single-seat all-metal aircraft. Northrop's first experimental "all-wing" machine of 1929. Powered by one 90-hp Menasco inverted in-line air-cooled engine (a version of the British Blackburn Cirrus III engine). Wingspan 30 ft 6 in (9.29 m), length 20 ft (6.09 m), max weight approx 1,750 lb (793 kg), longest known flight 45 mins.

NORTHROP N-1M JEEP

American single-seat experimental flying wing of 1940. Powered by two 120-hp Franklin 6AC264F2 six-cylinder, air-cooled engines. Wingspan 38 ft (11.6 m), length 17 ft (5.2 m), max weight 4,000 lb (1,814 kg). Aircraft underpowered and often towed to test height.

NORTHROP B35

American tail-less long-range bomber of 1946. Powered by four 3,000-hp Pratt & Whitney Wasp Major, R-4360-17 and 20 air-cooled, 28-cylinder radial engines. Wingspan 172 ft (52.4 m), length 53 ft 1 in (16.2 m), max speed 500 mph (804.6 kph), range over 10,000 ml (16,093 km), endurance 9 hours, empty weight 89,000 lb (40,368 kg), max weight 209,000 lb (94,800 kg). 15 crew.

NORTHROP T38 TALON

American Mach 1 two-seat trainer of 1959. Powered by two 2,680-lb (1,215.6-kg) thrust General Electric J85 GE-5A turbo-jets—3,850 lb (1,746 kg) with afterburn. Wingspan 25 ft 3 in (7.69 m), length 26 ft 4 in (14 m), max speed 850 mph (1,367.9 kph) at 36,000 ft (10,972 m), initial rate of climb 32,500 ft (10,728.9 m) per min, ceiling 53,500 ft (16,306 m), range 1,140 ml (1,834 km), max weight 11,820 lb (5,361.4 kg).

NORTHROP B2

American two-seat tail-less "stealth" bomber of 1990. Powered by four 33,000-hp thrust GE F118-GE-100 turbofans with afterburner. Wingspan 172 ft 9 in (52.43 m), length 69 ft (21.03 m), max speed 627 mph (1,010 kph), Mach 0.85 at 50,292 ft (15,239 m), ceiling 50,000 ft (15,240 m), range 6,960 ml (11,200 km), max weight 352,739 lb (160,000 kg), armament 16 nuclear bombs or variety of other ordinance.

NORTH AMERICAN F 86A SABRE

American single-seat fighter. Prototype first flown in 1948. Powered by one 4,859-lb (2200-kg) General Electric J 47-1 engine. Wingspan 37 ft 1 in (11.31 m), length 37 ft 6 in (11.43 m), max speed 675 mph (1086 kph), Mach typically 0.92, ceiling 50, 000 ft (15,240 m), initial rate of climb typically 8,000 ft (2,438 m) per min, range 850 ml (1,368 km), max weight 16,223 lb (7358 kg), armament six 0.5 Colt machine guns, two 1,000-lb bombs or eight rockets or two Sidewinder missiles.

PEARSE MONOPLANE

New Zealand monoplane of bamboo, metal, and calico designed by Richard Pearse. Powered by a 24-hp horizontally-opposed, two-cylinder, air-cooled engine. A 60-hp engine also installed. Wingspan about 27 ft ((8.2 m) length about 17 ft (5.1m), max weight 500 lb (226.7 kg) with Pearse aboard, speed approx 20 mph (32 kph). Made hops of about 75 ft (22.8 m) to about 15 ft high (4.5 m), exact dates unknown but reported as between 1903 and 1909.

PERCIVAL GULL IV

British 3-seat touring monoplane of 1932. Powered by one 130-hp Gypsy major, or Cirrus Hermes IVs, four-cylinder, inverted in-line air-cooled engine. Wingspan, 36 ft 2 in (11 m), length 24 ft 9 in (7.54 m), max speed 145 mph (233 kph), range 640 ml (1,030 km), max weight 2,450 lb (1,110 kg). Kingsford Smith fitted an extra 60-gall (270-ltr) fuel tank into the cabin of his Gull IV for his 1933 England to Australia record, and the engine was a 130-hp De H Gypsy Major inverted in-line air-cooled engine.

PERCIVAL MEW GULL

British single-seat racing monoplane of 1939. Powered by one 205-hp De Havilland Gipsy six series II six-cylinder, in-line air-cooled engine. Wingspan 24 ft 9 in (7.54 m), length 21 ft 11 in (6.7 m), max speed 247 mph (397.5 kph), cruising speed 235 mph (378 kph), total weight 2,350 lb (1,065.9 kg), range 2,000 ml (3,218.6 km), rate of climb approx 1,400 ft (426.7 m) per min. Data for the Mew Gull flown on Cape Town record flight.

PERCIVAL GULL SIX

British three-seat touring aircraft of 1934. Powered by one 200-hp De Havilland Gypsy six inverted six-cylinder, in-line air-cooled engine. Wingspan 36 ft 2 in (11.02 m), length 24 ft 9 in (7.54 m), max speed 178 mph (286 kph), range 640 ml (1,030 km). Long-range aircraft such as Jean Batten's were fitted with extra fuel tanks to give a range of 2,000 ml (3,220 km).

PILCHER'S GLIDER

Scottish monoplane glider of 1896. First of the pioneer gliders to be fitted with a wheeled undercarriage. Wingspan 23 ft 4 in, weight 50 lb (22.6 kg), weight with Pilcher as pilot 195 lb (88.5 kg), fatal crash from 30 ft (9.1 m).

PROGRESS AIR DISCOVERY

American two-seat kit plane circa 1992-3. Powered by one 180-hp Textron Lycoming 360 horizontally-opposed, air-cooled engine. Wingspan 30 ft (9.14 m), length 17 ft 10 in (5.5 m), max weight 1,750 lb (793.8 kg).

RYAN NYP (NEW YORK-PARIS)

American single-seat long distance mono-plane of 1927 specially designed for Charles Lindbergh. Powered by a single 223-hp Wright J-5 Whirlwind nine-cylinder air-cooled radial engine. Wingspan 46 ft (14 m), length 27 ft 7 in (8.4 m), max speed 128 mph (205 kph), ceiling about 11,000 ft

Major inverted in-line air-cooled engine.

(3,352 m), range 4,650 ml (7,483 km), weight 4,495 lb (2,038.8 kg), fuel capacity 425 gal (1,608 ltr).

SANTOS-DUMONT 14 BIS

French single-place flying machine of 1906. Powered by one 50-hp Antoinette six-cylinder in-line engine. Wingspan 36 ft 9 in (11.3 m), length 31 ft 10 in (9.7 m), max speed 25 mph (40.3 kph), max weight 661 lb (300 kg). First powered flying machine to fly in Europe, it flew 722 ft (220 m) in just over 20 seconds.

REP-1

French single-engine monoplane of 1907. Powered by one 30-hp REP seven-cylinder, air-cooled radial engine. Wingspan 31 ft 5 in (99.6 m), length 22 ft 3 in (6.9 m), speed unknown. First successful use of modern-style ailerons for lateral control, also first use of seat belt.

RUTAN VOYAGER

American two-seat experimental long-distance aircraft of 1986. Powered by one specially designed 117-hp Teledyne Continental IOL 200 liquid-cooled engine as main cruise engine and one standard 130-hp Teledyne Continental air-cooled engine. Wingspan 111 ft (34 m), cruising speed 110 mph (175 kph), range 37,000 ml (59,545 km), weight of airframe 939 lb (426 kg), fuel load 7,000 lb (3,200 kg), ceiling more than 20,000 ft (6,000 m).

SAVOIA MARCHETTI S-16TER

Italian five-passenger flying boat of 1923. Powered by one 400-hp Lorraine-Dietrich engine. Wingspan 50 ft (15.24m), length 32 ft (9.75 m), max speed 120 mph (193 kph), cruising sped 93 mph (149.6 kph), ceiling 9,800 ft (2,987 m), range 850 ml (1,367 km). De Pinedo used the passenger cabin as a workshop and for extra fuel storage. Two crew.

SAVOIA MARCHETTI S 55

Italian twin-hulled flying boat of 1933. Powered by two 18-cylinder 750-hp Isotta-

Fraschini Asso 750R 18 engines. Wingspan 78 ft 9 in (24 m), length 55 ft (16.8 m), max speed 173 mph (279 kph), ceiling 13,780 ft (4,200 m), range 1,245 ml (2,000 km), max weight 16,975 lb (7,700 kg), armament four machine guns and 4,409-lb (2,000-kg) bomb/torpedo load. Crew, two pilots and various gunners. Airliner versions carried five passengers in each hull. De Pinedo's machine was powered by two 500-hp Isotta Franschini engines which gave a max speed of 127 mph (204 kph), range 1,350 ml (2,172 km).

SEVERSKY P 35
American single-seat fighter of 1937. Powered by one 950-hp Pratt & Whitney R-1830-9 Twin Wasp 14-cylinder, air-cooled radial engine. Wingspan 36 ft (10.97 m), length 25 ft 2 in (8.17m), max speed 281 mph (453 kph), ceiling 30,600 ft (9,330 m), range 1,150 ml (1,850 km), max weight 6,295 lb (2,855 kg), armament two machine guns and 300-lb (136-kg) bomb load.

SHORT S 23 C CLASS FLYING BOAT
British 24-passenger long-range flying boat first flown in 1936. Powered by four 920-hp Bristol Pegasus XC, nine-cylinder air-cooled radial engines. Wingspan 114 ft (34.75 m), length 88 ft (26.84 m), total weight 40,500 lb (18,380 kg), max speed 200 mph (322 kph), cruising speed 164 mph (264 kph), rate of climb 950 ft (290 m) per min, ceiling 20,000 ft (6,100 m), range 703 ml (1,300km), endurance 4.5 hours.

SHORT SINGAPORE I
British maritime patrol flying boat of 1934. Powered by four 730-hp Rolls-Royce Kestrel V-12 liquid-cooled engines. Wingspan 90 ft 10 in (27.7 m), length 64 ft 6 in (19.65 m), max speed 144 mph (233 kph) range 1,740 ml (2,800 km), max weight 31,526 lb (14,300 kg), armament six 7.69 mm machine guns and 1,984-lb (900-kg) bomb load. Cobhams' machine carried no armament.

SHORT VALETTA
British floatplane transport of 1931. Powered by two Bristol Jupiter XI F nine-cylinder, air-cooled radial engines. Wingspan 107 ft (32.6 m), length 70 ft 5 in (21.5 m), payload, 7,388 lb (3,351 kg), cruising speed 100 mph (160.9 kph), range 500 ml (804.6 km), total weight 23,000 lb (10,432 kg). Six crew on survey flight to Africa.

SIKORSKY S 2
Russian single-seat biplane of 1910. Powered by one 25-hp Anzani three-cylinder air-cooled radial engine. Wingspan 26 ft (7.9 m), length 26 ft (7.9 m), speed unknown, total weight 727 lb (329 kg). Igor Sikorsky's first successful aircraft.

SIKORSKY MOURAMETZ
Russian four-engined bomber—several variations with differing engines, such as Salmson, Sunbeam, Renault—of between 150 and 220 hp—produced. World's first four-engined aircraft. Wingspan 97 ft 9 in (29.8 m), length 56 ft 1 in (17.1 m), max speed 75 mph (121 kph), ceiling 9,843 ft (3000 m), range 340 ml (550 km), max weight 10,130 lb (4,495 kg), armament varied, up to seven or more machine guns.

SIKORSKY S 29A
Russian 14-seat passenger transport of 1924. Powered by two 300-hp Hispano-Suiza and later two 400-hp Liberty V-12 water-cooled engines. Wingspan 68 ft (20.7 m), length 48 ft (14.6 m), max speed 115 mph (185 kph), total weight 12,000 lb (5443 kg).

SIKORSKY S 38
American 10-passenger amphibian of 1928. Powered by two 450-hp Pratt & Whitney Wasp C air-cooled radial engines. Wingspan 71 ft 10 in (21.9 m), length 40 ft 4 in (12.3 m), max speed 110 mph (177 kph), max weight 10,480 lb (4,754 kg) payload 1,650 lb (748 kg) with up to 10 passengers. Two crew.

SIKORSKY S 40
American 33-44 seat amphibious passenger

transport. First flown in 1931. Powered by four 660-hp Pratt & Whitney T2 D1 seven-cylinder, air-cooled radial engines. Wingspan 114 ft (34.7 m), length 76 ft 8 in (23.4m), max speed 155 mph (249.4 kph).

SIKORSKY S 42
American long-range passenger flying boat. Powered by four 700-hp Pratt & Whitney Hornet nine-cylinder, air-cooled radial engines. Wingspan 114 ft 2 in (34.8 m), length 69 ft 2 in (21.1m), max speed 170 mph (274 kph), range 1,200 ml (1,931 km), take-off weight 42,000 lb (19,050 kg).

SIKORSKY VS 300
American single-seat helicopter. First flown in 1942. First main rotor/tail-rotor helicopter. Powered by one 75-hp four-cylinder, horizontally opposed, air-cooled Lycoming engine. Main rotor diameter 30 ft (9.14 m), length 27 ft 10 in (8.48 m), max speed 50 mph (80 kph), range 75 ml (120km), max weight 1,290 lb (585 kg).

SIKORSKY R4, HOVERFLY
American two-seat military helicopter of 1942. Powered by one 180-hp Warner R-550 Super Scarab air-cooled radial engine. Main rotor diameter 38 ft (11.6 m), length 35 ft 3 in (10,7 m), max speed 75 mph (121 kph).

SIKORSKY SEA KING
Amphibious-hulled multi-role military helicopter. First flown in 1959. Powered by two 1,400-hp General Electric free turbine turbo shaft T5 8-10 engines, roles included anti submarine warfare, reconnaissance, mine sweeping, rescue gunship and commando operations, and civilian passenger transport. Licensed to Britain's Westland Aircraft with two Rolls-Royce Gnome free turbine turboshaft engines, similar performance figures. Main rotor diameter 62 ft (18.9 m), length 72 ft 8 in (22.15 m), max speed 166 mph (267 kph), initial climb 2,200 ft (400 m) per min, ceiling 14,700 ft (4,480 m),

range 625 ml (1,005 km), armament variable.

S.I.M.B. BERNARD FERBOIS V2
French single-seat racing monoplane of 1924. Powered by one 550-hp Hispano-Suiza engine. Max speed 278.5 mph (448.2 kph)—an absolute speed record in its class for eight years. Designed by M. Hubert, it was superbly finished in a thin wood-veneer. Engine employed an evaporative steam cooling system, using underwing radiators.

STEARMAN C3 MB
American single-seat mail plane of 1927, sometimes known as the C3 Special. Wingspan 35 ft (10.6 m), ceiling 17,500 ft (5,334 m), range 560 ml (901.2 km), max weight 2,380 lb (1,283.6 kg).

SOPWITH ATLANTIC
British two-seat, long-range transport transatlantic type of 1919. Powered by one 350-hp Rolls-Royce Eagle V-12 in-line liquid-cooled engine. Cruising speed 168 mph (270 kph) at 10,000 ft (3,048 m), endurance 22 hrs, fuel 3,000 lb (1,360 kg) capacity 400 gal (1,800 ltr).

SOPWITH CAMEL
British single seat fighter. First flight in 1916. Powered by a single 130-hp Clerget nine-cylinder, air-cooled rotary engine. Wingspan 28 ft (8.53 m), length 18 ft 9 in (5.72 m), max speed 113 mph (182 kph), initial climb 1,000 ft (305 m) per min, ceiling 19,000 ft (5,790 m), range typically 250 ml (400 km), max weight 1,453 lb (659 kg), armament two 0.303 Vickers machine guns.

SOPWITH TABLOID
British single-seat fighter and two-seat reconnaissance biplane of 1914. Powered by one 80-hp Gnome Rhone nine-cylinder rotary engine or one 100-hp Gnome monosoupape rotary. Wingspan 25 ft 6 in (7.7 m), length 20 ft 4 in (6.20 m), max speed 92 mph (148 kph), initial rate of climb

1,200 ft (365.7 m) per min, ceiling 15,000 ft (4,600 m), range 315 ml (506 km), max weight 1,120 lb (508 kg).

SPACE SHUTTLE COLUMBIA

American seven-place orbiter of 1982, manufactured by international Rockwell. Powered by 3 main engines of 375,000-lb (170,250-kg) thrust, operating for eight minutes, consisting of a central rocket flanked by two combusters. Solid rocket boosters 5,800,000-lb (2,633,200-kg) thrust for 2 minutes at liftoff and jettisoned at 31-ml (50.2-km) altitude, fuel capacity 1,500,000 lb (681,000 kg)—520,000 gal (2,366,000 ltr) liquid oxygen— jettisoned at 59 ml (95.6 km) up, 44 small thrusters to control attitude during orbit. Orbit speed 15,200 kts, rate of descent 15,000 per min, approach speed 650 kts at 52,000 ft (15,860 m), 290 kts at 1,800 ft (549 m), gear down at 270 kts, touch down 190 kts.

SPERRY FLYING TORPEDO

American unmanned flying bomb of 1922, developed in secret by U.S. Navy and U.S. Army. Controlled by a Sperry autopilot and based on Alfred Verville's Sperry Messenger design. See Sperry Messenger for more data.

SPERRY MESSENGER

American single-seat ultra-light fully aero-batic military communications aircraft stressed to 6-G (!). First flown in 1920. Powered by one three-cylinder Lawrence L 4 air-cooled radial engine. Wingspan 20 ft (6.3m), length 17 ft 9 in (5.4 m), max speed 86 mph (138 kph), max weight 862 lb (390 kg).

SUPERMARINE S4

British single-seat racing seaplane designed for Schneider Trophy of 1925. Powered by one 2,600-hp Napier Lion VII twelve-cylinder, inverted arrow in-line water-cooled engine. Wingspan 30 ft 7 in (9.3 m), length 26 ft 7 in (8.1 m), max speed 231.4 mph (372.4 kph), max weight 3,191 lb (1,447 kph).

SUPERMARINE S6 A

British single-seat racing seaplane designed for Schneider Trophy of 1929. Powered by one 2,350-hp Rolls-Royce R 12, V-12 liquid-cooled engine. Wingspan 30 ft (9.1 m), length 28 ft 10 in (8.8 m), max speed 332 mph (534.3 kph)—a world record for 1929, total weight 6,086 lb (2,760 kg). Machine shown as an S6 took part and was disqualified for turning within a turning point. It was modified to an S6A to become a reserve aircraft for the 1931 races.

SUPERMARINE SEAGULL III

Three-seat British spotter-reconnaissance amphibian of 1926. Powered by one 450-hp 12-cylinder Napier Lion water-cooled engine. Wingspan 46 ft (14 m), length 37 ft (11.2 m), max speed 108 mph (173.8 kph), rate of climb approx 450 ft (137 m) per min, takeoff weight 5,668 lb (2570.9 kg), armament one 0.303 Lewis gun.

SUPERMARINE STRANRAER

British maritime patrol flying boat of 1937. Powered by two 920-hp Bristol Pegasus nine-cylinder, air-cooled radial engines. Wingspan 85 ft (25.9 m), length 54 ft 10 in (16 .7 m), max speed 150 mph (241 kph), 165 mph (265 kph) at 16,000 ft (4,876 m), rate of climb 1,350 ft (411.4 m) per min, range 1,000 ml (1,609 km), endurance 9.5 hr, max weight 19,000 lb (8,618 kg), armament three 0.303 machine guns and 1,000-lb (453-kg) bomb load.

SUPERMARINE SPITFIRE MK1

British single-seat fighter. Prototype first flew in 1936, the Spitfire Mk 1 entered service by 1938. Powered by one 1,030-hp Rolls-Royce Merlin II V-twelve liquid-cooled engine. Wingspan 36 ft 10 in (11.23 m), length 29 ft 11 in (9.10 m), max speed 364 mph (586 kph), ceiling 31,500 ft (9,601 m), range 395 ml (636 km), max weight 5,800 lb (2,631 kg), armament eight 0.303 machine guns.

SUPERMARINE SPITFIRE V

British single-seat fighter of 1941. Powered by one 1,478-hp Rolls-Royce Merlin 45 V-twelve liquid-cooled engine. Wingspan 36 ft 10 in (11.23 m), length 29 ft 11 in (9.12 m), max speed 369 mph (594 kph), ceiling 36,500 ft (11,125 m), max weight 6,417 lb (2,911 kg), armament Va model eight 0.303 machine guns, Vb model two 20-mm cannon with four .0.303 machine guns, Vc model four 20-mm cannon.

SUPERMARINE SPITFIRE XI

British single-seat high altitude photographic reconnaissance aircraft. First flown in 1942. Powered latterly by one 1,650plus-hp Rolls-Royce Merlin 70 V-twelve liquid-cooled engine. Wingspan 36 ft 10 in (11.23 m), length 31 ft 3.5 in (9 54 m), max speed 422 mph (679 kph), ceiling 44,000 ft (13,411 m), range 1,200+ ml (1,930 km), no armament.

SUPERMARINE MODEL 224.F.7/30

British single-seat experimental fighter of 1934, often referred to (wrongly) as the "first Spitfire." Powered by one 600-hp V-12 Rolls-Royce Goshawk II. Wingspan 45 ft 10 in (13.97 m), length 29 ft 5 in (8.9 m), max speed 228 mph (367 kph) at 15,000 ft (4,543 m), rate of climb 1,578 ft per min (480.9 m per min), ceiling 38,800 ft (11,826 m), max weight 4,743 lb (2,151 kg), armament four 0.303 machine guns.

TUPOLEV TU144

Russian 140-passenger Supersonic transport of 1969. Powered by four Kuznetsov N-K 144 turbofans of 44,090-lb (20,000-kg) thrust with afterburning. Wingspan 94 ft 6 in (28.8 m), length 215 ft 6 in (65.7 m), cruising speed Mach 2.35m, max weight 396,830 lb (180,000 kg), range 4030 ml (6,500km). Three to four crew.

VICKERS VIMY

British heavy bomber. First flown in 1917. Powered by two 360-hp V-12 liquid cooled Rolls-Royce engines. Wingspan 68 ft (920.73), length 43 ft 6 in (13.27 m), max speed 103 mph (166 kph), ceiling 12,000 ft (3,660 m), range 900 ml (1,448 km), max weight 12,500 lb (5,570 kg), armament up to four machine guns and up to 4,804 lb (2,179 kg) bomb load.

VOUGHT F4U CORSAIR

American single-seat carrier-based fighter. First flown in 1940. Powered by a single 2,450-hp Pratt & Whitney R-2800-18W two-row 18-cylinder, air-cooled radial engine. Wingspan 40 ft 11 in (12.47 m), length 33 ft 8 in (10.26 m), max speed 446 mph (718 kph) ceiling 45,0000 ft (12,650 m), max range 1,560 ml (2,511 km), max weight 14,670 lb (6,654 kg). Armament six 0.5 machine guns plus two 1,000-lb (454-kg) bombs or eight 5-in (12-mm) rockets.

WRIGHT GLIDER NO. 1

American single-place biplane glider of 1900. Wingspan 17 ft 6 in (5.3 m), length about 13 ft (3.9 m), wing area 165 sq ft (50 sq m), weight 52 lb (23 kg), speed about 25 mph (40 kph).

WRIGHT GLIDER NO. 2

American single-place biplane glider of 1901. Wingspan 22 ft (6.7 m), length about 13 ft 7 in (4.14 m), wing area 290 sq ft (88 sq m), weight 98 lb (44.4 kg), speed about 25 mph (40 kph), longest flight down-slope 390 ft (118.8 m) in 17.5 secs.

WRIGHT GLIDER NO. 3

American single-place biplane glider of 1902. Wingspan 32 ft 1 in (9.8 m), length 16 ft 1 in (4.9 m), speed unknown but probably about 30 mph (48 kph), longest flight down-slope 600 ft (183 m), endurance over one min, more than 1,000 flights made.

WRIGHT *FLYER*

American single-place biplane of 1903. Powered by one 20-hp Wright four-cylinder, water-cooled, in-line engine weighing 150 lb (68 kg). Wingspan 40 ft 6 in (12.3 m), length 28 ft (8.5 m), speed about 35 mph (56 kph), total weight 750 lb (340 kg). Made the world's first sustained, controlled powered flight.

INDEX

References to illustrations
are in *italics*.

ACKNOWLEDGMENTS

It is an onerous task to remember who to thank when a work has taken a decade or more to come to fruition. Inevitably there will be someone out there I have forgotten to include—to you, I offer my humble apologies. It is also difficult to prioritize the list, except to say that without doubt, my patient and supportive wife, Jean, gets first billing. Without her, this publication would not have happened.

So, with that said, I have elected to list my many benefactors in alphabetical order. My grateful thanks go to David Baker for his analysis of the death of the Red Baron in his book *Manfred von Richtofen*, upon which one of my paintings is based; Bruce Brown for help in locating material for the Gatty story and Mike Gatty for supplying photographs; the Civil Aviation Historical Society of South Australia for the gift of their photographs; Colin Cruddas and Daryl Carmichael of Cobham Plc Ltd for their informed comments and generous use of photographic material used in the story on Sir Alan Cobham; Glenn Appel and Lynn McDonald at the Cradle of Aviation Museum, New York, for their diligence and perception in helping me complete the details of Jackie Cochran's P-35; Luc Berger at Dassault Aviation for his helpful review of the story on Dassault; the Deutsches Museum in Munich for invaluable information on Reinhold Platz; Cmdr. David Hobbs for last-minute assistance with details of aircraft in Britain's Fleet Air Arm Museum; John Hudson Fysh for the use of material from the Hudson Fysh Archives; Lt. Cmdr. Bob Geale R.A.N. Retd of Australia's Museum of Flight and Lt. Cmdr. Peter Nelson R.A.N. for help with the Sea King episode in the Sikorsky story; the Goble family for allowing access to their family records and photographs; Dr. Philippe Grasse of the Musée de l'Air et de

l'Éspace le Bourget, Paris, for unraveling my tortured French and for supplying background material for several stories—Lawrence Sperry to name but one; Ralph Strong of the National Air and Space Museum Smithsonian Institution for his help with several stories, notably Chubbie Miller, Lawrence Sperry, and Harold Gatty; Jeffrey P. Rhodes and the team at the Lockheed Martin organization for their generosity in supplying archival photographs; the late Bill Mann for his contribution to the Lancaster details in the story on Roy Chadwick; Ian Debenham of the Powerhouse Museum, Sydney, for his help searching out historical facts; Peter Davison at the Science Museum, London, for investigating aircraft details; Frank Hunter at the Igor I. Sikorsky Archives for detailed information on early Sikorsky aircraft; Peter Dimmick and D. G. Upward of the Southampton Hall of Aviation for information which contributed to the completion of the story on R. J. Mitchell; Peter Smidmore of the Aviation Historical Society Inc. (N.S.W.) for allowing me to rifle his collection of material on Anthony Fokker and Howard Hughes; Phil, Mary, and Mark Taylor for the use of their studios and the talent of photographer Stephen Mather; Lena Kaljit at the U.S. Department of Defense (Marine Corps) for help to complete the story on John Glenn; Nancy Bird-Walton, unwavering in her support and enthusiasm, and for access to her photographs; Jeff Watson, a walking encyclopedia on our spy in the sky Sidney Cotton; Kevin Weldon, flyer and philanthropist, for his encouragement and support over many years. Finally, to my coauthor Bruce Harris— what can I say? Your professionalism, energy, and way with words endowed this project with life and allowed it to see the light of day.

DAVID MARSHALL

It has been a joy to work with David Marshall again—years after we worked together in advertising. His unfailing good humour, extraordinary patience, intimate knowledge of his subject, and the ability to recreate aviation history made our collaboration exhilarating. Thanks, too, to Jean Marshall for the splendid victuals she supplied, along with her obvious support during the many days we worked together at their Bayview retreat.

My own wife, Shirley, provided the care and support that allowed me to stay hunched over the computer in my "box" for days, nights, and weeks at a time. Her patience with my variable behavior over the years has only been equalled by her enthusiasm as the project progressed.

I also wish to acknowledge the assistance and advice of John Ferguson, that contemporary member of an Australian publishing dynasty, given both in Sydney and after he moved to California. He encouraged us to prepare, polish, and persevere. His friend and co-worker, Denise Barnes, also provided valuable publishing insights and helped us make contact with Henrietta Silver in the U.K. as well as Myles Archibald, who made some invaluable suggestions.

We also salute the guidance of Colin Brown, on matters digital and on how to harness state-of-the-art photography to ensure that easel acrylic paintings and delicate watercolors, depicting aircraft and dramatic aviation events, would be faithfully reproduced in our book.

Finally, the pleasure of having the enthusiasm and encouragement of Gordon Cheers and Margaret Olds of Global Book Publishing, with the creative arts of designer Stan Lamond and editor Jayne Denshire lifting our work to a satisfying combination of style and assurance, made the years of effort worthwhile.

BRUCE HARRIS

PHOTO CREDITS

The Publisher believes that permission for use of the historical photographs in this publication, listed below, has been correctly obtained. However if any errors or omissions have occurred, Global Book Publishing would be pleased to hear from any copyright owners.

Boeing Archives: p96 bottom, p100 top, p100 bottom, p101 top, p103 top.

Reproduced courtesy of Nancy Bird-Walton: p190 bottom.

Reproduced courtesy of the Civil Aviation Historical Society of South Australia: p84 bottom, p86 left.

Cradle of Aviation Museum, Garden City, NY: p192 bottom.

C. Cruddas/Cobham Archive: p52 bottom, p53 top left.

Hudson Fysh Archives: p88 bottom.

Reproduced courtesy of Mike Gatty: p63 top left, p63 bottom.

Getty Images Pty Ltd: p24 bottom, p45 top, p48 top, p122 bottom, p144 bottom, p165 bottom, p168 right, p180 top.

Glenbow Archives: p62 top.

Hachette Filipacchi Associes: p134–135 top.

Lockheed Martin Archives: p44 top, p128 bottom, p132 top, p132 bottom right.

David Marshall: p56 left, p59 right, p62 left, p74 bottom, p104 bottom.

© Musée de l'Air et de l'Éspace/Le Bourget: p26 left, p28 left, p70 bottom, p72 bottom, p73 top left, p78 top (both), p146 bottom, p177 bottom, p178 bottom.

National Air and Space Museum, Smithsonian Institution: p12 right, p16 top, p19 top, p20 bottom, p21 bottom left, p21 bottom right, p82 top, p152 bottom, p160 bottom, p162 bottom, p196 bottom.

By permission of the National Library of Australia: p148 bottom, p151 bottom left, p151 bottom right, p153 bottom.

Reproduced courtesy of the Powerhouse Museum, Sydney: p14 left, p173 top right.

Igor I. Sikorsky Historical Archives Inc.: p34 left, p35 right, p37 right.

San Diego Aerospace Museum: p107 bottom.

State Library of New South Wales: p114 bottom, p154 bottom, p173 top left.

State Library of Queensland: p64 bottom, p156 bottom, p159 top.

By permission of the United States Department of Defense (Marine Corps): p204 bottom left (DOD(USMC) #A3469), p204 bottom right (DOD(USMC) #A348551).